DAILY LIFE IN

Pre-Columbian Native America

D0071891

Recent Titles in
The Greenwood Press "Daily Life Through History" Series

DAILY LIFE IN

Pre-Columbian Native America

CLARISSA W. CONFER

The Greenwood Press "Daily Life Through History" Series

GREENWOOD PRESS
Westport, Connecticut • London

Library of Congress Cataloging-in-Publication Data

Confer, Clarissa W., 1965–
    Daily life in Pre-columbian Native America / by Clarissa W. Confer.
       p. cm. — (Daily life through history, ISSN 1080–4749)
    Includes bibliographical references and index.
    ISBN-13: 978–0–313–33743–7 (alk. paper)
    1. Paleo-Indians.   2. Indians of North America—Antiquities.
    3. North America—Antiquities.   I. Title.
    E61.C74   2008
    970.01—dc22   2007035362

British Library Cataloguing in Publication Data is available.

Library of Congress Catalog Card Number: 2007035362
ISBN-13: 978–0–313–33743–7
ISSN: 1080–4749

First published in 2008

Greenwood Press, 88 Post Road West, Westport, CT 06881
An imprint of Greenwood Publishing Group, Inc.
www.greenwood.com

Printed in the United States of America

The paper used in this book complies with the
Permanent Paper Standard issued by the National
Information Standards Organization (Z39.48–1984).

10 9 8 7 6 5 4 3 2 1

For John, Mom, and Muffet – thanks for all your help and support.

Contents

Introduction

This book attempts to offer readers a view of the daily life of ancient North Americans. In most cases, daily life was an ongoing struggle for survival. Not all cultures were on a knife edge between living and dying, but in terms of existence they probably lived closer to the edge than do today's North Americans. Some areas, such as the Arctic and Far West, barely supported human life; others offered more of a buffer against starvation. Severe shortages, however, were never out of the range of possibility for any group. Because starvation is often not a concern of today's readers, the life of ancient American Indians may seem far removed from modern life with its consistent food supplies. On the other hand, many of the concerns of human life have changed little over the millennia. Family life, economic pursuits, religious beliefs, social activities, and artistic expression are all aspects of life that are common to people's experience. Although today's readers may never bring down an animal with a spear, or grind their own pigments for paint, the people in these pages should not seem too unfamiliar.

The scope of this work encompasses pre-Columbian American Indians. This includes all inhabitants of the present-day United States before the arrival of Europeans. Although Columbus arrived in the Caribbean in 1492, most areas of the North American continent did not see Europeans for another century or more. Obviously, this book covers a huge span of time, stretching back at least 10,000 years, and describes a huge span of territory that includes much of a continent. Thus the picture of people in that vast continuum can be at best a snapshot, a glimpse of a moment frozen in time. At worst it is an unexposed photograph with no image at all. Readers must accept that there are many people who lived in this world that will never be known. There is simply no physical record of their time on earth. Their daily lives have been lost to the vastness of time. The knowledge that does exist relies a great deal on incomplete evidence, educated guesses, and plausible theories. Archaeology is the key provider of most of the evidence on which our understanding is based, and it certainly has its limitations.

It is important to keep a few things in mind when reading this volume. One is the nature of the archaeological evidence. An archaeological site can provide substantial information, but it yields only a fraction of the complete story. The excavated and studied sites represent a very small proportion of the areas of human settlement or resource exploitation. Many important coastal sites were lost millennia ago during rising sea levels, and many other ancient use areas have been destroyed by modern development. Experts draw the best conclusions they can from the available evidence, but each new discovery, each new archaeological site, can offer a wealth of often startling new information. Our understanding of ancient peoples can change quickly and dramatically at any time. That said, anthropology is a fairly traditional discipline and challenges to the accepted wisdom are rarely immediately embraced. This work stays close to the established anthropological rationales while remaining open to alternate viewpoints.

Another unique aspect of this subject matter is the lack of written historical record. Writing, as both a means of communication and as a method of recording important events for the future, is critical to Western culture. This is especially true in the American culture of the twenty-first century. Traditionally, historians rely heavily on written documentation to relate the story of the past. The items of our country's past that we value most highly tend to be written documents such as the Declaration of Independence and the Constitution. These are tangible, seemingly incontrovertible proof of events in the distant past. So a problem arises in dealing with cultures that did not create and preserve documents, letters, diaries, or literature. Cultures indigenous to the Americas did not have a form of written language. They did not write to communicate or to record. This leaves historians bereft of one of their main resources for investigating the past.

Some forms of recording, primarily in the form of representative pictures, existed and can shed light on a culture's experience. Most of these nonliterate peoples relied on oral communication to support their culture. They passed down histories, taboos, customs, humor, and other cultural aspects orally. Typically, an oral culture values and thus enjoys a far greater memory retention than a literate culture. Thus oral traditions, often described merely as storytelling, are an important aid to understanding native cultures. This volume, however, addresses a period far removed from the present, so the availability of oral traditions is quite limited. The exception is the use of creation stories to illustrate indigenous peoples' understanding of their ancestors' place in this world.

Another point to keep in mind is the incredible diversity of indigenous peoples in North America. When Europeans arrived on the continent, hundreds of distinct groups of people were living there. Language, subsistence, religion, social and political organization, housing, and clothing styles differentiated these people from one another. Some would have been somewhat similar in culture; others would have been extremely different. The most important idea to remember is that there is no one Native American culture or experience. Indigenous Americans were, and are, very diverse.

The book covers the main cultural groups in North America in the area currently defined as the United States. There were no political divisions in pre-Columbian times. The distinction that anthropologists use is cultural area, which divides people by the way they adapted their life to their surroundings. The four primary divisions are subsistence pursuits, settlement patterns, housing style, and clothing. These in turn are adaptations to ecosystems or climactic regions. Humans in the woods of Pennsylvania lived differently from those in the desert canyons of Arizona. Scholars divide people along somewhat arbitrary lines of regional adaptations such as Northeast, Arctic, or Southwest. This volume is organized in a roughly east to west scheme, moving from the Northeast across the Plains to California and then north to the Arctic. There are certainly other ways to present the subject matter, but this follows the most common anthropological organization. Most culture area maps show essentially the same regional divisions. These divisions mark changes in adaptations of humans to their environment. There are clearly commonalities between the divisions, however, and some elements, such as a hunting and gathering lifestyle, are seen over and over again across the country. There are always exceptions to the rule, but the material here focuses on the norm rather than the rarity.

HISTORICAL OVERVIEW

The term *pre-Columbian* is used here to define the period before European settlement in America. Christopher Columbus is a well-known figure to non-native Americans. His name conjures up stories of daring and adventure and perhaps the oft-repeated rhyme of 1492 when "Columbus sailed the ocean blue." Pre-Columbian, of course, is a phrase that would mean absolutely nothing to the subjects of this book. Europeans, and later Americans, regarded America as a story of conquest and discovery. Columbus became the name that represented the beginnings of that tale for those connected to the Old World. The millions of people living in the New World in the fifteenth century obviously had no sense of being discovered. They would never hear of a sailor named Columbus until their descendents learned of him centuries later in Euro-American education systems.

We often call Native Americans "indigenous" people in recognition that they are the original human inhabitants of the continent. We know, however, that these people did not develop here, but rather arrived on the continent as modern *Homo sapiens*. There is no fossilized record of primitive humans in the Americas. Thus the human population must have come from somewhere, and we know from physical and cultural characteristics, as well as new studies of DNA, that the somewhere was Asia. The story of how humans made the journey from Siberia to North America is both well established and constantly changing. New archaeological studies, as well as new approaches such as use of dental records or linguistic characteristics, provide us with new information that must be assimilated into the existing knowledge base. The major trend of new research has been to push the date of humans' arrival in America earlier and earlier.

The majority of any scientific work in this area is being conducted by non-Indians. The theory is the most widely accepted version of indigenous peoples' past, but not the only one. Most cultural groups in North America have their own set of beliefs that explain their origin. These origin stories answer questions that all humans ask: Who are we? Where did we come from? What is our place in the world? These cultural explanations of origin are just as "real" to native people as scientific explanations are to non-natives. The revered oral tradition that passes this collective identity down through generations often includes explanations of the group's physical setting, relationship to animals, and interactions with natural phenomena. These are sacred stories cherished by indigenous people.

The following creation story of the Iroquois people from the Northeast includes the role of gods and animals, the importance of water, and other elements shared in many indigenous explanations.

Before there was an earth there was only water and sky. In the sky was a great tree, full of fruits, flowers, and seeds. One day, prompted by a dream, the Great Chief pulled up the tree, which left a big hole in the sky. His wife, Skywoman pregnant with a child, peeped through the hole, and leaned over too far. She slipped through, grasping a handful of seeds from the branches of the tree as she fell.

The animals of the waters saw her falling toward them and felt anguish, because they knew she couldn't live in the waters. The swans flew up and caught her and supported her with their wide wings. The muskrat dove deep and brought up mud, which the Great Turtle held on his back. In this way they made the Earth. The swans brought the Sky Woman to live on this Earth and bear her child there, from whom came all people. The seeds in her hand fell into mud, sprouted, and grew up into all the living things of the land.[1]

The peoples of the Northwest Coast have their own story that explains their origin and reveals the connection they feel to the ocean.

Raven was so lonely. One day he paced back and forth on the sandy beach feeling quite forlorn. Except for the trees, the moon, the sun, water, and a few animals the world was empty. His heart wished for the company of other creatures. Suddenly a large clam pushed through the sand making an eerie bubbling sound. Raven watched and listened intently as the clam slowly opened up. He was surprised and happy to see tiny people emerging from the shell. All were talking, smiling and shaking the sand off their tiny bodies. Men, women, and children spread around the island. Raven was pleased and proud with his work. He sang a beautiful song of great joy and greeting. He had brought the first people into the world.[2]

Indian people, certainly those who lived before the arrival of Europeans, lived in the knowledge that their creation story was the real story of their origins. What is now understood as the scientific explanation for human habitation of America came to be only in the last few hundred years and it is still evolving.

MIGRATION

The world was much different at the beginning of American Indian history. The Pleistocene epoch was a major Ice Age lasting from 1.6 million to about 10,000 years ago. Much of the world was covered with glacial ice. The expanding and retreating ice sheets at times stretched over Greenland, Canada, and the United States as far south as a line drawn westward from Cape Cod through Long Island, New Jersey, and Pennsylvania, along the line of the Ohio and Missouri Rivers to North Dakota, and through Montana, Idaho, and Washington to the Pacific. The ice carved and shaped the earth to create the landscape we know today. Areas not covered with ice, including the arid and semiarid parts of the western United States, had periods of increased rainfall and lessened evaporation that allowed for the spread of vegetation and the formation of many lakes. Heavy precipitation in the West was responsible for two great lakes: Lake Lahontan of Nevada and Lake Bonneville of Utah (today the Great Salt and Utah Lakes). Other massive forces were at work such as the volcanic activity on the Pacific Coast and the erosion of the Grand Canyon. Entirely different species roamed the moving continents, including North America. Among the characteristic Pleistocene mammals of North America were at least four species of elephants, including the mastodon and the mammoth, true horses (of the same genus as the domestic horse but not the same species), saber-tooth cats, large wolves, giant armadillos and ground sloths, bisons, camels, and wild pigs. Among the arctic mammals that ranged far south in the glacial stages was the musk ox.

In the Pleistocene epoch, with much of the earth's water locked up in glaciers that covered one-third of the earth, the sea levels dropped precipitously and exposed new land areas. The Bering Sea, named after Danish navigator Vitus Bering who died there in 1741, is fairly shallow. The decline in ocean water 30,000 years ago revealed a flat land mass that scientists have named Beringia. The size of this vast open land changed with the water levels, varying from 100 to 1,000 miles across. It would have appeared as a permanent tundra region to people and animals. The large herbivores populating the region would have been lured onto Beringia by the new grass and other food sources growing there. People, in turn, followed the animals that were their food source across the land

mass. It is unlikely that people or animals had a conscious sense of migrating; they simply followed food sources to ensure survival. Once across the temporary continent, they continued survival patterns, moving with food sources farther into the interior of North America. At times of warmer climate, the ice melted, seas rose, and Beringia disappeared, ending the migration route. As the cycle continued, the land reappeared and migration resumed. For this reason, the peopling of the Americas should be seen as a series of movements, rather than as one mass migration.

Although the migrants to North America may have come inadvertently, they were prepared for what they found. They had lived in similar climates in Siberia and had honed the requisite skills for providing shelter and obtaining food and other necessities of life. The New World they inhabited did not differ markedly from the old one.

The tundra they lived on was a vast, treeless expanse of low-growing plants. This ecosystem supported large megafauna, both herbivores and carnivores. Animals such as ground sloths, mammoths, mastodons, saber-toothed cats, and dire wolves roamed North America. The large plant eaters such as the mastodon became the favored prey of early hunters. Such a large animal could supply meat for many individuals for many days, as well as provide raw materials for many other needs. Large bones became roof supports; small bones tools; hides clothing, blankets, and door coverings. Creativity and necessity led early hunters to incorporate nearly every part of their prey into their survival strategy.

Hunting large mammals required skill and bravery and the cooperation of others. No one man could bring down a mammoth or mastodon, so the very nature of their food supply forced early paleo-Indians to live and cooperate in small groups. These groups were likely bands made up of four to ten related families who worked, hunted, and migrated together seasonally. Bands lived in isolation much of the year, but to fill needs of finding mates, social interaction, and companionship, the bands collected at times of food abundance. They would have enjoyed normal recreation like talking with others, seeking company of the opposite sex, playing games, showing off skills, gossiping, and generally enjoying the company of others like themselves. Upon dispersal of the larger group, those young women who had agreed to marry would travel with their new husband's band. This arrangement reflected the emphasis on hunting skills, which would be passed from father to son. Thus the men maintained their kin group, hunting collectively and perpetuating

their specialized knowledge through generations. Women's tasks were less communally oriented so they could change dwellings more easily.

Overall, the hunting bands who migrated from Siberia successfully adapted to life on the new continent. They spread outward from Beringia and modern Alaska, following game animals and continuing traditional subsistence patterns. Little evidence of these people remains today. All that survives from their occupancy are a few material remains of their activities. In 1932, archaeologists found stones that clearly had been altered or shaped by humans. In reference to the area Clovis, New Mexico, anthropologists named the people who made and used these stones the Clovis culture, considered the earliest demonstrable cultural complex in North America. Sites containing Clovis materials date from 9500 to 8900 B.C. The existence of Clovis culture is well documented; however, several other sites such as Meadowcroft Shelter in Pennsylvania and Monte Verde in Chile may have revealed very early dates of human habitation. This subject is an ongoing debate among the archaeological community.

Little survives from the life of the Clovis people, but they probably had few possessions. Because they traveled extensively, objects had to be effective, lightweight, and portable. The basic tools with which they hunted and butchered included fluted projectile points, as well as cutting and scraping tools. The points referred to as Clovis points are three to six inches long, sharpened stones chipped from larger pieces of rock, referred to as cores. A hammer stone delivered the precisely aimed blow to the core, breaking off small flakes, and creating a taper from a sharp end to a blunt, wide base. Further modification fine-tuned the shape of the point and the sharpness of the edges, yielding a spear tip or cutting blade. Clovis points are marked by a central channel extending one-third of the way from base to tip. This channel provided a secure resting place for the spear or knife handle and is considered an important technological advance. The whole piece could be ruined by one errant blow, so flint knapping had to be a highly prized skill to early hunters. Not all rock made acceptable points and Clovis people both traveled and traded to get the material they wanted.

Not surprisingly, most of these points are found at kill sites, where animals fell to human hunters. Large mammals died of wounds from the stone points that were thrust or thrown at them. Clearly, many such stabs would have been required to bring down a huge

Clovis Points. BigStockPhoto.com

animal. The atlatl represents a major advantage for human hunters. It is a spear thrower that increases the leverage of the human arm. A wooden or bone shaft has a hook for holding the spear on one end and a handle on the other. The hunter holds the atlatl with spear attached and snaps his arm forward, sending the spear on a straighter, faster, and more powerful arc. In use in both Siberia and Mexico, atlatls may well have aided the Clovis hunters.

With or without the spear thrower, a mammoth with eight-foot tusks posed a formidable challenge to stone age hunters. The animals probably moved in herds like modern elephants and in predictable patterns. Kill sites are often found near water sources where the animals may have been caught off guard with limited mobility. Although challenging to kill, such a large animal rewarded the hunter with plentiful supplies of meat, fat, tusks, bones, and pelts for myriad uses. The large Ice Age bison also provided an important food resources for early hunters.

Although large mammal hunting clearly provided critical protein supplies to the tenth century B.C. Clovis hunters, evidence suggests

they had a broad-based economy. People may have exploited small mammals such as raccoons, badgers, and mice, as well as reptiles and reptile eggs. This diversification would prove increasingly critical to North American residents as climate changes altered their world. The lush conditions of the earlier glacial period gave way to a drier period when springs and lakes dried up. The increasing drought conditions reduced the carrying capacity of the region and concentrated prey species at water sources, thus maximizing human hunters' success. The climatic change, perhaps coupled with increased hunting pressure, pushed the large fauna species to extinction.

As smaller animals, such as bison, replaced the larger species, so too did people known as Folsom, from the site in New Mexico, replace Clovis hunters on the landscape from the Southwest throughout the Great Plains. Folsom projectile points are smaller, more completely fluted, and of more refined workmanship than Clovis. They were used to hunt the ancient bison (*Bison antiquus*) that thrived on the expanded grasslands of the Midwest, referred to as the "Great bison belt." Bison were nomadic and so too were their predators. Folsom people moved in small family groups, leaving little trace on the land, but returning often to favored spots like Lindenmeier, Colorado. Hunters exploited the bison's herd instincts, stampeding large groups toward natural obstacles such as cliffs or sand banks, where they could be exploited. Driving a herd over a cliff or into a canyon corral required intimate knowledge of the area, careful planning, and cooperation. Men came together to take advantage of this rich resource and women waited out of danger of the confused and frightened beasts, ready to help with butchering and preparing the products of the hunt. After a successful drive the long process of butchering began. Meat, hide, internal organs, hoofs, and horns came off the carcass for use by humans. Virtually every part of the animal offered something to people, from important protein to material for spoons and sinews for rope. Thus the bison were important to these early hunters. Like the Clovis culture before them, however, Folsom people also ate duck, deer, pronghorn, rabbit, turtle, wolf, prairie dog, mountain sheep, and marmot. A diverse diet enhanced their chances for success, as the availability of prey could vary seasonally and annually, so varied food sources often meant sustainability.

Life for the early Clovis and Folsom people was much more than mere subsistence. These people had a social, political, and probably

spiritual life. It is more difficult to find concrete evidence about these cultural aspects, but we can build some picture of their lifestyle by considering the cultural traits of more contemporary hunting groups such as Inuit in the Arctic or Naskapi Indians of Labrador.

The family would have been the unit of reference for early Americans. On a daily basis, that small group would be each person's reference, their source of identity as husband and father or wife and mother. Each family member's position reflected their contribution to the group. Because hunting provided the main source of food, and without a hunter a family faced failure, males in the prime of life held positions of power and authority in the family and the band. Bands consisted of perhaps five or more families, probably related by blood, who hunted and camped in the same territory. Males spent their young lives training for the role of provider and political leader that they would assume at adulthood. Boys learned to know the landscape and to understand, predict, and respect the animals they hunted. Years of play with weapons honed skills necessary on the hunt. By the time a male reached maturity, he knew his home territory and its inhabitants intimately. That accumulation of knowledge was a great achievement that directly affected a man's, and thus his family's, chance of survival. Therefore social practices protected that asset by keeping men in their home territory after marriage and requiring women to relocate. Most cultures, including these early Americans, avoided incest by requiring marriage outside of the band. As a result girls found themselves moving away from family and the territory of their childhood to start a new life among strangers.

Like social organization, spirituality supported survival. Because hunting success equaled human success, the spirits that controlled the hunt were important to people. Groups that rely on the hunt for survival often give respect to the spirits of the animals. Animals must not be disrespected by wanton killing, waste, or disrespectful treatment. Hunters would pray to the animals' spirit hoping to appease the animal so that its brothers would allow themselves to be killed and so that its own spirit would be renewed. To that end, the carcass had to be treated reverently, butchered properly, and certain parts disposed of ritually. Clovis and Folsom hunters may have regarded prey mammals as kin who gave their lives for the continued life of humans. If so, they likely treated the animals with kindness in return.

The world of hunting, ritual, and frequent travel that Clovis and Folsom hunters developed did not last that long. Major climactic changes swept through America as the Ice Age ended after 10000 B.C. The resulting landscape was both familiar and yet drastically altered as familiar plants and animals once used as food sources now disappeared. The extinction of the megafauna changed human life forever. Mammoths, mastodons, dire wolves, saber-tooth cats, sloths, and giant bison were unable to successfully exist in the new landscape. They gradually died out, to be replaced by more viable species. The enormous mammals of the Pleistocene epoch did not adapt to the post-Ice Age world; their predators did, simply turning to different prey for subsistence.

As ancient Americans turned the corner from the glacial to the nonglacial world, from the Pleistocene to the Holocene epochs, their culture changed. They could not live the same way they had before in a world without mastodons. They had to adapt their hunting skills, technology, and migration patterns. These adaptations depended increasingly on the availability of local resources. Equipped with basic technology and flexibility, these people, referred to as Archaic Indians, spread out across America and conformed their lifestyle to the region around them. About 10,000 years ago, they began to develop distinct regional cultural adaptations that can be loosely grouped according to ecosystem and are here divided into seven areas. Ancient Americans would continue to face periods of environmental change. One such period was the Altithermal, a time of increased temperatures and reduced rainfall that occurred across the continent from around 5000 B.C. to 3000 B.C. This climate change affected each region differently, encouraging settlement in some areas while dooming it in others. As people adapted to new challenges, they became more distinct and developed unique adaptations. In many cases these adaptations persisted nearly unchanged right up to the period of European contact. This is the story of the peoples of ancient North America.

NOTES

1. Demus Elm and Harvey Antone, translated by Bryan Gick, *The Oneida Creation Story* (Lincoln: University of Nebraska Press, 2000).

2. Raven finds the First Men. This site retells native creation stories. http://eldrbarry.net/rabb/rvn/first.htm.

FURTHER READING

Coe, Michael, Dean Snow, and Elizabeth Benson. *Atlas of Ancient North America*. New York: Facts on File, 1996

Fagan, Brian M. *Ancient North America*. London: Thames and Hudson, 1991.

Gibbon, Guy E. *Archaeology of Prehistoric Native America: An Encyclopedia*. New York: Routledge, 1998.

Haynes, Gary. *The Early Settlement of North America: The Clovis Era*. Cambridge: Cambridge University Press, 2002.

Jablonski, Nina, ed. *The First Americans: The Pleistocene Colonization of the New World*. Berkeley: University of California Press, 2002.

Madsen, David B. *Entering America*. Salt Lake City: University of Utah Press, 2004.

Native Americans. This Web site has a wide range of information organized by tribe as well as several sections on early inhabitants. http://www.kidinfo.com/American_History/Native_Americans.html (accessed September 1, 2007).

Paleoamerican Origins. This is the Smithsonian Institution's scholarly discussion of the origins of early Americans. http://www.si.edu/Encyclopedia_SI/nmnh/origin.htm (accessed September 1, 2007).

Peregrine, Peter N., and Melvin Ember, eds. *Encyclopedia of Prehistory*. Vol. 6: North America. New York: Kluwer Academic/Plenum, 2001.

Pringle, Heather. *In Search of Ancient North America: An Archaeological Journey to Forgotten Cultures*. New York: Wiley, 1996.

Thomas, David Hurst. *Exploring Native North America*. New York: Oxford University Press, 2000.

Turnmire, Robson Bonnichsen, and Karen L. Turnmire, eds. *Ice Age People of North America*. Corvallis: Oregon State University Press, 1999.

West, Frederick Hadleigh, ed. *American Beginnings: The Prehistory and Palaeoecology of Beringia*. Chicago: University of Chicago Press, 1998.

Chronology

28000 B.C.	Humans living on Santa Rosa Island, off coast of California
28000–10000	Late Pleistocene exposes Beringia, wave of migration
12000	Paleo-Indians settle nonglacial areas of the Americas
11000	Evidence of paleo-Indian settlement in Colorado
10000	Paleo-Indians live in Saugus, Massachusetts for the next 11,000 years, only to be destroyed by the Puritans in the seventeenth century.
10000–7000	Last Ice Age floods Beringia and cuts off further land-based migrations
11000–6000	Paleo-Indians live in North America
9200–8200	Clovis hunters
9000	Danger Cave, Utah; Meadowcroft Rockshelter, Pennsylvania occupied
8800–8200	Folsom hunters
8000–1000	Fishing, shellfish economy dominate southern California
8000	Arctic microblade tools

7000	Climate change drastically alters the lifeways of paleo-Indians by removing large mammals and creating vast grasslands and forests
6000	Paleo-Indian adjustments to new environment includes diverse food gathering techniques using specific tools such as stone points, bone whistles, scrapers, fish hooks
	Sea mammal hunters live on Aleutian islands
	Salmon runs on Columbia River cease and resume after landslide A.D. 1265
5500	Encinitas culture in southern California; food-grinding implements appear
5000	Maize first cultivated in Tehuacan Valley in central Mexico
	Athabaskans migrate south from Alaska into western sub-Arctic
	Algonquians migrate into eastern sub-Arctic from northeastern woodlands
4500	Watson Brake mounds: oldest circular monument in North America
4000	Koster site in Illinois: permanent hunting base camps
	Danger Cave artifacts similar to those of historic period
3000	Red Paint Archaic culture
	Aleut and Inuit migrate from Siberia to western Alaska
2500	Evidence of Archaic fish traps in Northeast
2000	Inuit small tool tradition; Aleut sea mammal hunting
	Poverty Point, Louisiana residents cultivated four crops
	Great Lakes inhabitants mine and work copper
	Coastal California develops maritime subsistence patterns
1500	Southeastern Indians produce fired earthenware
	Mounds built at Poverty Point, Louisiana

1400	Adena cultures develop: first burial mounds
1000	Archaic cultures wane in East
	Inuit small tool tradition gives way to local cultures
	Ancestral Northwest Coast cultures evident
800	Dorset culture develops in Arctic
750	Ohio Valley: Adena and Hopewell cultures build large temple mounds; extensive burial objects show refined artistic skills
700 B.C.–A.D. 1500	Woodland tradition in Northeast
500 B.C.	Norton culture develops in Arctic
300	Arizona: Hohokam farm Gila and Salt River region
200	Mogollon culture develops
100	Hopewell build effigy mounds in shape of serpent
	Mounds built at Etowah, Georgia, Spiro, Oklahoma, Moundville, Alabama
	Early Anasazi develops
A.D. 1	Cedar canoe carving in Northwest
	Arizona: Hohokam culture begins extensive irrigation projects near Phoenix
100	Dorset Eskimos colonize Newfoundland
200	Adena cultures wane
300	Ipiutak culture evolves from Norton in Arctic
400	Settlement of Four Corners region (Arizona, Colorado, Utah, New Mexico) by Anasazi
400	Plains Woodland culture emerges
500	Hohokam build ball courts styled after Mesoamerican courts
	Sinagua culture develops from Anasazi and Mogollon migrants
	Northwest Coast emphasis on wealth; stratification well established
550	Hopewell cult wanes
600	Early Mississippians build large mounds at Spiro, Oklahoma

700	Mississippian culture develops: temple mounds, painted pottery
	Anasazi pueblo period begins
750	Plains Woodland culture wanes
800	Mogollon culture in Arizona produced elegant Mimbres pottery
825	Apache bands break from northern Athabaskans and migrate south
900	Plains village culture develops
900–1250	Height of Mississippian culture centered at St. Louis; highly centralized, agriculturally supported group produces elaborate grave goods and large platform mounds.
950	Anasazi centers at Chaco Canyon, Mesa Verde flourish
1000	Mississippian fully formed with southern ceremonial complex
	Fremont culture in Great Basin
	Thule culture in Arctic: traditional Eskimo technology—igloos, dogsleds, stone lamps
1025	Ancestral Navajo bands follow Apache south
1100–1300	Anasazi construct multistory dwellings in cliff openings in canyons
1119–1180	Anasazi create 500 miles of road to connect Pueblo Bonito to outside
1200	Hohokam build Great House at Casa Grande
1275	Anasazi culture stressed by drought and Athabaskans contracts
1300	Peak of indigenous population in North America: 12–15 million
1350	Mogollon abandon villages
1390	Haudenosaunee (Iroquois) unify in a league of friendship that will ensure their strength in the Northeast
1398	Last Hohokam settlement at Casa Grande destroyed by Apache
1450	Hohokam irrigation agriculture collapses
1470	Droughts cause contraction of High Plains villages

1

The Northeast

The area of the country that anthropologists designate as eastern culture extends from the Mississippi River east to the Atlantic and from the Gulf of Mexico northward to the Great Lakes. If the east is defined, as it is by some scholars, by the ability to grow maize, then it pushes a bit north of the lakes. In both ancient and modern times, because of the variation in climate resulting from latitude, we actually have two separate regions—the northeast and the southeast. The northern portion was strongly shaped by glaciations. After the Ice Age this area was characterized by heavy forests; thus the east supports essentially a woodland lifestyle throughout the region and so is often referred to as the eastern woodlands. The term *Woodland* refers to a period of culture that followed the Archaic tradition (after 1000 B.C.) in the east. This Woodland tradition is defined by three traits: agriculture, distinctive ceramics, and constructed funerary mounds. In some regions it was replaced by later cultures such as the Mississippian in the southeast, but in the northeast the Woodland way of life persisted up to the period of European contact. The Algonquian and Iroquois are the best examples of terminal Woodland lifestyles in the northeast.

FLORA, FAUNA, GEOGRAPHY

The eastern woodlands in the centuries before European arrival were heavily forested. Dense old-growth forest boasting huge

ancient specimens blanketed the land. Northeastern natives lived among dark woods with few openings except those they made themselves. In the mid-Atlantic region mostly deciduous species such as oak, maple, and hickory predominated; coniferous fir, pine, and spruce intermixed as the woods spread northward to the Arctic. The landscape of early native Americans was permanently shaped by the Ice Age, which covered most of the Northeast in glaciers. The ancient Appalachian mountain chain thrust upward in a slice running northeast, and in its northern section harbored the east's highest peak—*Agiocochook* (Mt. Washington, New Hampshire) at 6,288 feet. The north-south alignment of this important range allowed animals and humans to migrate easily. Species occurring in northern latitudes could move to southern latitudes at higher elevation and find similar conditions. The area is rich in water resources. Thousands of rivers, streams, and small creeks bisect the land, many following the north-south alignment of the mountains, again providing migration routes for humans and animals. The flowing water feeds lakes, ponds, and wetlands, which in turn support a wide variety of aquatic life. The Northeast is among the richest temperate regions, supporting hundreds of species of mammals, birds, fish, and reptiles in addition to abundant plant life.

The abundant variety of plants and animals, which translated into rich food resources for early Americans, appeared after the Ice Age. The northeastern topography, climate, and species had been forever altered by the effects of glaciation. When the Ice Age ended and the glaciers retreated, a new landscape was revealed. The ice sheet had sculpted, carved, and reshaped the land. A great deal of material had been removed to create areas like the Great Lakes, and in other places it had been deposited, as for example the arm at the end of Cape Cod. The end of the Ice Age also brought on rapid changes in climate and in flora and fauna species. The year could now be divided into four distinct seasons in the East, with increased seasonal extremes of both warm and cold. Initially, the postglacial changes would have been quite rapid. Numerous species went extinct and humans had to adapt to a rapidly changing environment. As prey species disappeared hunters had to either switch resources or change territories. In the northern forests there likely would not have been enough edible plant materials to support people. The only choice would have been to move territories. This can be a problematic strategy in areas of dense settlement where movement triggers conflict; however, early northeastern populations were light enough to

make movement practical. The paleo-Indian technology was easily transferable.

   Hunter-gatherers began moving to exploit resources, particularly
animal sources of protein. In the Eastern Archaic period before 5000
B.C., the residents of the Northeast followed the big game hunting
traditions, which sustained humans throughout much of the continent. This successful exploitation of resources led to a steady rise
in population. Deer to the south, caribou in the far north, and sea
mammals on the northern coast sustained human life for thousands
of years. After 5000 B.C., the regional diversity occurring across the
continent began to shape the Northeast. At this time the descendants of the big game hunters began exploiting the smaller game
species. Little remains of the lives of these hunters. A few rock
shards showing human use, scattered bones from a meal, charred
earth from a campfire are all that exists to tell us their story. One of
the most important sites for understanding the lifestyle of eastern
Archaic hunter-gatherers is the rock shelter in southwestern Pennsylvania known as Meadowcroft. The shelter was naturally carved
into the sandstone rock on the bank of Cross Creek 7 1/2 miles
from the Ohio River, near Pittsburgh, Pennsylvania. It must have
been a welcome shelter for hunter-gatherers traveling through the
area. Although it is now 49 feet wide and 20 feet deep with a 43 foot
ceiling, evidence shows that it used to be much larger. Its discovery and analysis challenge the common belief that humans settled
eastern America only by 10000 B.C. The main researcher of the site,
Dr. James Adovasio, believes his discoveries show people living at
this site thousands of years before accepted dates of Clovis people.
Some of the artifacts may date to as early as 17000 B.C. As archaeologists dug down to the level corresponding to 10000 B.C., they
found a three-inch spear point that was not fluted like the Clovis
points, which were believed to be the earliest evidence of human
weapons. There were points made from a variety of stone—West
Virginia chert, Ohio flint, and Pennsylvania jasper. From 13000 B.C.,
bones, wood, shells, basketry, and cordage remain. This shows that
people spent a considerable amount of time in this place and that
women, often responsible for basketry, were probably present. We
tend to know more about males than females in these early cultures
because their lives are associated with the less perishable stone artifacts, but it seems clear from the available evidence that people of
both sexes used the rock shelter over tens of thousands of years. The
Meadowcroft rock shelter remains somewhat controversial because
of its very early dates for human occupation of the Northeast.

Other sites have also challenged the accepted timeline of the New World. In southern Virginia at Cactus Hill, excavated tools appear to predate Clovis points. These quartzite blades, blade fragments, and spear points seem to have been made nearly 15,000 years ago. Such early dates always generate controversy among archaeologists, and there is rarely agreement on evidence that challenges the established understanding of early occupancy in a region. It seems likely that our perception of early humans in the Northeast will continue to evolve as more and more evidence comes to light.

There are other locations indicating early human habitation in the Northeast, including the Debert site in Nova Scotia dating to about 8500 B.C., the Bull Brooke site in New England, and the Plenge site in New Jersey. Elk, caribou, deer, and rodent bones were found in proximity to fluted points. These sites may have served as a sort of base camp for large groups of game hunters in the Paleolithic period. Archaeological evidence reveals a variety of Archaic Indian cultures. The Neville culture was located in New England around 6000 B.C. and has left behind examples of polished stone. Neville sites along river beds indicate that people relied on fish and other aquatic creatures to supplement their diet. As with most Archaic cultures, only artifacts of durable material such as choppers, axes, and scrapers remain to indicate what was once a thriving society.

As people continued to live successfully through the generations, their world changed around them. The sea level that had been affected by glaciation had stabilized by 4500 B.C. This allowed shellfish beds to grow along the shore, which would provide an important resource for coastal residents. As the temperatures warmed, other food sources expanded their ranges, such as the hickory tree whose nuts fed both humans and game animals. Fish species like salmon, smelt, shad, sturgeon, and herring thrived in the waters of the Northeast. In one spot on Penobscot Bay, Maine, late Archaic people used deer, moose, mink, seal, walrus, beaver, river otter, fisher, bear, swordfish, cod, sturgeon, sculpin, mallard, black and oldsquaw ducks, geese, loon, eagle, and shellfish. Such an abundance of resources naturally encouraged relatively dense populations.

One group that thrived in the late Archaic, around 2000 B.C, was named Lamoka after a site in central New York. Archaeological work revealed a substantial village of 27 rectangular houses. The Lamoka culture enjoyed success hunting deer, pigeons, and turkeys, as well as catching fish in small lakes and streams. They made stone adzes, chisels, mortars, knives of beaver tooth, and even tools of copper. Their burial sites reveal shell pendants, combs, and turtle shell flutes,

which suggests a society with the time and inclination to enjoy personal decoration and music. It also allows us a window into their belief system, which must have included a journey or afterlife for the deceased. Corpses were buried with red ocher and artifacts of daily life, and even cremated remains received burials with objects. Some objects were buried without any human remains, which may have been part of a renewal ritual held when acorns and hickory nuts ripened. Burial pits heavily sprinkled with red ocher have been found in coastal northern New England, prompting the name red ocher culture. The sites also contained tools for heavy woodworking, most likely to construct dugout canoes. These people used stone tools for heavy work, but they also used slate for thin, smooth knives and spear points, as well as copper in pendants, beads, and bracelets.

The Lamoka obviously were not the only ones who held strong beliefs about the dead. The Orient lived in present day Delaware, New Jersey, and Long Island around 1200–750 B.C. They cremated their dead and placed the remains in large pits, containing numerous personal effects, and sprinkled with red ochre. Pottery decorated with cording imprints served as containers for food and valuables. Another group, the Owasco people, lived in New York around A.D. 1000–1300, near Owasco Lake, for which they are named. Their camps were found on higher ground or near marshes, which facilitated access to hunting and fishing. They were also early cultivators of corn, beans, and squash, a surplus of which could be stored in the Oswego's distinct pottery vessels. The Oswego immediately predate the Woodland cultures that dominated the Northeast up to and beyond European contact.

These traditions, or cultures, as anthropologists refer to them, naturally developed gradually and at different rates in each area. A region like the far Northeast, on the Canadian Shield, was characterized by boreal forest and tundra. Agriculture would never thrive here so inhabitants remained reliant on game hunting, especially caribou. Fish and an unreliable supply of edible plants rounded out an economy that could not support large numbers of people. So an area like this continued to exhibit late Archaic traditions; people to the south moved onto a more complex cultural pattern.

WOODLAND TRADITION

The Woodland tradition represents a change in ideology and subsistence and developed gradually out of the Archaic culture. Anthropologist Merwyn Garbarino identifies the Woodland tradition in

the Northeast as beginning about 1000 B.C., although others make it later at 700 B.C., when traditions of mounding burials with earth, intensive use of plants, and pottery creation can be seen. Similar developments, but of greater concentration, arose in the southeast around A.D. 1000 and resulted in temple moundbuilding and intensive corn agriculture. Charles Hudson describes it as probably the most distinctive, the most completely indigenous culture ever to exist in eastern North America. Woodland culture is generally recognized by characteristics such as the exploitation of local resources, widespread use of pottery, supplemental agriculture, and elaborate mortuary customs.

Anthropologists generally divide the Woodland tradition into three parts: early Woodland dating from about 700 B.C. to A.D. 700, middle Woodland from there to A.D. 1200, and late Woodland beginning about A.D. 1200 and continuing into the period of European contact. Distinct cultural changes eventually marked out a new era; however, old cultural practice also remained vibrant. For example, at the end of the late Archaic period, simple round cooking bowls were made of soapstone. They have been found in occupation sites that showed no evidence of permanent dwellings, suggesting a seminomadic people; however, the same sites have burials that include artifacts such as the soapstone bowls. The carved stone vessels would be replaced by the pottery of a sedentary people in the woodland period, and the burial of such artifacts would continue to be a persistent cultural tradition.

This appearance of pottery is the general marker of the transition from late Archaic to early Woodland culture. Throughout the Northeast, the so-called Woodland ceramic tradition of dark-brown, grit-tempered pottery existed throughout the Woodland period. The only similar pottery style occurring at the same time is in northwestern Europe and northern Asia. Early Woodland people also created tobacco pipes. They must therefore have cultivated tobacco plants to have a reliable supply of leaves for smoking. The desire to tend a patch of favored plants for recreational or spiritual use eventually transformed into a dependence on specific crops for a substantial portion of the community's food supply and thus a serious commitment to agriculture. This commitment transformed northeastern societies from mobile groups of hunter-gatherers or collectors to more sedentary groups of part-time farmers.

Adena

In the Ohio region, a group of hunter-gatherers slowly developed a unique lifestyle, beginning around 1000 B.C. Anthropologists have

dubbed this the Adena culture after a modern-day estate where evidence was discovered, near Chillicothe, Ohio. The Ohio valley proved to be a profitable area for the early stages of sedentary lifestyle and the people here thrived. The Adena made a good living from the abundant resources of the eastern forests. The richness of food and water allowed them the wealth and leisure to engage in trade as well as public building projects. We regard this as a culture because the developing Woodland tradition began to link villages into a social, religious, and economic structure.

The basis of the Adena's success was the environment. The rich flood plains and bottom lands of the Mississippi drainage system supported a wide range of flora and fauna. The woods provided excellent habitat for woodland animals. Here men could hunt large herds of white-tailed deer or the larger elk, flocks of turkeys, and black bear fattened on berries and grubs. They used stone tipped spears to kill their prey. The streams in the region also provided resources for the cooking pot. Turtles, mussels, and a variety of fish could be obtained with nets and snares. The protein segment of the Adena diet was supplemented by extensive gathering of seasonally available plants, such as walnuts and chestnuts in the fall, or raspberries in the summer. These people certainly could have made a viable living by hunting and gathering as their ancestors had done for millennia; however, that was always a somewhat unpredictable lifestyle so the certainty of food stuffs had a definite attraction. This desire to predict and to some extent control the availability of their food supply led early Americans to begin gardening. This was far from full-blown maize agriculture when it started as the sowing of indigenous plant seeds in lightly prepared spots close to villages. As their skill and dependence on horticulture increased, the Adena expanded their efforts, growing tobacco for smoking as well as edible plants. Maize, particularly cold-resistant varieties, would come to later residents of the region.

So the Adena people built a stable lifestyle in the Ohio River valley. They hunted, fished, gathered, and gardened fairly close to their villages. They did not construct the monumental, permanent dwellings of the early Southwest, but lived more simply. In groups of about a dozen, their round homes were built of posts supporting cane or other flexible material for walls. Thatch covered the roofs of these small homes intended for sheltering immediate family members. Central fire pits provided warmth and cooking, although much of the daily tasks would have been accomplished outside. The Adena must have been skilled in the use of fibrous plant materials, creating not only homes, but also woven mats, bags, blankets,

and clothing by finger weaving. They even decorated their pottery with the impression of cording.

Although they were self-sufficient, the Adena were not isolated. The relative bounty and prosperity of their lives allowed them to reach outward and engage in trade with outsiders. Much of what they sought in trade would be considered luxury items. Copper from the Great Lakes was beautiful and malleable and could be worked into various forms, primarily for decoration. Similarly, sheets of mica from North Carolina were too fragile for tool use, but created impressive decorative art. Even marine shells traded up from the Gulf of Mexico could be drilled, incised, and added to other exotic materials to create bracelets, gorgets, and effigies. These specialized items, made of valuable materials purely for enjoyment, became treasured objects to the Adena, which were usually buried with their owners.

The Adena must have believed in some sort of afterlife for their people because burials contained such items. Like many other native peoples who live close to nature, they thought that animals had spirits. Because they depended heavily on the availability of animals, the Adena sought to appease these spirits with ritual. Shamans wore deer antler headdresses and were buried with their ceremonial wolf jaws. Even stronger commitment to their belief in animal spirits is the effigy mounds they left behind. The range of intentionally constructed mounds at Adena sites goes from low hills piled over bones to the huge Grave Creek mound, 70 feet high. The existence of these large earthworks shows that the Adena had a common sense of purpose and probably effective leadership structure to organize and direct what must have been decades of construction by thousands of people. Burials occur in stages of a mound's construction, leaving us a sort of family history of the people over several generations. The style of interment reflects status in life. With space at a premium, only the rich and important could recline in death; ordinary people's bodies were curled up. Elite status could be determined even in death by the red paint and jewelry, masks, and ornamental objects crafted from imported materials. The other fascinating remnant of this early Woodland society is their effigy mound construction. These are not burial mounds, but rather three-dimensional renderings of animals. It seems that the Adena began working in this tradition, while later residents of the region developed a more intensive moundbuilding culture.

One of the most amazing and enduring testaments to ancient beliefs is the serpent mound of Ohio. This intriguing structure

stretches along a bluff of Brush Creek in southwestern Ohio. It has existed for centuries, yet the origins, construction, and intended use of the mound remain somewhat mysterious. It was originally thought that the Adena people constructed the earth work; however, recent dating has placed it in the eleventh century, in a culture known as the Fort Ancient tradition, which shared many characteristics with the Adena and Hopewell people. Far more than a simple pile of dirt such as a conical or even platform mound, this structure is clearly designed to represent a serpent. The snake shape twists and writhes along the ground, ending with an open mouth. The creature's mouth seems to grasp an elliptical object, perhaps an egg, or a symbolic eye, or even a heart. The snake's coils are sinuous and even, truly a work of art; however, this is art on a grand scale. The serpent mound is 5 feet high, 20 feet wide, and 1,254 feet long. These large proportions are impressive even in the age of machinery, but become more incredible when placed in a period of strictly human labor.

Excavations revealed that the shape of the serpent had been outlined with small stones and lumps of clay. This formal, designed outlined then guided the much larger task of building up the structure. Individuals would fill and carry woven baskets of yellow clay and dump each one within the markers, slowly creating the huge mound. This would have taken a long time, even with extensive human labor, and so its completion represents a major commitment to a single purpose and probably an effective organizational structure to manage the operation over time. Considering the effort required to produce the serpent should shed light on its purpose. It must have been important to many people, as well as to the culture as a whole, to command such dedication. Yet we still do not truly know why it was built.

Most experts assume it was an honoring or memorializing feature meant to impress a spirit. Some local Indians believed that it represented Ursa Major and Minor—Big and Little Dippers; however, its most impressive feature is also its most curious. At 5 feet high and more than 1,000 feet long, the serpent cannot be appreciated from the ground. From a human perspective it is not immediately impressive as are pyramids or platform temples that rise up majestically in front of the viewer. The average person confronts a long curving bank at about head level. The beauty and the actual shape of the serpent are revealed only from an aerial perspective, which is easy to obtain in the twenty-first century, but unknown in the eleventh. Thus these effigy mounds appear to confirm that ancient

Native Americans gave great importance to the sky and world above the earth.

The concept of producing monumental earthworks was not unique to the makers of the serpent in Ohio. This type of effigy moundbuilding apparently spread fairly widely around the region. A site named Azatlan in the southeast corner of Wisconsin yielded ruins of a 20-acre fortified riverbank center containing bird- and animal-shaped earthworks. One of the largest surviving concentration of mounds are the Great Bear, Little Bear, and Marching Bear groups now preserved at Effigy Mounds National Monument. This collection of clustered effigies lies along the bank of the Mississippi River on the Iowa border. More than 200 mounds built between the seventh and fourteenth centuries remain after centuries of farming, environmental changes, and other disruptions. Excavations of noneffigy mounds have yielded a rock altar, a great deal of charcoal, as well as burials, testifying to the ceremonial and sacred importance of the sites. Finding extended burials, bundled burials, as well as cremation remains reveals long-term use of the mounds as cultural practices changed. Numerous artifacts such as bone awls, copper and pearl beads, clamshells, eastern pottery, and a copper breastplate reveal an extensive trade network bringing luxury items to the area. Some of the most intriguing creations of the ancient builders are the 10 bears and 3 birds that appear to be marching across the landscape. Clearly conceived and planned for a reason, these effigies may have been territorial markers, boundaries of ceremonial lands, symbols of family affiliations to spirits, or representations of astronomical observations like the Big Dipper. The Adena and related cultures started a thriving lifestyle characterized by prosperity based on abundant natural resources, trade, and a growing ceremonial life. Future generations built on the successes of the Adena and embellished them.

A culture identified as Hopewell is such an example. Hopewell sites date to A.D. 200–700 and were long regarded as a separate group from the Adena; however, research now suggests that this represents a continuation of the previous culture. The Hopewell may be described as bigger, better, and more than their ancestors; they increased the existing trends of the cultures centered in the Ohio River drainage by engaging in more intense agriculture, religion, and artistic expression. The people lived in larger villages of more than 100 residents. People still subsisted on the richness of the resources, hunting and gathering mammals, birds, fish, fruits, and seeds in abundance. Solitary hunters seeking small mammals used such strategies as stalking, decoys, and traps and snares. As in

the past, males continued to take the role of hunters and fishermen, warriors, traders, and craftsmen. Women prepared foodstuffs both for consumption and storage by smoking or drying. They gathered most of the fruit and vegetable products consumed by the family in addition to caring for children and the home. Small gardens supplemented the wild supply, growing squash, marsh elder, sunflower, maygrass, and knotweed. Women made the pottery vessels used for cooking and storage, as well as the tanned skin or woven fiber clothing worn by both sexes. Men wore loincloths, women wore calf-length skirts without tops except in winter when everyone added fur and woven robes for warmth.

The bounty the Hopewell gained from the land produced surpluses, which in turn fed a more widespread trade network, bringing exotic materials from afar. The Hopewell became masters at using the waterways for transportation. Men paddled canoes along streams leading to the Missouri, Great Lakes, and eventually the St. Lawrence and Hudson River systems. From these far-flung contacts came obsidian, turtle shells, copper, and other rare substances. These luxury items had little practical use and are generally regarded as materials for the expression of art. Hopewell culture clearly had the wealth and inclination to support a class of artisans dedicated to producing ceremonial objects. Those that have survived as artifacts are truly impressive.

Religion and ceremony bound the Hopewell culture together. Moundbuilding on a large scale was clearly a group effort and some large projects must have served as ceremonial centers for several villages. At Hopewell, Ohio, 38 mounds occupied a 110-acre enclosure. This concentration probably was a ceremonial area to serve various villages. A road system may have connected outlying villages to the major religious sites, similar to that built in the Southwest for the same purpose. A society exhibiting extensive religious, economic, and social systems was stratified on the basis of wealth and power. The Hopewell chiefs who could direct large communal undertakings received honor in both life and death. Although most dead were cremated, the elite received full body burials along with numerous grave offerings. Typically, a chief's body was laid out in a specially constructed log mortuary house, alone or with the bodies of women and children, probably his relatives, and surrounded by the cremated remains of those who had died in service to him. Grave goods were added, then the entire structure was burned and heaped over with dirt to form a mound. The grave goods excavated from burial mounds show us the wealth and artistry of Hopewell society. Some bodies had been covered with freshwater pearls and

beads, more than 40,000 in one grave. Shell beads, silver nuggets, and copper jewelry also adorned the dead. Beautifully crafted stone pipes depicting various animals, effigy pottery, pounded silver, and mica silhouettes attest to the skill of Hopewell artisans. The burial of these highest forms of art and craftsmanship both honored the dead and guaranteed the continuation of the trade network and artistic traditions to supply future generations.

At Hopewell sites we see the increasing focus of the living on the rituals for the dead. This trend was to continue and reach its greatest expression in a cult of the dead that was the most defining aspect of a civilization known as Mississippian. The Hopewell themselves seem to have faced challenges that caused an abandonment of their trading and moundbuilding traditions by A.D. 400, but the individuals of the society remained in the region, serving as a bridge to the next great civilization in Middle America. As the most powerful examples of Mississippian culture occurred in the Southeast, they are discussed in Chapter 2.

AGRICULTURE

The lifestyle of inhabitants of the rest of the Northeast changed drastically with the arrival of agriculture. The inclusion of agriculture in the lifestyles of the region took longer than elsewhere because a species of maize had to evolve that withstood the harsher climate and shorter growing seasons. Maize appeared in the East in the period A.D. 800–1000, but an important new variety called eastern Flint arrived by A.D. 1200. These cobs with paired rows of kernels were probably domesticated in Guatemala and then spread north. This variety, which thrives in cool, moist climates, was perfect for the East. The Hopewell people discussed in Chapter 3 may have introduced agriculture to the Northeast. From their base in the Midwest Hopewell traders traveled on an extensive network that facilitated the spread of new ideas and objects. Seeds from new strains of maize could also have moved along these corridors of trade and commerce. Although residents of the Northeast never became as dependent on agriculture as those in the Southwest, it did provide an important component of their diet and slowly altered their lifestyle patterns. In general, the farther north, the shorter the growing season and the less dependent on agriculture were the residents.

After good soil and the proper amount of sun and rain, the main requirement of growing maize is attention. Maize fields need atten-

tion to yield a successful crop. As northeasterners enjoyed more and more benefits from a reliable crop, they accepted the changes necessary to achieve that. The key requirement was to remain fairly sedentary, at least during the growing season. Thus northeastern natives settled into quasi-permanent village life. These northeastern villages did not resemble the large ceremonial centers of the Southeast, but sheltered several hundred people, most of whom were related. It appears that collections of people grew as their cultures matured all the way up to the European contact period. The village sites were chosen for their proximity to both good farmland and reliable hunting and gathering areas. This was not a difficult requirement in much of the Northeast, so people could move their villages fairly frequently. The same group of people might move their village several times within a person's lifetime to take advantage of fresh soil for their crops.

Lifestyle Changes

Agriculture changed a seminomadic people who moved seasonally with a regular pattern, to a fairly sedentary people tied to the location of their fields. At first agriculture was a secondary food source, but as inhabitants became more successful, crops took on a larger significance in their diet. They began to maintain permanent villages along with seasonal hunting camps. Many changes came with this alteration of economic and social organization. A steady food supply, obtained in one location, allowed for increased population, and a corresponding growth in house sizes. Sedentary behavior also allowed for the development of other culture traits.

The adoption of an agricultural base in the Northeast shaped the culture around a few main crops. The triad of maize, beans, and squash became the focus of subsistence for many groups. These three crops worked well together with beans returning nitrogen to the soil, which had been absorbed by growing corn. Still, fields could be played out within a decade of consistent farming. There were many more varieties of these foods than we currently use today, but they played a similar role in diets. Corn proved to be a major staple in Woodland life. It stored well and provided a stable food supply for lean winter months. Nearly every group in the Northeast that could grow maize did so. Indians ate it nearly daily, as corn cakes, corn bread, corn porridge, corn soup, and a brew made with parched corn. Some of the meals they enjoyed are still around today. For example, boiled beans and corn is what we

call succotash. Washing corn with wood ash loosened the hulls and created hominy, still prepared today. Berries, fresh, cooked, and dried, added flavor to meals, as did spices such as wild onions, ginger, and maple sugar.

Pottery was one of those distinct developments that marked the Woodland tradition. Pottery vessels can be used for storage as well as cooking, but do not lend themselves to a nomadic lifestyle. Pottery is far too fragile, bulky, and weighty to be moved frequently. Those who develop a sedentary lifestyle, however, find pottery to be a useful addition to their repertoire of tools. Women in the Woodland tradition made pottery from local sources of clay. They dug clay, formed it into a variety of vessel shapes, decorated, dried, and fired it. Throughout numerous generations the styles shifted and changed. The basic shape of the objects did not vary widely, although toward the end of the period the pots began to have shoulders, necks, and collars. The aspect of design that changed the most was decoration. Typically, pottery was decorated by marking the outer surface. Early pottery was marked by pressing a cord into the wet clay. By the early middle Woodland period, dentate decoration (toothlike impressions), as well as stamped designs, adorned the outside of vases. Still later, potters wrapped a stick with cord and pressed that into the clay to create parallel, horizontal, or vertical rows. Throughout the period, pottery decorations tended to be lineal or geometric rather than any kind of impressionistic designs. Pottery was widely distributed and traded frequently among groups so that particular styles might be found throughout the Northeast.

REGIONAL DISTINCTIONS

Throughout much of the Northeast the climactic and geographic conditions were similar. People living in the Northeast had far more in common than they would have with others outside the region. As a result of geography and reaction to changing conditions, however, distinct cultures arose in the Northeast. The major cultural groups can be loosely identified by language, as well as cultural adaptations. Although there were three distinct geographic areas of the East—the Northeast, the Southeast, and the Western Great Lakes—there also were three language groups. The Algonquian speakers lived from the western Great Lakes across to the northeast coast and then down the coast. Iroquoian speakers inhabited the eastern Great Lakes and Appalachian region, as well as isolated

areas farther south in the interior. Also, a small group of Siouan speakers lived south of the Iroquois.

Iroquois

The Iroquois probably trace their heritage to the Owasco cultural pattern of the eleventh century. Initially similar in culture and dialect, the Iroquois eventually clustered into five village groups that became known as the Mohawk, Onondaga, Oneida, Seneca, and Cayuga. The Iroquois became the dominant group in the area of modern-day New York and maintained that position for hundreds of years. The daily life of the Iroquois people changed little in the several hundred years before European contact, which enables us to draw a fairly complete picture of these northeastern residents.

The Iroquois, like other northeastern Woodland Indians, supported themselves by hunting, gathering, and agriculture. The forests, lakes, and streams around them teemed with a wide variety of plants and animals. Their geographic location allowed for fairly successful crop yields in most years, which provided a balanced diet. As the Iroquois became more dependent on crops, their lifestyle changed to accommodate that need. They became sedentary, residing near their fields and traveling to other resources. The Iroquois wholeheartedly embraced agriculture, coming closest to the Mississippian system of the Southeast (described in Chapter 2) of any group in the Northeast. They were basically the northeastern frontier of agriculture, and like the Mississippians, would come to play a dominant role in the trade and politics of the region.

The Iroquois lived in year-round villages. These were usually located at the fork of two streams, offering both a secure water supply and fishing and easy transportation. Each contained numerous longhouses and was surrounded by wooden palisades. Everyone resided within the palisade walls, but much of the surrounding area belonged to the village. Daily tasks such as hunting, fishing, gathering, farming, or quarrying stone drew people to the local resources; raiding might take men much farther away. Trails led toward other villages whose residents were also members of the tribe. The open space around the longhouses was used for activities such as drying meat, sweat lodges, and cooking fires. Everyone used the common space of the village, and clearly the village was a close-knit community. Most people were related, and everyone was known from birth to death. Many of these villages could get quite large. The Draper

This drawing depicts the European view of a
palisaded native village. Library of Congress.

site north of Toronto, Ontario, occupied from A.D. 1450–1500, spread
over 20 acres and housed 2,000 people in 37 longhouses.

The Longhouse

The Iroquoian longhouse is one of the most iconic native structures in the United States. It does not differ much in construction
from other eastern dwellings as it uses sapling and bark construction, but it does have a characteristic size and shape. Longhouses
resembled large barns, but were quite tall and could be as long as a
modern football field. The supporting elm saplings stood upright
about three feet apart, and heavier posts alternated with slimmer
secondary posts. The entire frame was covered with sheets of bark
collected by skilled craftsmen. Straight windowless walls reached
up to domed roofs into which smoke holes had been cut. A clever
system of shutters allowed the opening to be partially blocked
in inclement weather, thus offering a measure of protection to
inhabitants.

The longhouse structure was in fact a good design for comfortable shelter. Several fires running down the middle of the long axis provided heat and light to an otherwise dark structure. The fires, combined with the body heat of dozens of people, kept the longhouse fairly warm. In the winter, the proximity of bodies helped to warm everyone. Residents also bundled up in fur robes and blankets on raised platforms around the walls of the house. These elevated berths kept sleepers away from the coldest air collecting on the floor. The sleeping robes could be put away during the day when the platforms turned into day couches. Items needed daily could be stored under the benches for easy retrieval. In fact, most everything that residents needed was close at hand. Cooking containers, spare skins for clothing, weapons, and tools could be stored on shelves along the wall while drying foods hung from rafters and poles.

The longhouse was such an important concept that the Iroquois identified themselves as *Haudenosaunee* or "people of the longhouse." This communal structure represented the values of the people. Everything about a longhouse spoke to a communal society. Several families lived in each building and each family consisted of several generations. This proximity established close ties on every level. Children grew up in a house full of relatives to love and guide them. Their lives unfolded in a dynamic world that included birth, sex, illness, and death experienced first hand. Children were not treated as adults, but neither were they kept separate from the realities of life.

All children grew up in longhouses, but not all remained in the same one throughout their lives. The Iroquois were a matrilineal culture, passing kinship and ownership rights through the mother's lineage. Thus in each longhouse lived related women and their children, tracing ancestry through the clan mother, the oldest women in the house. A girl could expect to remain in the home of her mother and maternal grandmother throughout her life until it possibly passed to her to be clan mother. A boy, on the other hand, grew to manhood in his mother and sisters' home, but left upon marriage to reside in the longhouse of his wife and her female kin. It makes sense then, as males were the transients and females the residents, that the actual structure belonged to the women. Women owned the longhouses and the possessions within that sustained life. Men moved into their new residence with just the clothing and weapons they carried.

Family and Gender

The ownership of dwellings and possessions by women and weapons by men reflected the gender divisions within society.

Women bore and nurtured children and thus associated with the lifegiving forces of the earth, whether gathering or agriculture. They maintained stable home lives that ensured the success of the next generation. They controlled access to foodstuffs, cooking vessels, clothing, and other necessities of daily life. Men, on the other hand, protected the group and provided valuable protein in the form of wild game or fish. Their occupations necessarily required long distance travel, hardship, and danger. So males, who could be quickly lost on a hunting trip or raid or be away from home for months, did not have responsibility for maintaining home life. Males, of course, did play an important role in family life, primarily acting as disciplinarians and advisors to children. Men taught the next generation of boys the skills necessary for adult life. They served as role models and mentors, guiding young men on their journey to becoming warriors, hunters, and leaders. In this matrilineal culture, however, men were responsible for the upbringing of their sisters' children. Their own offspring would be similarly governed by their mother's brothers. Thus society relied on the bonds of blood and kinship rather on the far less permanent bonds of marriage to ensure the future.

Marriage was a somewhat fluid concept to the Iroquois. Young men sought the hand of the girls they admired, but the match had to be approved by clan mothers. Taboos prevented the marriage of close relatives or clan members, but little else restricted an individual's choice. Similarly, little prevented an unhappy marriage from dissolving. What we know as divorce was a simple matter of the man moving out of his wife's family dwelling. The children stayed with their mother and continued to have their maternal uncles in their lives, thus ensuring the continuity of life. Many people married for life, but many others changed partners frequently.

Adult men and women moved in distinct, but harmonious spheres. In a world predicated on harmony and equality of forces, lopsidedness in any aspect of life was to be avoided. Each gender had its assigned roles from which they gained their status and power. The Iroquois relied on agriculture as an important part of their diet, and women were solely responsible for the produce of the fields. They grew corn, beans, and squash—known to the Iroquois as the *Three Sisters* and to anthropologists as the North American triad. Grown together these three crops work in remarkable harmony, both in the ground and in the human diet.

This produce formed the basis of the Iroquois's food supply, and a bad year in the fields could mean a bad year for society, so

farming was a very responsible position. Iroquois women did more than just labor in the fields. They controlled the use of the fields, deciding what would be planted and when it would be planted and harvested. Women worked communally in fields controlled by their kinship group. They planted, fertilized, weeded, scared away the birds, and harvested; men were typically only invited to share in the heavy labor of initial field clearing. The reward for all of this work was control of the produce. Women oversaw the storage and distribution of the village's yearly crops. They even made the pottery vessels used for cooking and storage. In addition to agriculture women also gathered the fruits of the forests. They collected and stored nuts, berries, fruit, roots, and herbs that would later be used in cooking. Thus females were directly responsible for obtaining and keeping all the nonmeat portion of the Iroquois diet. This storage and redistribution of foodstuffs are important powers. Women literally held the life of the village in their hands and could wield considerable influence through this control.

Iroquois men excelled at hunting and warfare. Those two pursuits were the means to achieve honor, fame, and power, and there were plenty of opportunities to participate in both. White-tailed deer were an important species to the Iroquois, and they routinely burned the underbrush in the forests to improve habitat and hunting opportunities. Deer provided venison, which could be eaten immediately, cooked later in stews, or dried for jerky. Deerskin was favored for garments and was desired for its flexibility and softness. The less common black bear was valued for its meat, fur, and immense stores of fat. Bear fat pounded with dried fruit created pemmican, a staple food for long-distance trips.

Individuals knew their expected roles in society from the start of life. Childhood served as training for future adult roles. Iroquois children enjoyed considerable freedom to explore, play, and learn. After spending their early years in a cradleboard on their mother's back or near her as she went around her daily activities, young children essentially had the run of the village. In due time they would come to learn to be as brave, hardy, honest, uncomplaining, and self-disciplined as the rest of their people. As they grew up, children began engaging in gender-specific play. Boys played with small bows and arrows, ran foot races, and developed the skills needed to be a successful hunter and warrior. Girls mirrored their mother's activities, learning gathering, food preparation, and childcare. When she passed puberty, an Iroquois girl was ready to marry and enter into the responsibilities of womanhood.

Spirituality, Festivals, and Rites of Passage

Puberty marked the departure from childhood for both sexes. The Iroquois did not have the elaborate ceremonies marking this passage that were characteristic of other native groups. Girls left the household at first menstruation and continued to follow this practice each month. Boys generally went off into the woods to prove themselves worthy of their new responsibilities. They were to display honor, courage, strength, and fortitude. The trips were overseen by an older man who could attest to their worthiness, and this solo trip often produced a vision of the boy's guardian spirit that remained with him for life.

The world of the Iroquois was full of invisible spirits; humans were just one type of creature that inhabited the world and not necessarily the most powerful. Good and evil occurred in the world and the trick was to keep them in balance. Great care was taken not to irritate spirits who might harm humans, and it was important to thank them for their beneficence. Several festivals throughout the year served as thanksgiving ceremonies to recognize that the creator had continued to give the people great things. The Maple Ceremony celebrated the fact that sap flowed in the trees each spring, and the strawberry festival that the plants bore berries again. Several rituals reflected the importance of agriculture in Iroquois life. The planting and harvest festivals, and particularly the Green Corn Ceremony, gave thanks for a successful crop each year. The most important ceremony, Midwinter, concluded the old year and began the new. Held during the darkest, coldest period of the Iroquois year, this festival beseeched the spirits to smile favorably on the people for another year. The six days of the ceremony included a variety of activities such as sacrifice of the white dog, dances, and games.

In addition to scheduled ceremonies, the Iroquois also had spiritual societies. One of the best-known was the False Face Society, which concerned itself with curing and healing. Members gained their power by wearing elaborately carved, sometimes grotesque, wooden masks. The figure for the mask came to the wearer in a dream. The mask contained powers and had to be ritually cared for, oftentimes by being "fed." Society members performed rituals at the home of sick persons who became members of the society upon their recovery. It is important that the obligation for receiving a healing was to spread the gift and cure others in society. Most aspects of Iroquois religion, such as ceremonies and societies, were communal.

Political Structure and Warfare

In a sense, Iroquois politics were also somewhat communal. Like most other eastern tribes, the Iroquois operated on a basis of consensus. Everyone with an interest in an issue should have input into dealing with the situation. There was little anyone could do to coerce an Iroquois to do something; rather, honor and shame, responsibility, kinship and community motivated peoples' actions. This was a fairly pure form of democracy. That is not to say that everyone was equal. Men held offices and participated in public life but women did not; however, it would be a mistake to dismiss women's influence simply because they did not officially have titles. In fact, clan mothers had the responsibility of nominating men to serve as chiefs to represent the clan. What they created they could also destroy, so female elders could reprimand and remove chiefs who strayed from representing their interests.

Women also affected tribal decision making in other ways. The chiefs, or *sachems*, chosen by the women acted as first among equals. They did not have unlimited or exceptional power. Younger men accorded them honor and some privilege because of the achievements, which gained them elected position. These men had great responsibilities: to uphold the law, to collect and redistribute tribute, to declare war, and to provide for widows and orphans. This was the general structure of government throughout the Northeast, but the Iroquois created a unique adaptation—the Iroquois Confederacy governed by *Kainerekowa*, the "Great Law of Peace."

Anthropologists point to the Confederacy as a practical solution to ongoing intertribal rivalry that strained resources and weakened all participants. The Iroquois have a far more remarkable understanding of the origin of their Confederacy. There are many versions of the founding of the league, but all agree on the basic outline of the story. At a time of seemingly unending conflict and bloodshed between the tribes, a holy man or possibly a spirit, named Deganawidah, sought an end to the violence. His plan was to unite the Iroquois people, replacing blood feuds with ritualized payments, thus ending the cycle of retributive murders. Hiawatha, a Mohawk man who had lost his whole family to the violence, became his spokesman and traveled widely, spreading the word of the new peace initiative. After much effort the chiefs of the five tribes came together and created the Confederacy, giving each of the nations its symbolic place in the great Iroquois longhouse. From that point, the Seneca, Cayuga, Onondaga, Oneida, and Mohawk

remained at peace with one another and turned their considerable energy outward enabling them to dominate the region. By the time Europeans arrived in their midst, the Iroquois Confederacy was thriving.

One of the greatest achievements of the Confederacy was the maintenance of peace. This is remarkable in light of the importance Iroquois men placed on warfare. A man's purpose in life focused on fighting. Honor, bravery, and skill in combat summarized male success. Warfare was fairly individualized. A chief might announce an attack on a traditional enemy, but more often an individual would indicate his desire to fight and followers would join him. Traveling light with only dried food, bows and arrows, ball-headed war clubs, and flint knives, a war party could move quickly and quietly toward their enemy. Men did not engage in protracted, large-scale conflicts: warfare in the Northeast was frequent but brief. Generally waged to avenge an insult or to gain status, the fast, guerrilla-style raid served the purpose. Before the creation of the Confederacy, the Iroquois tribes engaged in an endless cycle of retribution for deaths that continued to escalate. Raids often resulted in the death of the enemy and thus the honor of the warrior, but they also resulted in captives. The capture of enemy men, women, and children provided unique opportunities for Iroquois society.

Captives' fate ran the spectrum from intense torture to adoption. Presumably, the raid had been made to avenge a wrong, and slow, methodical torture provided satisfactory revenge. Male captives were stripped, forced to run a gauntlet of beatings, and then the real cruelty began. Villagers tore out hair, broke bones, pulled out fingernails, sliced off flesh, and removed sinews from their captives, all before burning them alive. A brave man who bore his pain stoically might be honored with ritualistic cannibalism at his death. This was done at the behest of women who had the right to demand revenge for the losses. It was understood that mothers and wives suffered the greatest loss from deaths in warfare. They lost providers, protectors, and loved ones so the women of the village decided the fate of captives. Mothers whose sons were killed could choose to have a captive tortured and killed in revenge, or they could adopt a captive to replace their loss. Women controlled the fate of their captives, forcing them to live like slaves, or granting them nearly equal status. Few captives at the mercy of Iroquois women would deny females' inherent power in their society.

Iroquois dominated northeastern native culture through a combination of successful economic, political, and social organization.

They learned to exploit the natural resources that characterized the northeastern woodlands in the precontact period. Other peoples also successfully used the natural bounty of the land; however, the Iroquois's particular unity and focus served them well. They did clash with other groups and contested over land and resources with them, but maintained power up to and beyond European arrival. Other groups in the northeast also carved out successful lifestyles, but none so dominant as the Iroquois.

The Huron

In general, the Iroquois clashed with any outsiders. One of their traditional enemies was the Huron. The name Huron came from a French word, which is an insult. Originally, the people called themselves Wendat meaning "Dwellers on the Peninsula" to describe their homeland surrounded by lakes and rivers. Although related linguistically to the Iroquois and sharing similar cultural traits, the Huron considered those neighbors to be traditional enemies. The Huron also lived in longhouses; had matrilineal clans; grew corn, beans, and squash; and hunted and fished extensively, but cultural differences could be seen in their villages. The Huron lived in close proximity to one another, which would prove disastrous when European diseases swept through their people. Community was very important to the Huron, so much so that the dead resented being parted from it. Their souls hung around the villages, living a similar lifestyle of hunting, fishing, and farming. Living Huron built temporary "homes" for the dead bodies, an elevated framework of poles that might hold a body for a decade. They would remain there, part of village life until the next Feast of the Dead. An elaborate, multiday ceremony of feasting and dancing prepared the dead for their journey to the next life. At the end of the celebration the physical remains of loved ones were buried in a large common pit and covered with beaver robes and other presents. Thus the dead went on in a communal state just as their living kinsman dwelled in a unified community.

Algonquian

In the century before European contact, Algonquian language speakers lived throughout the East. They inhabited a wide arc from the Great Lakes, sweeping across the far Northeast and down the coast to the region of Virginia. Anthropologists recognize linguistic similarities among Algonquians, and the tribes also shared similar

lifestyles. Although they often had a common enemy such as the Iroquois, these tribes did not necessarily think of themselves as part of a larger group or even as allies.

Groups of seminomadic Algonquians inhabited the northern interior sections of the Northeast. This was a harsh world of mountains and rocky shorelines with a sub-Arctic climate. Because corn would not grow, agriculture was not an option. The seminomadic residents had to find other ways to make a living. The Abenaki and Penobscot survived in Maine by moving frequently to pursue deer, bears, moose, wild ducks, and fish. Moose was an important part of the hunter's diet. This animal lives a mostly solitary life wandering from food source to food source. Indigenous hunters studied animal patterns and developed techniques to harvest them. They would lure the moose by reproducing a mating call and get close to an individual by dressing in skins and antlers. Once close enough, a hunter could bring down a moose with a bow and arrow. Moose could also be taken by means of an overhead snare that was triggered by the animal's weight, or they could be chased down in a heavy snow where the hunter had the advantage of snowshoes.

Beaver was another important species to northern hunters. Their meat could be eaten and their pelts provided water-repellent furs. The dams built by beavers also created ponds that attracted species like moose who fed on the willows growing there. Beavers could be seized from their houses or trapped along their trails and in the water. White-tailed deer provided another important source of protein, as did black bear with their valuable fatty meat.

Northern hunters were not dependent on mammals for food. Abundant lakes, streams, and coastlines offered access to plentiful fish. Fish could be speared or trapped in weirs and birchbark nets. They collected shellfish and occasionally even harvested marine mammals along the coasts. Birds migrating along the shoreline, as well as in the interior, were also used. Much of this meat would be preserved by smoking for future use.

Animals provided much more than a critical part of the Indians' diet. Animal skins were the main source of clothing. The same attributes that served the animals well also served humans well. Warm and waterproof, a skin cut from the animal with the forelegs intact, created a sleeved garment. Because of the weather, most of the year both men and women wore skins covering their body. Brief spells of warm weather had people stripped down to breechclouts and deerskin shirts. Both men and women cared about their appearance and often wore clothing decorated with quills, feathers, and shells.

Housing and Settlement

Because they exploited so many resources, these northern hunters had to move frequently. Their lifestyle dictated portable, comfortable housing and they chose the wigwam style. Four saplings bent into the center quickly created a frame over which were placed long strips of bark sewn together. An inside lining of swamp grass both insulated and absorbed moisture, and animal skins hanging at the one low entrance blocked cold air. There was no furniture in this portable dwelling, but fir branches covered with skins acted as beds to insulate sleepers from the cold earth. A constantly burning fire in the middle kept the whole place fairly warm. This well-designed dwelling was common throughout the Algonquian culture area.

Farther south along the northeast coast, groups used the diversity of natural resources. People like the Wampanoag could choose from a wide range of food sources. They could collect fish and shellfish along the rocky coastline, grow crops in fertile fields along the river valleys, or hunt and gather in the vast inland forests. The Indians routinely burned the underbrush of the forests to keep them open, easy to travel through, and inviting to game animals. The woods held mature oak, hickory, and chestnut trees that were heavy with nuts in the fall and provided fire wood and timber year-round. Sheets of chestnut bark covered their homes in the summer; chestnut wood fires kept them warm in the winter. Furs from forest animals protected people in the winter and their meat provided critical protein. The Wampanoags, as other northeast dwellers, carved out a successful adaptation to the northeastern landscape.

A chain of Algonquin communities grew up along the Atlantic seaboard, stretching from the Gulf of St. Lawrence to the Chesapeake Bay. In the north the groups maintained their seminomadic lifestyle. They had contact with others to the south through a regular flow of trade. Trade goods, gossip, news, and shared cultural similarities passed along this trade route. Thus more southerly Algonquians differed from their brethren in the north only to the extent of their adaptation to regional climate. One major change was the adoption of agriculture in regions with a growing season that allowed for it. Corn, beans, and squash grew well all through the East and provided a stable diet when supplemented by hunting and fishing.

The Delaware/Lenni Lenape

An Algonquian people that whites know as the Delaware numbered over 10,000 people in the period before European contact.

They inhabited a loose network of villages spreading west from Delaware to New Jersey, New York, and Pennsylvania. Like most native people they called themselves "the people" or Lenni Lenape in their language. They maintained three divisions based primarily on geography—Munsee, Unami, and Unalactigo—each of which used a different dialect. Their sense of themselves as Lenape stemmed from the shared matrilineal clans occurring in each group. Often described as "peaceful," the Lenape had none of the formal organization or system of warfare common to their northern Iroquois neighbors. This does not mean, however, that the people would not fight to defend their families and homeland.

Lenape family groups inhabited scattered villages that were always located near water along streams and rivers. This afforded them access to the fertile fishing spots that provided much of the protein in their diet. The men of the community hunted deer, turkey, small mammals, and waterfowl. Travel was mostly on foot or in a dugout canoe. They also fished, using spears, nets, and weirs, depending on the season. Women provided the rest of the family's diet by gathering chestnuts, wild berries, and other fruits of the forest. Women also tended gardens and fields near the village, which yielded corn, beans, and squash, those staple crops often eaten together as succotash. Because they also cultivated sweet potatoes and tobacco, a village's fields often covered more than 200 acres.

This Woodlands lifestyle was comfortable and afforded the Lenape time for other pursuits, including attention to personal well-being. All villagers participated in sweat house purification. A low, windowless hut held hot stones over which water was poured. The resulting intense heat and steam produced copious sweating that was thought to rid the body of impurities. Followed by a swim or roll in the snow, the Lenape were purified. One reason for the repeated cleansing was the common practice of body painting. The Lenape loved to mix berry juice and minerals to form a red substance that could be applied as an adornment to face and body. Men painted bold designs; women used the ocher more like modern-day makeup. Both sexes also tattooed their bodies for decoration. Appearance was important. Men spent hours tweezing out the hair on their faces and heads, and young men typically left only a tuft of long hair to be adorned by a single feather. Women kept their hair longer and usually braided and decorated. Bodies were covered only for comfort, leggings and skirts of deerskin in summer with turkey feather robes or fur mantles in the winter. Women decorated clothing with beads and quills or even hammered copper ornaments.

The descendants of the Lenape encountered by Europeans were described as tall, powerfully built people with great pride in their appearance and bearing.

The Lenape followed matrilineal descent and societal organization. Women owned the wigwam and contents, which she passed on to her daughters. In the case of divorce, which was as easy as parting company, the mother kept the children. Children grew up surrounded by examples of the adult roles they would assume. Young boys typically undertook a rite of fasting in the woods known as the Youth's Vigil, which brought the dreams and visions of forces to guide and protect a warrior and hunter. The matrilineal clans were represented by a male sachem who performed ceremonial functions and negotiated harmony after conflict. This individual could only govern by persuasion, as the Lenape were a particularly democratic society. Consensus was required for any major undertaking. All members of the community were involved in the government of the people. Children listened to the adult deliberations so they could learn the ways of their society, and elders were accorded high honor and consulted on important issues.

After a full life, a Lenape elder could expect to travel to a place of harmony after death. Burial would be in a shallow grave individually or in groups. The people believed in a Great Spirit, common to the Algonquians, who oversaw the spiritual forces inherent in all natural things. These forces had to be respected and appeased throughout life, and spiritual leaders could help interpret dreams in which the spirits revealed their wishes to men. Other holy men dedicated themselves to healing. The Lenape held ceremonies during the year including the big house ceremony, a 12-day ritual held at a specially designed building that was symbolic of the universe. This was a world renewal ritual that re-created the original creation saga and strengthened the ties between community members. As a community, the Lenape renewed their ties to each other and to the spiritual world, thus ensuring success and harmony in the coming year.

The Powhatan

The Lenape lifestyle was similar to many Algonquian people. Those we know the most about are those encountered by non-Indians who recorded cultural practices. Societies are of course fluid and dynamic; however, many core beliefs and traditions remained unchanged for hundreds of years. One Algonquian group for which

we have eyewitness accounts was the Powhatan, a name taken from the dominant village in the seventeenth century. This collection of tribes living along waterways of eastern Virginia shared many cultural traits with their northern neighbors. They pursued a varied economic strategy of hunting, fishing, gathering, and farming with clear gender divisions for each activity. They located their communal villages near waterways for easy access to water and fishing. Men left the villages, particularly in the fall, on extended hunting trips, primarily for white-tailed deer. Women farmed fields of corn, beans, and squash located nearby the villages. They differed from northern tribes mostly in their political organization. By the European contact period the Powhatans had a chiefdom level leadership. One paramount leader attempted to control foreign policy, warfare, and collect tribute from other groups within his sphere of influence. Thus the Virginia Indians shared more aspects of the ancient Mississippian system of the southeast than did northern Algonquian groups.

Algonquian Tribes of the Great Lakes

Other Algonquian groups shared similarities with most others of their language family; however, they often made regional adaptations to their lifestyles. One obvious change was the exploitation of local resources. We can see this clearly demonstrated in the Great Lakes region. Here people who would be known as the Ojibwa or Chippewa, Ottawa, Menominee, Potawatomi, Cree, and others expanded their economic strategies to make use of conditions. This northern area had been strongly shaped by glaciation. It had a myriad of waterways, lakes, ponds, streams, and marshes that could be an important resource for transportation as well as food. In the Archaic period the short growing season in this northern area precluded a reliance on agriculture. As the climate warmed by 1000 B.C., however, it was possible to grow the maize, which was traded up the Mississippi River from southern residents. So, as elsewhere in the East, a nomadic people settled down along fertile valleys and floodplains to tend a corn crop.

A LIFE OF ABUNDANCE

Northeastern America provided a rich setting for early inhabitants. The diverse resources enabled a variety of lifestyles to thrive in the region. The coastline provided marine fish and shellfish, the dense forests yielded endless wood products, and along with

clearings and meadows supported a rich array of plants and animals useful to humans. The most important aspects of the northeast-ern Woodlands for early Indians were the soil, rainfall, and grow-ing season suitable for corn, bean, and squash agriculture. With the ability to produce reliable harvests of crops, eastern Indians supported permanent settlements. Yet there was enough diversity in the Northeast to allow hunting and gathering lifestyles to suc-ceed. Even those communities committed to growing the North American triad did not abandon the foods of forests. White-tail deer remained an important source of protein for most easterners. Other animals, ranging from black bear to turkeys and squirrels, offered meat, fur, and feathers which had a variety of uses.

Males in the societies acted as hunters and warriors. Some groups, like the Iroquois, placed great emphasis on raiding and warfare. The conflicts were generally brief and targeted, but could be quite vicious. They yielded honor for participants and often valuable captives to augment local populations. Women in the eastern Woodlands farmed, gathered, and raised children. Their roles as lifegivers, both of children and crops, granted them essen-tially equal status with men. Most of these early societies organized on a matrilineal basis, giving women control of residential prop-erty. Children raised within the embrace of their mother's family enjoyed a fairly free childhood. All the youngsters of a village were highly valued. At a young age they began learning the expectations and skills of their adult roles. Bravery, strength, honor, and respon-sibility were expected of everyone in society.

Woodland people had varied belief systems; however, most emphasized harmony within the community and with the natural world. One great power and many lesser spirits inhabited the indigenous world. Illness and misfortune were caused by dishar-mony. Shamans, as well as religious societies, helped individuals stay in the proper relationship to the spirit world. A belief in the afterlife led communities to build funerary mounds thousands of years ago. Ceremony and ritual tied the living to the other powers that existed. Some of the art of the eastern region centered on rit-ual, such as the creation of special masks. Other artistic expression served more mundane purposes like pottery vessels. Pottery was a hallmark of the sedentary Woodlands culture. There was some variety in the Northeast, especially in language, but the overall cul-ture shared many similarities. The two major language groups—the Iroquoian and Algonquian speakers—used local resources in comparable ways. The eastern Woodlands lifestyle that developed

after the Archaic period was so successful it continued well into the postcontact period.

FURTHER READING

Axtell, James, ed. *The Native American People of the East.* West Haven, CT: Pendulum Press, 1973.

Bragdon, Kathleen J. *The Columbia Guide to American Indians of the Northeast.* New York: Columbia University Press, 2001.

————. *The Archaeology of North America.* New York: Viking Press, 1976.

Calloway, Colin G. *Indians of the Northeast.* New York: Facts on File, 1991.

Delcourt, Paul A., and Hazel R. Delcourt. *Prehistoric Native Americans and Ecological Change: Human Ecosystems in Eastern North America since the Pleistocene.* New York: Cambridge University Press, 2004.

Iroquois History. This is part of a very complete summary of information on 240 different tribes. http://www.tolatsga.org/iro.html (accessed September 1, 2007).

The Iroquois of the Northeast. The Carnegie Museum of Natural History maintains this site focusing on Iroquois people. http://www.carn egiemnh.org//exhibits/north-south-east-west/iroquois/index. html (accessed September 1, 2007).

Kallen, Stuart A. *Native Americans of the Northeast.* San Diego, CA: Lucent Books, 2000.

Sita, Lisa. *Indians of the Northeast: Traditions, History, Legends, and Life.* Milwaukee, WI: Gareth Stevens Publishers, 2000.

Snow, Dean. *The Iroquois.* Cambridge, MA: Blackwell Publishers, 1994.

2

The Southeast

The southeastern region of the United States bears strong resemblance to the Northeast. The geography, topography, and climate are much more similar east of the Mississippi River than to the west, so the cultures of people living close to the land, heavily influenced by natural surroundings, share many similarities.

The southeastern portion of America has long been a desirable place to live. In the early years of human habitation of the continent, this region offered more abundant and diverse resources even than at the present time. In the Pleistocene period, while much of the continent was glaciated, the Southeast boasted mixed forests and large prairies. Such a desirable combination of vegetation supported a wide range of animals, including mastodons, sloths, deer, capybaras, and giant armadillos in the far south. Humans would naturally have been drawn to the abundance of plant and animal resources and livable climate in the region; however, it has been difficult to find evidence of human habitation. Unlike the Southwest, material remains are not well preserved in the Southeast's humid, warm climate, which encourages rapid decay. The region is heavily influenced by water, another difficulty for archaeologists. Rivers and streams that may have attracted humans have for thousands of years flooded and deposited silt over the settlements. Similarly, humans undoubtedly used the extensive coastal areas of the Southeast, miles

of which are now underwater. As the glaciers melted and ocean levels rose, many sites of human occupation disappeared under the sea. Some evidence of fluted projectile points from the late Pleistocene has been collected, but the story of humans in the Southeast really begins in the Archaic period.

We know that hunters crafting small, triangular points lived along the Savannah River in Georgia about 8000 B.C. The points are made of chert, which the people quarried from the outcroppings along the fall line. Not surprisingly, humans seem to have followed a typical adaptation of animals, moving from lowlands in the winter up to higher, cooler elevations in the hotter weather. Like other early Archaic peoples, hunting and gathering wild plants would have been the basis of their economy. Tools found at a probable winter settlement include flaked stone knives, cobblestones used for grinding plant material, and stone adzes, possibly for wood working.

With sea levels continuing to rise until 4000 B.C., the coast would have been a difficult place to live as forests flooded and fluctuating shorelines compromised other resources. At this time the western interior sections of the Southeast seemed a more promising area. Evidence of settlement along the Tennessee River reveals an Archaic lifestyle. Dwellings appear to have been constructed of upright posts, packed clay floors, and probably some sort of plant material covering. Residents hunted turkeys and large mammals, especially prizing deer, which provided both meat and hides and bones for clothing and tools. They must have valued dogs because they buried some like humans. The evidence that remains was nonperishable, like bone beads, but there must have also been clothing, basketry, and wooden items that met the necessities of daily life. At a site in present-day Kentucky, more than 1,200 graves have been excavated, yielding artifacts that reveal the culture's prized possessions—those worthy of burial with loved ones. Stone projectile points and bone fishhooks show the primacy of hunting and fishing for survival; pestles and nut-cracking stones indicate that nuts and other plants supplemented residents' diet. Some people were buried with more exotic goods obtained in trade such as decorated shells and worked copper. These small pieces of ornamentation must have been valuable to their owners who wore them at burial.

FLORIDA

Telling the story of early habitation in the Southeast is a bit like working on a jigsaw puzzle with major pieces missing. Almost

nothing is known of residents' political, religious, or social organization, and from an archaeological perspective, the missing pieces are usually items made of plant materials. Florida archaeology has been the wonderful exception to that general rule with several unique sites where valuable artifacts have been preserved for millennia in anaerobic underwater conditions. These finds in Florida springs, ponds, and rivers have proved intriguing and enlightening for the study of early southeastern culture. The anaerobic conditions at the wet sites have preserved remarkable pieces of history from 5000 B.C.

At both Little Salt Springs and Windover, burials remain intact. The bodies yielded fascinating samples of twined cloth as well as wooden bowls, diggings sticks, stone, and bone artifacts. A wide variety of animal teeth and bone—shark, wolf, bobcat, deer, and manatee—served Archaic Indians as tools. Little Salt Springs served as the final resting place for a thousand corpses that were laid on branches and wrapped in grass to protect them from the mud they were buried in. Nearby Fort Center, near Lake Okeechobee, boasted burial platforms erected over water and guarded by carved wooden effigies of an eagle, otter, bobcat and other animals that were probably clan totems. Clearly, elaborate care for and respect of the deceased was a part of early southeastern culture. This concern for the dead would be greatly intensified in the later Mississippian complex.

By 3500 B.C., human habitation in the Southeast was thriving. Stable communities built on hunting and gathering rich resources increased their population density. Deer remained the backbone of subsistence, supplemented by raccoon, otters, turtles, birds, fish, and shellfish. Beautifully carved stone weights for throwing spears attest to the skill of the hunters in preparing their weapons and tools. Bowls and jars made from stone and pottery indicate that people became increasingly sedentary, allowing for the use of heavier, more durable objects. In the following millennium people committed to cultivating plants. They cultivated native seeds of sunflowers, goosefoot, marsh elder, knotweed, little barley, and maygrass. Squash may have been grown in Missouri as early as 5000 B.C. The forests also provide hickory, acorn, and walnuts, as well as wild fruits like blackberry and blueberry.

Calusa

In some areas the rich abundance of wild resources provided enough bounty that people did not need to turn to agriculture to

support themselves. The Calusa in southwestern Florida were one such group. Archaeological evidence points to the development of the Caloosahatchee culture around 500 B.C. This society thrived on the abundance of shellfish in the gulf region. Evidence of the abundance of marine resources can be seen in the extensive midden piles of castoff shells that characterize Calusa occupation areas. A comfortable living could be made by hunting wildfowl, reptiles, deer, foxes, whales, seals, sharks, rays, and fish, as well as gathering roots and seeds. The extensive marine resources of Florida's west coast provided ample supplies to support a large and complex society. The Calusa did not turn to agriculture primarily because they did not need it.

Reliance on agriculture is often considered to be an attribute of those societies that develop sociopolitical organization, but the Calusa were an exception. The Calusa had a single chief, based in Estero Bay on Florida's west coast when the Spanish encountered him in the sixteenth century. This chief exercised political control over 50 other villages and enjoyed the benefits of power that Europeans recognized as "kingly." The Spanish also understood the system of ritual tribute by which the current chief Carlos kept power over distant peoples. Calusa divided their society into a class of nobility, from which the paramount chief, his advisors, and retinue emerged, and the rest of the people who were commoners. Even this lower class, which had no hope of obtaining political power, ranked above slaves who usually came to the village as war captives. In perhaps the ultimate display of power, the death of a powerful individual caused the sacrifice of the lives of his servants. In addition to social and political differentiation, the Calusa probably also supported a variety of economic pursuits. A few remaining artifacts give tantalizing glimpses into the level of artistry they achieved. Carved wooden heads of deer, dolphin carvings, and painted animal masks with shell inlay may have been the work of professional artists. The Calusa people clearly used their abundant resource base to create a stratified social, specialized economic, and centralized political system hundred of years before European contact.

Timucuan

The northern part of Florida was better suited to agriculture than the south, and the inland areas had less access to the coastal resources. The Timucuan culture began here around 500 B.C. They located villages of palmetto-thatched houses, public granaries,

and ceremonial plazas near fresh water. Small maize fields nearby yielded a dependable crop that the Timucuan augmented with deer, oysters, clams, fish, birds, berries, and acorns. Meat, including alligator, would be smoked over open fires to prepare it for winter storage. A portion of all the food collected went into public storage on which each family could draw when in need. Although not as stratified as the Calusa, the people of north Florida maintained clans of varying levels of prestige. Chiefs could be distinguished from others by adornments such as imported copper breastplates, bead jewelry, and special tattoos. Later European drawings depict Timucuan leaders with body decoration from head to foot. All the early indigenous peoples of the region seem to have been of large stature. When Europeans arrived, they continually remarked on the height and physique of Florida natives. This characteristic was apparently valued by the Timucuan because when the chief was ready to marry, he sought the tallest of the daughters of the principal men. The ensuing marriage ceremony would be replete with displays of wealth and dancing, and the union was likely to result in statuesque offspring

The Timucuan, like many other native groups, strove to maintain a balance in life. They had many rules and prohibitions that if broken could bring disharmony to the individual and the group. The goal was to maintain harmony and purity at all times. The effort to achieve purity centered on a purgative drink ritual. Florida natives created the liquid by drying and roasting the leaves of a holly species (*Ilex vomitoria*). They then brewed the leaves into a strong, dark, highly caffeinated liquid. The Indians called this white drink because of its connection to purity and harmony, but later European observers referred to it as black drink because of its color. The black drink was a prerequisite to meetings or discussions of tribal leaders. It often acted as a purgative and men frequently vomited, sometimes projecting the vomit up to eight feet and other times into specially carved bowls. Thus purified and stimulated by the caffeine, the male leaders could deliberate for hours.

WOODLAND TRADITION

The most southerly areas of the east, like the land of the Timucuan and Calusa, were distinctly different from the bulk of the region and thus continued with their own adaptations. Throughout most of the east a new lifestyle emerged referred to as the Woodland Tradition.

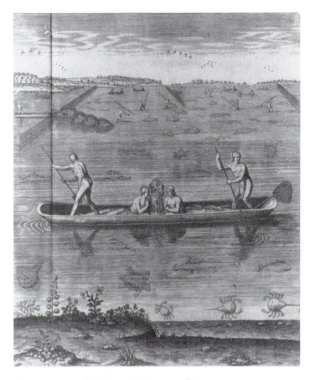

Timucuans fishing. Library of Congress.

In the Southeast this was centered primarily along the Mississippi and Ohio Rivers. This culture emerged around 1000 B.C. and lasted until A.D. 700, although aspects of it continued to be seen long afterward. This tradition developed gradually out of the Archaic culture, and represented a change in ideology and subsistence. In fact, one well-known scholar refers to the Woodland Tradition as probably the most distinctive and most completely indigenous culture ever to exist in eastern North America. Hunting and gathering was still the main source of subsistence; however, the period saw more refined techniques and better exploitation of local resources. Pottery became widespread and elaborate mortuary traditions including earthworks developed. Both traits would be exaggerated in the next culture to emerge in the area; however, the major change centered on agriculture. A new strain of maize appeared in the region by A.D. 1200. It was probably domesticated in Guatemala and spread northward. Called Eastern Flint, this variety thrived in cool, moist climates. When paired with beans, which also came into cultivation at this time, these crops provided a stable base for a thriving culture.

Poverty Point

Some southeastern groups developed fairly complex societies supported by rich local resources. An unusual site in northeastern Louisiana known as Poverty Point has prompted debate
among archaeologists for decades. Located at the confluence of the
Arkansas and Mississippi Rivers, the culture thrived here from
1500 to 700 B.C. Living from abundant fish as well as deer, birds,
berries, seeds, and nuts would not distinguish this group from
many other Archaic hunter-gatherers. The residents at this location, however, built an extensive set of earthen mounds that would
have required considerable organization and effort to design and
construct. The years of building resulted in a C-shaped figure
formed by six concentric artificial earth embankments. They are
separated by ditches, or swales, where dirt was removed to build
the ridges. This is no small pile of dirt. The ends of the outermost
ridge are nearly three-fourths of a mile apart, and if the ridges
were straightened and laid end to end, they would comprise
an embankment 7 1/2 miles long. Years of erosion have altered
them, but originally, the ridges stood 4 to 6 feet high and 140
to 200 feet apart. In addition to the "C" structure, which opens
onto a stream, there are several other conical mounds. One is
70 feet high with a base nearly 700 feet on each side. All of these
constructions clearly required a great deal of human power to
complete. Dirt had to be carried in baskets and placed precisely
in alignment with the plan of the mound. This construction technique used an abundant material, soil, rather than stone, which
had to come from sources in the Quachita, Ozark, or Appalachian
Mountains.

Found within the earthworks is evidence of both utilization of
local resources and items of long distance trade. The most numerous artifacts are balls of silt that have been formed by small hands,
often children's. Their shape varies greatly as one would expect
from the work of numerous craftsmen. It appears that these odd
objects are actually artificial "stones" made for cooking. Because
the area had few stones and millions would be required to heat
food, they just made a substitute. These objects have even been
found packed into fire pits as they would have been used. Archaeologists estimate that Poverty Point may have originally contained
24 million of these balls. Also in great supply were items made
from materials imported from as far away as the Great Lakes: copper, lead ore, and soapstone. Small figurines carved of jasper seem

to have been decorative, whereas stone plummets to sink fishing nets were a necessity. Clearly, these early southeasterners enjoyed a thriving, complex society based on the abundance of the region's resources, which allowed them enough surplus to trade for exotic goods. Although there are many unique aspects to the Poverty Point culture, some of the same features developed elsewhere.

MISSISSIPPIAN

The culture known as Mississippian may be the most remarkable product of early North America. It was a complex chiefdom that occupied an area the size of western Europe for more than 1,000 years. In so many ways it is the great ancient heritage of the continent, yet so few Americans know of it. A wealthy, complex, organized society in North America that existed centuries before the European invasion is a great heritage. The sophistication of art and ritual alone rivals contemporary societies from other continents. The physical remains of the civilization are like the Egyptian pyramids of America. It is therefore striking that this ancient lifestyle has attracted so little attention among nonspecialists. This fascinating culture reveals more depth and intricacies with each archaeological exploration of its many sites.

The phenomenon identified as Mississippian evolved and changed over several centuries, shrinking and growing in territory and influence. In general the term refers to farming societies thriving in the Tennessee, Cumberland, and Mississippi River valleys from A.D. 800 to 1500. It is generally characterized by maize agriculture, pottery production, stratified social organization with hereditary positions, long distance trade networks, a well-developed religious system, and the construction of flat-topped mounds. The extent to which groups reflected tendencies viewed as Mississippian varied with time and geographic location, but the ascendancy of the culture shaped the eastern United States for centuries, even into the European contact period.

The modern name for the ancient culture obviously reflects location. As Adena and Hopewell peoples centered on the Ohio River drainage, so later groups focused on the mightier Mississippi watershed. In the tenth century, residents of the interior of North America realized the same truth that Anglo settlers would discover 800 years later: the mighty Mississippi River and its tributaries are a nearly inexhaustible source of life. The greatest waterway system in the United States has supported a diverse mix of plant and animal

species as well as humans for millennia. The complex culture that grew up in and around this great watershed extended its influence over a vast scope of eastern North America. Mississippian societies stretched from northern Florida to southern Illinois and from the Atlantic coastal plain to eastern Oklahoma.

Humans would naturally be attracted to steady sources of water for survival, as well as to the plentiful game, fish, and a variety of plants that thrived in the Mississippi tributaries. And all this abundance was important; however, the Mississippian complex is associated with agricultural economies. The rich alluvial soil deposited along the banks of the streams and rivers in middle America proved to be some of the most fertile and productive in the country. It was able to support fairly large concentrations of people on a maize-based system of agriculture. The core of Mississippian culture was centered in the "American Bottom," the area of the confluence of the Mississippi, Missouri, and Illinois Rivers. It is a fertile region bounded by the Mississippi River to the west and the bluffs to the east that supported the largest Mississippian town—Cahokia.

Economy

Agriculture became the driving economic force of the Mississippian culture. It really is the factor that made the other aspects of the civilization possible. It created a stable, fairly predictable economy on which an elaborate lifestyle could be built. This was predominantly a corn agriculture; although other crops were certainly grown, corn remained the dominant food source. The varieties of maize that had developed since the plant's introduction to North America were critical to Mississippian subsistence. The earlier varieties grew well only in the forgiving climate of the Southeast, needing 200 days of growing season, but later types tolerated cold and short growing seasons of only 120 days enough to allow farming as far north as the Great Lakes. Corn suited the seasonality of the climate as well. Planting occurred in the rainy spring, followed by a long, warm summer, and then harvest in the drier autumn period. The crop grew well and fairly easily, but it also suited people well. It could be eaten fresh or dried, whole or ground; it could be incorporated into numerous dishes and stored well.

The greatest asset of maize agriculture for early peoples was that it produced surpluses. Corn grew so successfully that excess could be traded, stored, or used to increase population. In addition, the labor requirements were low enough that not everyone had

to participate in farming. In numerous ways the benefits of corn agriculture influenced the development of Mississippian civilization, and, in fact, made possible many of its unique features. It is clear that the increased reliance on maize as a major food source drove the population growth in the region.

Maize provided about 50 percent of the Mississippian diet; however, although corn was extremely important, the people did not give up their other types of foods. The location of Mississippian villages and farmsteads offered residents a choice of resources. They were generally located either in floodplains, on river levees, or on river bluffs overlooking the bottomlands. This gave access to the excellent soil of the floodplains, as well as the diverse species of plants and animals found in both the bottomland and upland environments. Varieties of squashes, beans, and other domesticated plants appeared in Mississippian fields. Crops were planted to maintain a harmonious balance—beans used the cornstalks for support and squash spread along the ground, choking out weeds and retaining soil moisture. Even with such a reliable harvest, native people did not lose touch with wild food sources. Their ancestors had been hunter-gatherers, so the knowledge had been passed through the generations. In addition to traditional knowledge, the Mississippians benefited from new technology, the bow and arrow, which increased their success. So the corn farmers also collected nuts, berries, seeds, and roots for food, flavoring, and medicine. Hickory nuts, persimmons, goosefoot, and knotweed seeds were important to these early gatherers. Streams also teemed with catfish, bass, and other fish, providing another important protein to their diet. The flyways of migratory waterfowl passed over the area, further diversifying sources of meat as well as feathers for decorative use.

The dependence of Mississippians on agriculture shaped their culture. The settlement pattern of the region reflected the agricultural focus with people living near their fields. The size of fields encouraged wide dispersal of homesteads but spread out hamlets had ties to fortified towns, so Mississippians lived in towns of varying size from a few hundred to the largest at 20,000 residents. The flat, fertile soil of flood plains required little human intervention to be suitable for planting. Any trees were girdled to kill them and the area was burned in preparation for planting. The village fields dominated the landscape and the structures remained fairly simple. For summer use near the fields, people built houses out of a basic frame of poles enclosed by cane or reed walls wattled with local clay. Gabled roofs of replaceable thatch created a watertight covering. Such housing was adequate, but not monumental or lasting

as seen in the Southwest. In the winter families moved to semi-subterranean lodges, a form that survived among the Mandan on the Plains. These eastern farmers moved frequently whenever the soil near the village was exhausted, so houses did not need to last too long.

Family and Gender

As in many indigenous societies the gender divisions that assigned specific duties and tasks to males and females governed daily life. Women and the young girls who served as their helpers held responsibility for the success of the village fields. This entailed planting seeds with digging sticks or hoes in fields cleared by the men. Each seed and resulting plant was precious and important to the welfare of the people so they had to be nurtured. It was important to keep weeds from competing for valuable moisture and sunlight, so fields had to be kept free of unwanted plants. Bean plants running along the ground between corn stalks aided the Mississippian women by making the ground unsuitable for weeds. In addition to the invaluable production of the maize crop, women also gathered other food sources to supplement the daily diet. Childcare, food preparation, and other household tasks also demanded women's attention. Men supplied protein to the Mississippian diet with the benefits of their hunting and fishing activities. They relied on an abundance of white-tailed deer, turkeys, raccoons, turtles, and various fish species. Men also protected family and village in times of conflict, serving as warriors in a sometimes volatile world. Perhaps most important, males served as priests and leaders, often overseeing the lives of thousands of regional inhabitants.

The average farming family in the Mississippian complex lived a fairly simple life, but the society developed stratification, which enabled a minority to live differently. As populations supported by maize agriculture grew, society turned to a hierarchical system to govern, protect, and guide the community. A ranked society developed that was characterized by the pervasive inequality of persons or groups. We identify the emergent sociopolitical organization as a chiefdom. Chiefdoms tend to be highly productive societies with economic, social, and religious coordination. Within this structure, certain family or kin groups enjoyed elevated status as social, political, and economic elites. They were socially ranked according to their genealogical proximity to the chief, thereby achieving a hereditary status so that society identified certain lineages as possessing

the rights to specific leadership roles and offices. Males of major lineages expected and received important positions in the community.

The Mississippian elite accounted for perhaps 5 percent of the population. Their increased status was most obviously seen in their unique lifestyles that were supported by the labor of the common farmers. Most obviously, they lived literally above the rest of the populace. Elite housing typically occupied a place of prominence on constructed mounds in the center of the village. These residences were set apart from and raised above the others. They would dwell in safety within the protection of a fortified town, while simple farmers lived beyond the palisades. Therefore in case of an attack, the more dispensable population would bear the brunt of the initial violence, giving the leaders time to organize defense. Life was not only safer in the elite neighborhood, it was also better in most material ways. The privileged classes ate more and better food, typically more meat, out of more valuable and ornate serving containers than commoners. Every aspect of the elite lifestyle was intended to convey the impression of wealth and importance. Elite individuals could be distinguished by the value of their clothing and jewelry, including some specific symbols of rank like axes. When they died the trappings of their position were buried with them, allowing archaeologists to gain a glimpse of the splendor of life at the top of Mississippian society.

Moundbuilding

The life and death of the highest classes of this culture are closely tied to the most striking feature of Mississippian life—the platform mounds. No other culture in the United States erected these striking monuments, many of which survive to the present. Built as they were on flat bottomlands of the Mississippi drainage, the earthen structures created a striking focal point for the surrounding territory. They were meant to impress, elevate, and separate. The mounds were built of earth, by hand, and in stages. The technique was simple and relied on the organization of thousands of individuals committed to the heavy labor of hauling basket loads of dirt to the chosen location.

The first construction yielded a flat-topped hill rising from the level ground. A wood and mud temple claimed the top spot so it could easily been seen by all, and could elevate prayers toward the gods. The chief priest reigned supreme here until his death at which time he would be buried in the temple, which would be burned

down and covered over with a new level of earth, and a new temple erected. Similarly, council houses and buildings housing other leaders came down after years of use and new earth was added to make a new platform. Thus the mounds grew in both height and breadth as the generations of leaders passed, sometimes reaching great heights in numerous stages over hundreds of years. Side platforms even sprang up on the sides of mounds, making multilevel pyramids. The mounds commanded a central location in the village and generally enclosed a plaza or open courtyard. This area served as an important public space for ceremonies, games, and gatherings held under the watchful eyes of the leaders. Ceremonies and ball games would have brought people from surrounding villages and farms to watch and participate. The Mississippians played a game similar to lacrosse as well as the "chunkey stone" game in which a pole was thrown through a hole in a rolling stone and the opponents were often rivals from different towns.

The existence of mounds in a town indicated that it was a major settlement and probably a ceremonial center. Not all places had mounds, however; there was diversity in settlement style across the Mississippian region. The social and political structure of a community would vary in complexity depending on its size. As the reliability of maize harvests fueled population growth, some villages evolved into regional centers. Such centers would have affiliated subsidiary villages and even farther flung farmsteads on the periphery whose residents provided food and labor and some level of loyalty to the leadership of the town. We can identity levels of complexity through archaeological research. For example, in the American Bottom there were varying sizes of temple-mound complexes. The largest in the area, indeed in the Mississippian world, was Cahokia with more than 100 mounds; the next tier of five sites had multiple mounds, and the last five contained only a single mound. Apart from these centers of political, religious, and social importance, people lived in dispersed farmsteads that were far more rural than the villages of an earlier period. So we see that as the Mississippian culture became more hierarchical and structured, it drove a change in resident patterns from all villages to either concentrated towns or isolated farms.

Political Structure and Warfare

The concentrated towns were centers of political spheres of influence that dominated surrounding production areas. They served

as hubs for the economic, religious, and social life of the region's residents. Although they were not numerically dominant, they wielded extensive power over the lives of Mississippians. We know of several major ceremonial centers of the Mississippian culture from which the ruling class wielded its considerable political and religious power. Such regional centers had formal plazas, earthworks, and other structures of civil and religious importance. They thus left the strongest physical evidence from the period. Several of these have been excavated and extensively studied, providing our best window into Mississippian life.

Moundville

The chiefdom located in west central Alabama at Moundville was large and important. At its height in the thirteenth and fourteenth centuries, it covered 370 acres and included two dozen mounds. The location on a bench along the Black Warrior River was well chosen to use local resources. People had inhabited the area for millennia and had begun relying on maize agriculture, but the outlines of a centralized town do not appear at the site until around A.D. 1050. The population density grew rapidly until by A.D. 1250 Moundville had emerged as a regional center of some importance. By this time maize provided 65 percent of residents' diet, supporting a stable residential society. The emergence as a major location in the Mississippian world seems to have come quickly. From A.D. 1200–1250, construction began on all the mounds, as well as the palisade. This work defined the outline of a four-sided central plaza that had been laboriously leveled before mounds were laid out in the cardinal directions. There were square and oval mounds ranging from 3 to 58 feet high. An east-west symmetry paired residential mounds with mortuary temple mounds. A palisade enclosed the plaza on all but the river bluff side, and it was protected by square-towered bastions along sections of walls.

Perhaps concern over security is what encouraged people to move from the outlying farms to within the these protective walls. As people began moving from farmsteads to Moundville, the density increased. About 1,000 people in nuclear families built square wattle-daub houses. Even with the rapid growth, the distinction between public and private areas of the town was maintained. The plaza area held the residences of the elite atop mounds. More flat-topped mounds north of the plaza contained high-status burials. The central portion of Moundville was clearly dominated by

the powerful leaders; however, their lives depended on tribute, often in the form of maize, from the commoners. Secondary satellite centers grew up between the main town and the farmlands to administer and regulate tribute flow. In addition to this localized trade in foodstuffs, the residents of Moundville also engaged in long-distance trade by importing chert, greenstone, mica, copper, and marine shells.

Life in Moundville continued growing in complexity until about A.D. 1300. Then over the next 150 years, the population moved away from the center town; however, farmers, tradesmen, and artisans did continue to provide tribute and remain engaged with the leaders at Moundville. Over this time the palisade fell into disrepair so perhaps the threat of attack declined and people no longer desired the security of town life. Moundville's previous high population density may have overtaxed natural resources so that dispersal was the only option for continued success. The departure of most of the commoners left only the elite and their sacred areas. Moundville became a city mostly of the dead as cemeteries were established in abandoned residential areas. Because the number of dead outnumbered the living, bodies must have come from the surrounding region to be buried there. This system could not and did not remain sustainable for much longer. By the time of DeSoto in the 1540s, there was little left of the ranked centralized society that had thrived here in the thirteenth century. A combination of military defeat and disease that accompanied European invasion doomed the remnants of Moundville's society.

Spiro

The Spiro complex in eastern Oklahoma was one of the most impressive Mississippian centers. Unfortunately, it is also one of the most destroyed by time and looters. This location shows the impressive reach of the Mississippian culture outward from its core. In general the cultural traits weakened as they extended toward the periphery of the sphere of influence; however, at Spiro a full-blown manifestation of the ranked chiefdom clearly existed.

Spiro covers about 140 acres along the Arkansas River. Like other temple centers, it spread along a terrace, giving it elevation as well as access to the fertile floodplains for agriculture. The nearby Ouachita mountains benefited the location by providing the resources of a temperate forest environment. It would have been physically arranged and politically organized similarly to other ceremonial

centers. Like those towns Spiro contained several mounds, but one stands out for its size and the wealth of burials found within it. The mound with the modern day name Craig Mound is a bit unusual in its construction. It began as a series of small mounds, about 15 feet high, that were laid out in a straight line and connected by low saddles. A final mound reached 33 feet and completed the 400-foot long line. This large mound represented a long accretion of material used in burial mounds—mats, bark, burials, and earth fill. Several charnel houses or houses of the dead had been built and destroyed on this spot. The last of these sacred spaces remained intact so that excavations revealed the process of burials. The bodies of high-ranking individuals arrived at the sacred area borne on woven mat litters, which remained under the bodies. An impressive array of goods was heaped over each body, many made from exotic materials such as marine shells and copper, as well as basketry and fiber. All this opulence clearly marks these bodies as those of the powerful elite who were accorded honor and respect in death as well as life. The grave goods also reveal Spiro as the center of an extensive trade network. Like Moundville, this vibrant religious, political, and economic center gradually declined and became a vacant town, occupied only by the revered dead of elite status. Also like other ceremonial centers, Spiro was abandoned by 1450. People did not leave the region, and scholars believe that the Caddo and perhaps Wichita tribes are Spiro descendants.

Cahokia

The Mississippian culture left many remarkable towns and mounds with fascinating artifacts. It was obviously a widespread set of shared cultural attributes. The premier Mississippian site, however, is clearly in the heart of the American Bottom, near present-day St. Louis. Cahokia, as we call it today, was the largest town in North America before European arrival. In fact, it was five times larger than any other town. The location covers five acres of some of the richest land in America, predicting success in a agriculturally based society. This territory supported a large population that probably exceeded 15,000 people in the town and many thousands more in the surrounding countryside.

The population and power centered at Cahokia grew quickly around A.D. 1000. The town began to take on the characteristics of a Mississippian center with mounds, plaza, sacred spaces, and precincts for the elite. This intense growth followed a model of concen-

tration of power in the hands of a hereditary aristocracy holding the allegiance and support of a large rural majority. The rural population labored at agriculture, which successfully supported a dense settlement pattern and generated impressive wealth.

Cahokia boasted both the largest collection of mounds in North America, nearly 120, and the largest constructed earthwork in the Americas and perhaps the world. Monk's Mound, named for its nineteenth-century association with a monastery, dominates the landscape at Cahokia. It covers 17 acres, rises 100 feet, and contains 22 million cubic feet of earth. Although the mound reached these proportions over several centuries, the 900 by 650 foot, 20-foot tall core was built quickly, as it was clay and had to be covered rapidly to prevent shrinking. We can imagine a huge workforce that traveled from outlying areas to participate in the project. Once constructed, the mound was topped by a temple for the priests. Temples contained the symbols of power, strands of pearls, turkey feather headdresses, copper and shell pendants, as well as figures representing revered ancestors. When an important official died, he would be buried within the building, which was destroyed and covered over to create a new sacred space.

Other mounds also contained burials that tell us more about the society at Cahokia. Excavations at Mound #72 reveal the power that the elite held over the populace. One powerful man was laid to rest on top of 20,000 shell beads, along with 400 arrows, 19 chunky stones, and bushels of exotic raw materials such as mica and copper. All of this wealth was created specifically for this purpose. In addition, six people were apparently sacrificed to be buried alongside the leader. An even clearer statement that rulers held the ultimate power of life and death over the populace is seen in another grave containing the bodies of 50 young women and 4 decapitated men. All of the burials were accompanied by large amounts of grave goods.

Some mounds did not contain burials; more likely they served to enclose a sacred place or to provide orientation to the cardinal directions (compass points) and the powerful sun. All the measurements and alignments of the mound construction are incredibly accurate. Another remarkable engineering feat was the construction of the woodhenges. These are precisely laid out circles of tall wooden posts. Scholars cannot agree on the purpose of these circles, which may have been created to track solar positions; but considering the planning and labor they required, Cahokians clearly valued them. Another construction project that would have required considerable

commitment of labor was wooden palisades that at times surrounded
the heart of Cahokia. By A.D. 1150, inner and outer stockades ringed
the sacred center in an effort to improve security for the rich and
powerful.

The whole system of hierarchical power, extensive trade, and
massive building projects was supported by agriculture. The successful cultivation of maize and other supporting crops provided
the sustenance and the wealth of the Cahokian population. The
residents of the sacred city, especially the elite, relied on the labor
of the rural farmsteads in the surrounding region. The political and
religious leaders sought to control agricultural production through
their authority over fertility symbolism and ritual. Examples of
the relevant symbolism were unearthed in the temple complex at
Cahokia. Two stone figures of goddesses portray females with symbolic corn, squash, and hoes, clear references to the importance of
the bounty of Mother Earth. Artifacts such as these testify to the
importance of religion among Mississippian peoples.

Southeastern Ceremonial Complex

It appears from the physical evidence remaining from Mississippian culture that religion played an integral and critical role in
society. It is hard to reconstruct or analyze what must have been a
vibrant, evolving belief system shared by thousands of people over
a long time. Artifacts can tell only a small part of the story. Anthropologists have added to our understanding of the ancient lifeways
of the American Southeast by examining the practices of historic
native residents of the area and this technique has informed much
of our projections about Mississippian religion. Several Mississippian centers existed, although in reduced form, when Europeans
arrived. The Natchez, Calusa, Cofitachequi, and the Powhatan peoples retained elements of the hierarchical chiefdoms that previously
dominated the region, particularly in respect to religious beliefs and
icons. We know from archaeological and historical accounts that the
belief in powerful beings who affected human life dominated native
thought. Southeastern natives divided the world into dualistic categories. These were two opposing systems and each had considerable power. In this case they were probably the Upper World and
the Under World. Humans spent a great deal of time and energy
trying to strike a balance between these two forces. The idea was
that men could not change the power of each entity but could miti-
gate their impact in this world. Therefore people had to be aware of

the power of spirits and be prepared to appease them or at the least not offend them by improper behavior or lack of reverence.

One way to repair and maintain harmony within a powerful system would be to hold ceremonies honoring the gods. These events would be prescribed, specific undertakings to which the whole community subscribed and in which they participated. They would have been held on a regular cycle throughout the year. Ritual observances could have included initiating the new year with a new fire ceremony, celebrating the spring reappearance of plants, the summer maturing of maize, and of course the life-sustaining harvest season. In addition to large elaborately planned ceremonies, religious leaders supervised rituals to ensure successful planting and harvest. Supernatural forces were thought to affect every phase of human activity and so great care was taken to ensure proper conduct at all times.

In many ways the religious patterns of southeastern natives were not remarkable or unusual: many cultures have seasonal ceremonies to ensure harmony with spirits. It is the extent to which Mississippian beliefs permeated their lives (and deaths) and the level of intensity with which they practiced their religion that makes them the object of much scrutiny. The term *southeastern ceremonial complex* (also *southeastern cult*) refers to the incredibly rich outpouring of ceremonial art that is tied to trade and the hierarchical organization of Mississippian society. It is so widespread, over such a large area, that it suggests the existence of a common religion throughout the Mississippian world. Again, we have only the material objects with which we can try to reconstruct an elaborate worldview. This artistic expression of powerful beliefs is also closely linked to the trade, social organization, and political power. Some scholars regard the southeastern ceremonial complex as a network of exchange and interaction as much as a religion.

The finest examples of the symbolism of the southern ceremonial complex are found in burials. Interments of powerful individuals offered an opportunity for conspicuous display of special or ceremonial items. Hundreds of objects might be buried with a revered leader and most would have been created solely for that purpose. The grave goods showed the wealth of the person, but might also contain symbols that served as insignia of office, thus proclaiming the position and status he held in life. Some depicted ancestors, a group Mississippians held in high regard; others depicted supernatural beings, also an important force. We can discern what was important to people in their lives by what they chose to send with

their dead. Most grave goods focused on religion and ritual. Implements used in public ceremony included rattles, fans, and scarifiers (to inflict ritual scars), and crystals usually used for personal rituals were also included. The decorations on many objects show figures with maces or axes clutching severed heads, which is a clear reference to bold, decisive, often violent action that must have been a positive trait in Mississippian society. Similarly the inclusion of arrows shows the importance of hunting, whereas stones from a popular game indicate that recreation had its place in society.

The symbols of the southern ceremonial complex have long fascinated observers. Several motifs appear frequently and are also found in earlier Hopewell sites and occur across the region, showing their widespread importance and longevity. Although they differ in execution, there seems to be a pan-southern set of symbols including weeping and forked eyes, elaborate crosses, the sun circle, human eyes on open hands, and the arrows with attached lobes. These might be displayed on their own or as part of a representation of a human form. Human figures were often depicted wearing ear spools, necklaces with conch shell pendants, forelocks threaded with beads hair knots at the back of their heads, belts with tassels, and pointed aprons. Animals indigenous to the region also appear including raccoons, falcons, woodpeckers, serpents, and others. Powerful animals or those with admirable skills were clearly highly regarded. For example, the central ritual area at the Mississippian site of Okmulgee, Georgia, is an earthen platform 40 feet in diameter shaped like a bird of prey.

The common motifs are usually depicted on artifacts found in burials. They could be incised onto thin sheets of copper, engraved on marine shell or stone, and painted, etched, or shaped into pottery. The majority of the artifacts occur at major ceremonial centers at Etowah, Georgia; Moundville, Alabama; and Spiro, Oklahoma. The widespread use of the symbols indicates an interconnectedness to Mississippian life; however, the materials used in the artwork reveal even more about the society. Most of this skilled art relied on materials from outside a town's immediate vicinity, thus proving the existence of a vast network of trade.

The Mississippian world obviously stretched widely across southeastern America. The objects found in homes, temples, burials, and trash piles reveal a great deal about the values, economy, and organization of a culture. By analyzing the physical remains of artifacts, archaeologists can determine the source of raw material. The Mississippians traded copper from the Great Lakes region, marine

shells from the Gulf of Mexico and Atlantic Ocean, and flint from various sources. They obviously moved a wide range of raw materials and finished items over long distances. Only the nonperishable materials have survived, but it is possible that the network also moved food and salt throughout the region.

Trade

The existence of long distance trade routes throughout the Mississippian world tells us about their society. The ongoing demand for exotic luxury materials must have been driven by a wealthy and powerful elite. Demand was sustained by the fact that the materials were interred with the dead, thereby removing the items from future consumption. Some members of society apparently dedicated much of their time to the long journeys required for trade, whereas others organized and controlled the trade, and still others grew the food to sustain nonagricultural citizens. Trade routes were well established and probably valued. Cordial relationships had to be maintained both with the sources of the trade and the areas in between through which traders must pass. Traders would have needed to be multilingual to accomplish long distance travel. Aside from the practical measure of security, there would have been social interaction among traders, thus spreading ideas, beliefs, customs, and other aspects of culture.

The extent of the trade and its ongoing nature would have provided Mississippian centers with an important conduit for the exchange and dissemination of ideas. This contact would have aided the dispersal of religious beliefs and symbolism that we recognize as the southern ceremonial complex.

The complex world created by the Mississippians eventually began to collapse. In center after center, archaeologists find evidence of decline and abandonment. Of course, we cannot know what brought on this disintegration of the highly structured society that had thrived for centuries. Experts, however, do put forth various theories to explain the end of the Mississippian world, which can be divided into categories of materialistic and ideological crises. Environmental instability is an obvious material explanation. Rising populations, especially at a large center like Cahokia, may simply have overtaxed the available resources in the region. Consider the number of trees required to build and rebuild woodhenges, palisades, and temples, and to fuel heating and cooking fires. Such requirements would have ensured the areas surrounding the towns were

stripped of woods and planted with crops. Without the natural tree cover, the uplands began to dump water and sediment on the fields below with each storm event. Flooding could have posed a serious problem. Certainly this was the case at Cahokia where leaders attempted to solve a water shortage by diverting a local creek to the center of town, which only worsened the danger of floods. The unpredictability of increased flooding pushed residences up onto the bluffs, away from the sacred town centers. Experts also point to a changing climate that posed new challenges to the existing agricultural system.

All the ecological changes would have severely taxed the Mississippian leadership who responded poorly, which in turn drove the ideological decline. The elite, especially the priests, were supposed to maintain the peoples' relationship with the spirits that governed natural forces. The problems of the early thirteenth century showed the populace that the priests had failed, thus sparking a crisis of confidence in the leadership. In response, leaders at Cahokia had a two-mile palisade built around the central plaza that separated their space from the public, at a cost of 20,000 trees. This event had to increase tensions within the hierarchical political and social system. People may have decided that the benefits of the centralized society had waned to the extent that they moved outside the power sphere of the former rulers.

At Cahokia, nature gave the last exclamation point to the town's demise—an earthquake. The quake apparently destroyed part of the premier earthwork, Monk's Mound, and subsequent failed repairs show the golden age of skilled workers had passed. Cahokia could not recover from the combination of factors that stressed the Mississippian society. Some archaeologists even believe that the society devolved into a civil war that destroyed its very fabric. We do know that Cahokia, as most major Mississippian ceremonial centers, was almost empty by A.D. 1350, more than a century before Europeans' arrival.

Archaeology can tell us that the major urban areas of the core Mississippian culture fell apart by the mid-fourteenth century. We also know, however, that the people did not all disappear but rather dispersed and moved away from the hierarchical, structured society of the past. In fact, descendants of Mississippian people were everywhere in eastern woodlands when Europeans arrived. In many places the social complexity was lost, but some features, especially the dependence on agriculture, continued.

We can surmise the look of the post-Mississippian Southeast by examining the observations of Europeans who encountered native

peoples within the next century. Some of the same cultural traits we have identified as Mississippian remained in sometime weakened forms throughout the south. For example, the settlement pattern of pre-Columbian southeastern natives was similar to the rural Mississippian households. High status households among the Chickasaw and Creek tribes had several buildings, including those for storage, cooking, and residence. The Virginia countryside observed by the English explorers included fortified villages that may have looked similar to the fortified Mississippian towns in the American Bottom.

Natchez

The group that best reflects the faded glory of the Mississippian culture was the Natchez of modern-day Mississippi. The Natchez proudly kept alive the moundbuilding tradition until the French nearly wiped them out in 1731. Despite their earlier devastation by European-introduced diseases, the Natchez still impressed French explorers with their rich ceremonial life and recognizable hierarchical structure. Not surprisingly, the Natchez economy centered primarily on the cultivation of maize. This focus led the people to worship the sun, the force on which a successful harvest depended. The premier ruler was revered as the Great Sun who dwelled on the main temple mound and was attended by lesser Suns, probably from his lineage. The society was further stratified into a noble class, honored men, and finally the commoners whose labor supported the whole system. In one odd custom that was perhaps a reaction to the problems that challenged earlier Mississippian hierarchies, all noble classes had to marry from the common class, or "Stinkards," which ensured a constant renewal of blood lines, as well as eternal hope for betterment from the lower classes.

Ceremonial Life

The Natchez ceremonial life was rich, including temples, idols of stone and clay, and animal remains. Periodic feast days brought people to the temple to honor their ruler who was borne on a litter or walked on mats at all times. DeSoto would report similar reverence for the leader of Cofitchequi in South Carolina lasting into the early sixteenth century. In imitation of Mississippian ancestors, the burial of a Great Sun involved the sacrifice of several of his relatives and servants. The spouse of the leader, siblings, close associates, and trusted servants knew it to be their duty to express their devotion by

dying with the leader. Other individuals actually volunteered to be sacrificed, considering it an honor for their spirits to accompany that of the Great Sun to the next world. Thus a funeral of a high-ranking Natchez leader triggered numerous deaths, which caused a considerable disruption in the immediate society. The funeral itself was a lavish affair, which we learn from French accounts of the death of the Great Sun's brother, the Tattooed-Serpent. The body lay in state for three days, bedecked in finery of elaborate clothing and a feathered headdress, along with his weapons and symbols of his office and accomplishments in life. It was then carried to the temple where the people to be sacrificed sat on mats and ingested tobacco to stupefy them. Relatives then hooded the victims and strangled them to death. All the bodies were buried in accordance to their rank. Months later the bodies would be dug up, the bones cleaned and stored in baskets inside the temple. Although the Natchez's elaborate mortuary ceremony was the last in the Southeast to strongly reflect the Mississippian culture, the basic concept of ancestor worship remained widespread. Europeans reported seeing bones stored in temples throughout the region, including among Pocahontas's people. Other aspects of distinctive mortuary practices continued to characterize southeastern natives into the contact period.

The era of politically united, religiously focused chiefdoms ended before European contact with native Americans. The remnants of the past practices evident among the Natchez and other southeastern groups intrigued and confused whites who encountered them in the fifteenth and sixteenth centuries. Evidence of the glory, power, and wealth of indigenous peoples was generally dismissed by Europeans. White male observers did not believe the stories passed through the generations that revealed the past. Even concrete evidence such as remaining mounds failed to break through the Europeans' conviction of cultural superiority. Euro-Americans continued to deny indigenous construction of the mounds into the modern era. So the greatest native flourishing of religion, politics, and economic success faded from America's memory and is only recently reemerging as a powerful part of the country's past.

The American Southeast witnessed some of the most complex and wealthiest of pre-Columbian cultures. Those in the Mississippi River drainages used agriculture to develop complex societies with hierarchical social and centralized political systems, elaborate religious beliefs, extensive trade networks, and diverse economic stratification. The moundbuilding traditions of the Mississippian

Europeans found native villages supported by agriculture throughout the Southeast. Library of Congress.

peoples remain a highpoint of North American history. Others, like the Calusa of Florida, developed thriving communities complete with hierarchies and tribute systems without agriculture. The richness of the Southeast, from coast to forest to mighty rivers, allowed early inhabitants to prosper.

FURTHER READING

Archaeology of Cahokia. Cahokia Mounds State Historic Site maintains a complete web page about the mounds. http://www.cahokiamounds. com/archaeology.html (accessed September 1, 2007).

Hudson, Charles. *The Southeastern Indians.* Knoxville, TN: University of Tennessee Press, 1976.

Legend of the Tlanuhwa and the Uhktena. The Cherokee of California maintain this page dedicated to Cherokee history. http://www.powersource. com/cocinc/articles/tlanuhwa.htm (accessed September 1, 2007).

Milner, George. *The Moundbuilders: Ancient Peoples of Eastern North America.*
    London: Thames & Hudson, 2005.
Pauketat, Timothy R. *Ancient Cahokia and the Mississippians.* New York:
    Cambridge University Press, 2004.
Townsend, Richard F., ed. *Hero, Hawk, and Open Hand: American Indian Art
    of the Ancient Midwest and South.* New Haven, CT: Yale University
    Press, 2004.

3

The Plains

The Plains is a large region occupying the very middle of America. It is the great grassland of the American continent. Before the area was settled with permanent structures, first-time visitors were overwhelmed by the huge expanses of vegetation. The vastness of the vistas still sparks wonder. You can see farther across the unfolding landscape here than anywhere else in the country.

Like most geographic regions, the Plains is hard to define. The western border is accepted as the Rocky Mountains, but the mountains are not a solid line. In some areas ranges, such as the Black Hills or the Bighorn Mountains, stand separately; however, the Rockies do make a fairly coherent western border. On either end the Plains has no clearly defined edges. To the north the grasslands gradually transition into the Canadian sub-Arctic and to the south into the Mexican desert. On the east the Plains abut the Eastern Woodlands and again a strong border is hard to discern. In general a line paralleling the Mississippi River to the west from Louisiana, Arkansas, Missouri, and Iowa to Minnesota can serve as a division betweens woods and Plains. Along that rough boundary the trees begin to taper off and occur only in river valleys and the "sea of grass" begins to dominate. Rivers here generally flow easterly to meet the mighty Mississippi. Several important river systems—the Platte, Missouri, and Red—drain the Plains into the Mississippi

basin. The Missouri was especially important to prehistoric peoples. As it cuts southward through the Dakotas, the river bed marks the border of glacial deposits and delineates a sharp difference in soils to the east and west. The river's floodplain provided the only thinner soils that could be successfully exploited by farmers without metal tools and draft animals; the sod on the rest of the grasslands was too thick to exploit. So sedentary villages were concentrated along the banks of the Missouri. The river also created a barrier to travel and tended to separate peoples east and west of its path.

CLIMATE AND ENVIRONMENT

The Plains are composed primarily of northern temperate grasslands. The western portion is higher and drier, which supports shorter grasses like buffalo and gama grass. Yucca, cactus, and sage also grow thickly in some areas. The only trees are confined to ridges where juniper and pine grow or to valleys whose greater moisture supports willows and cottonwood. Small valleys and channels fill quickly after a storm, but are not permanent water sources. Where streams have cut down to the bedrock, springs come up and then berries and other edible plants can grow there. The mammals on the Plains tend to be grazing or burrowing species. Bison, pronghorn antelope, mule deer, white-tailed deer, elk, black bear, grizzly bear, and coyote have made the region their home. Smaller species exploited by early humans included prairie chicken and grouse. During the Ice Age the Plains hosted a wide variety of amazing animals such as ground sloths, giant beaver, musk oxen, dire wolf, and saber-toothed cats. The iconic image of Indians hunting bison on horseback that is so connected to the Plains in modern thought was only partially realized in pre-Columbian history. The bison thrived on the pre-Columbian Plains, but the horse had died out after the Ice Age and would not be represented in the Americas until the Spanish reintroduced the modern horse.

There are some unusual environments within the greater Plains region. In the western Dakotas the Badlands are heavily eroded, steep-sided hills barren of vegetation that have an other worldly look. In Nebraska there is an area of sandhills. These stationary sand dunes are covered with grasses, yucca, and cactus. They included marshes and ponds, which provided important habitat for migrating birds that could be exploited by early hunters. Millions of swans, ducks, terns, plovers, and other birds fly south from their arctic breeding grounds and can provide a fairly reliable, seasonal food source.

The eastern section of the Plains is lower and wetter and thus dominated by tall grass species and can be distinguished from the high Plains by referring to it as prairie. A wide variety of plants produce seeds, tubers, and roots for human consumption; however, it is not as rich as the eastern woodlands. The Plains were not well suited to horticulture and, in fact, cultivation developed elsewhere and was then imported onto the prairies by experienced cultures. This occurred in distinct sections of the Plains like the Missouri River valley.

Anywhere on the Plains the weather can be a challenge to human existence. The region experiences extremes of both heat and cold. The same area can be 32 degrees below zero in the winter and soar to 114 degrees Fahrenheit in the summer. The region receives considerable, but unpredictable rainfall. Summer thunderstorms can be intense and local, flooding one spot while a few miles away the ground is dry. The yearly rainfall varies widely presenting distinct challenges to human habitation.

PALEO-INDIANS

The Plains has been one of the most misunderstood regions in the country. For many years experts believed it was uninhabitable before the arrival of the horse. They reasoned that the animals living there could not be exploited by humans without the aid of a horse. Subsequent archaeology has disproved this theory, and we now know that humans have lived on the Plains for more than 10,000 years, beginning in the Ice Age. In the Pleistocene period, life on the Great Plains followed the pattern of much of the continent. From 9000 to 6000 B.C., the region was used by big game hunters who moved frequently in pursuit of megafauna such as mammoth and giant bison (*Bison antiquus*). Winds blowing off the continental glaciers to the north cooled the region and provided rainfall to create a lush environment perfect for these large herbivores. Archaeologists can point to the existence of big game hunters on the Plains through excavations of kill, work, and camp sites. There have been findings of Clovis hunters with lanceolate points.

Hunting

This culture hunted mammoth with groups of men. Hunters were probably members of different kin groups who came together to exploit the large mammals that they could not handle alone.

Herbivores moved fairly slowly as they grazed, but humans needed some advantage over these behemoths. Men sent out scouts and when animals were sighted they stayed downwind and got as close as possible. They then waited for mammoth group to enter a compromising situation such as a spring or pond where the animals' feet might become entrapped by mud. To increase their chances, the human hunters followed the practice of other carnivore hunters by singling out young or female animals. Although there was more meat in a bull, it was not worth the risk to attack a large, aggressive animal in his prime. In a period long before emergency medicine, when an entire extended family might rely on the skills of one or two men, each risk had to be carefully weighed. It would do no good to take down the biggest animal if a man was injured or maimed in the process.

When the herd was surrounded, all the hunters hurled spears at the animals whose movement was restricted by their surroundings. The result was usually chaos, as frightened animals reacted to the intrusion and sudden pain. Hunters had to be careful not to get trampled in the chaos of a panicked herd. If they were successful, the stone spear points punctured the mammoths' thick hide and brought one down. This was clearly not the task of one person and required a social structure that could accommodate communal work.

Once the animals were dead the men commenced butchering, once again a huge task requiring shared effort. The foreshaft of their spears detached with the points from the main shaft to make a knife. After word reached the rest of the band, families arrived to set up camp near the kill site. It took a great deal of work to process a mammoth carcass. Meat had to be removed and prepared by drying or smoking. Of course some meat would be enjoyed immediately by the people who may not have had meat for weeks. Sinew was saved for sewing and lashing, and bones became useful tools such as scrapers. Mammoth skin was too thick for clothing but could be used to make durable foot coverings valued by a nomadic people.

As the climate on the Plains changed at the end of the Ice Age, people had to adapt. They had become adept at using the large animals for their survival, but now the megafauna was dying out. Hunters had to adjust their skills to take advantage of available smaller game animals. The Folsom culture showed remarkable skill in flint knapping by creating a sophisticated fluted point. These were lighter and easier to carry than Clovis

points. In addition, the points could be produced more easily and sharpened repeatedly. Folsom people had cultural ties to the Clovis but represent a continuation and evolution of the hunting tradition. Their carefully flaked points were designed to bring down animals like the extinct species of bison and mule deer that populated the Plains 10,000 years ago. A site in Alberta, Canada revealed evidence that early hunters exploited the ancient species of horse as a prey animal, as well as hunting bison and musk ox. Folsom sites occur all over the Plains and clearly record a successful cultural adaptation.

The Plano culture replaced the older Folsom tradition in the Plains as elsewhere around 6000 B.C. They created a different, distinctive style of points that varied throughout the country. These styles are named for their locations and those in the Plains include Hell Gap, Agate Basin, Scottsbluff, and Eden. Like those hunters before them, the Plano moved around in pursuit of nomadic game animals that provided critical protein in their diet. Plano sites, however, have also yielded evidence of grinding tools used to process vegetative materials, thus providing rare evidence of gathering to supplement a hunting economy. The Plano people's exploitation of a variety of resources marks the transition into the next phase of early civilization.

One of the favorite game animals of the time was the bison. Pre-Columbian hunters knew the animals well and used their skittish herd instincts. Hunters generally chose a naturally favorable location like a cliff or dead end canyon. They then used communal techniques to drive the animals toward the goal. Once they startled the prey, the animals tended to panic and hurtled forward without reason. In such a state hundred of animals could quickly fall over the cliff or be penned into a natural corral. At a cliff site the fall generally killed or maimed most animals. Because the hunters could not easily control the number of animals that fell over the cliff, this technique was somewhat wasteful. At a corral site the first animals ran into the natural barrier while those behind careened into them. Stretching skins or some other barrier behind the herd prevented escape. Hunters took advantage of the animals' confusion and panic to dispatch them at close range with spears. The Indians took as much meat as they could process and carry, but inevitably some waste occurred. Later hunting techniques that singled out individual animals were more efficient; however, the bison jump was certainly successful and offered a high return with low level technology.

PLAINS ARCHAIC

As the Ice Age finally released its hold on the Plains, life changed drastically for humans. Around 7000 B.C., the temperature climbed, land dried out, and the grasslands spread. Gone now were all the large game animals that hunters had relied on for huge amounts of meat. Plant species also changed as the climate became drier and warmer. People had to diversify and adapt their hunting and gathering techniques to the new realities, and that adaptation ushered in the Archaic period. There is a period referred to by scientists as the Altithermal when the west went through a drier, warmer period than present-day conditions. This would presumably have taxed both animals and humans in their delicate balance for survival. There is less evidence of human occupation in this period, suggesting that hunter-gatherers migrated to adjacent regions to compete successfully.

By the early Archaic period, around 5500 B.C., the new culture began to take shape. People now hunted and gathered more than previously. Foraging people tended to occupy sites for longer periods of time than big game hunters. They spent more time in one area exploiting a variety of resources and thus tended to leave a bit more evidence of themselves. By 4500 B.C., the smaller bison species thrived in the region and as they moved north and east, the people followed. In some areas humans relied on more than bison for meat. They also hunted pronghorn antelope and mule deer extensively. This both broadened their diets and made them less dependent on the availability of one species. Hunters added waterfowl and fish to their meat supply when they could. All of these animals also provided other necessities of daily life. In the Missouri River area we have found bird bones that have been purposely modified. The bills of whooping crane and raven appear to have been used in a ritualistic manner. In addition to meat, the women of the groups gathered nuts, berries, roots, and seeds to supplement daily meals.

We find evidence that indicates that local communities had developed specialized subsistence strategies and new tools to adapt to local conditions. It made sense to specialize to more effectively exploit the resources at hand. Archaeology reveals evidence of new stone points with notched sides, which allowed stronger and tighter binding of point to spear handle and thus more reliable hunting. Archaic hunters used the atlatl or spear thrower to improve velocity of their weapons, perhaps indicating the pursuit

of a quicker species than the lumbering mammoths of the Pleistocene. The aesthetic quality of points, however, seems to have begun a long decline never to be regained. Perhaps toolmakers were making a larger quantity of points more quickly to exploit the increased numbers of smaller animals. Other hunting techniques were also used. Archaeologists have found a net woven by hand from 1.25 miles of twisted juniper bark fibers. This enormous investment in time and labor captured bighorn sheep and deer. There was also an increase in the use of grinding stones, which suggests greater reliance on plant materials.

Economy

Bison continued to be an important game animal of the American Plains. During the Ice Age the giant bison (*Bison antiquus*) roamed the Plains; after it died out an intermediate species *Bison occidentalis* emerged, and then finally the modern species *Bison bison*. It is clear from the archaeological record that hunters exploited all three of these species. For thousands of years the bison jump was a reliable method of capturing this important food source. More than a hundred of them occur throughout America. Probably the best documented and most famous is Head-Smashed-In site in southern Alberta. This site was used from 3500 B.C. to the nineteenth century, a clear indication of the success of this hunting technique. The location is most closely associated with the modern-day Blackfoot people and must have been used by their ancestors. More than 100,000 bison met their deaths here and excavation has told us much about the people who used the site.

The use of the bison jump, and thus the killing of bison, was not taken lightly by people who depended on the animal for food. As the bison became an integral part of the Plains Indian life, it became the object of more and more ritual. Each group had a specific ritual of songs, charms, dances, offerings, and prayers. For example, they might offer prayers to cloud the minds of the animals or to charm them into the trap. The animals themselves were honored through songs and dances during which people might wear buffalo skins as tribute. The use of the bison jump took a great deal of planning and communal effort, so preparation was essential.

The Head-Smashed-In site covers 1,470 acres and consists of three major activity areas: the gathering basin, the kill site, and the processing campsite. First, bison had to be lured to the site. There was a 15-square mile creek drainage, which was lush with springs,

streams, and grass that would naturally attract the herds. The challenge began with moving the herd toward the desired spot. Buffalo runners were sent to locate the herd and drive the bison. These men wore bison and wolf hides to get closer to the animals and often bleated like a calf in distress to interest the females. They would gather bison from several valleys and drive them five to eight miles to the gathering location. It might take days to get the herd into position and so took great patience. The Indians built stone cairns or rock piles to create drive lanes leading from the grazing spots to the cliff edge. The nearsighted animals naturally shied away from the piles and thus concentrated in the middle of the lanes. These might go for miles and generally formed a "V" with the point at the top of the cliff. More than 4,000 have been found at the site and would once have been piled high with sticks and branches. To help stampede the herd men jumped from behind the brush covered cairns waving and yelling. Once the bison began to run, it was difficult for them to stop. Even as the front animals may have sensed danger the momentum of the frightened animals behind them pushed them on. Before they could stop, hundreds of animals had hurtled over the 35-foot sandstone cliff. The bodies piled up at the bottom, many dead or maimed. In fact, the cliff could have once been more than 100 feet high, but the base has been built up over time by bison bones. Archaeologists have excavated bones to a depth of 35 feet.

After the drive the real work began. A stampede might kill 200 to 300 bison, which now had to be butchered. Below the cliffs on the prairie was an open flatland, which served as a campsite and butchering area. Men would quarter the carcasses at the kill site and then drag them to the camp. Everyone would pitch in to prepare the meat and other parts of the bison for storage and use. With no refrigeration people could enjoy fresh meat for only a few days. They ate delicacies like the tongue and heart immediately. The meat would be sliced very thin and then dried on racks. Or it could be pulverized with fat, bone grease, and dried choke cherries to make pemmican, a long-lasting staple of Native American diets. Stripping and preparing the meat alone was a huge task; however, there was much more to do. Bison skins could be used for warm clothing with the hair left on or for lighter weight coverings with the hair removed. Different parts of the animal had different uses. For example, a thick bull neck hide would make a war shield, a hind leg skin a pair of boots, or a green untanned hide could become a kettle. Every part of the bison yielded something useful for humans from tail hair braided into ropes, to spoons made of horns, and shoulder

blade scrapers. All this production took some time and it is clear from the remains at the campsite that people lived there for weeks while they reaped the benefits of the kill.

Apart from extended stays at resource sites, Archaic hunter gatherers moved frequently. Some anthropologists believed that a group of people moved every other day in the summer, but less in the winter. On the Plains there was little use of water transportation like canoes as there was in the east. People walked everywhere they needed to go and carried their belongings with them. They probably were assisted with some of the burden by their dogs, which they domesticated around 2000 B.C. A travois (a later French word) consisting of two poles crossed over the dog's back with the ends dragging on the ground supported a hide platform. Small ones could be pulled by dogs and larger ones were later adapted to the horse. A dog could pull about 75 pounds, which may have determined the size of the tipi. Obviously, when you carried everything, weight and bulk were major concerns, which guided the design of Plains cultural items. These groups never adopted pottery, as it was too heavy and fragile for a nomadic lifestyle. Rather they used stiff untanned hide to create waterproof containers for cooking and food storage.

Housing and Settlement

The most obvious adaptation to this mobile lifestyle was the characteristic Plains dwelling—the tipi. It was so perfectly adapted to conditions that it remained the housing style through the end of the nineteenth century and is still a traditional icon of the West. The tipi consisted of a framework of poles set up in a conical shape with the tops resting on one another. Over this a light hide covering of sewn, tanned bison skins created a dry, warm dwelling. The genius of the design was in its portability. A woman could pitch it in an hour after arrival at camp. The poles could be used to form a travois on which the skin covering was carried. New hides replaced worn sections to maintain the tipi for many years. At each campsite families made a circle of stones to hold down their tipi bottoms. They probably returned to the campsite over and over, reusing the circles. Campsites often contain rock-filled pits that we believe were used in the preparation of vegetables. A bed of hot coals and stones was laid down in the pit to hold the heat and roast the food. These types of hot rock pits might also have heated the living spaces. Other pits served as cache or storage areas to protect food from animals.

Tipis were often set up near a source of water. Library of Congress.

Sometimes people camped in river valleys where bison foraged in winter; other months found camps on top of ridges where winds dried meat quickly and chased away insects. Each camp was chosen for its proximity to something the people needed and conditions on the Plains required exploitation of many resources. Sedentary lifestyles were not an option.

Most of our evidence of the Archaic lifestyle comes from such nomadic campsites. Obviously little remains except stone, bone, and a few other resilient substances. There are few traces of people's religious, political, or other cultural beliefs; however, we can infer something of their belief system from certain findings. For example, at a winter campsite in northwestern Wyoming, mule deer skull caps with antlers attached were found in what appears to be a ceremonial arrangement. In another area a likely ceremonial structure was built near a bison corral. Ritual treatment of important food source species fits with our understanding of hunter gatherer cultures. Burials appear to be isolated, suggesting that people were buried where they died. Only a few have been found and of those some had grave goods like projectile points and shell beads, but others did not. A nomadic people working hard to acquire the daily requirements for life had little time or resources to spend on the deceased.

One major change in the life of Archaic Plains Indians was the introduction of the bow and arrow. This weapon probably came to the region from the Athapaskan speakers migrating south from Canada. New innovations were adopted only if they provided advantages over existing technology. The bow and arrow quickly replaced spears and atlatls. The bow and arrow allowed a hunter to remain crouched and concealed and to fire several times in succession while a thrown spear was a one shot attempt from a standing hunter. The arrow tended to have the same velocity as the spear points, but was far more accurate. The bow and arrow improved a hunter's kill rate and thus were quickly adopted throughout the Plains. Archaic hunters continued to quarry considerable amounts of stone to produce these new arrow points.

The hunters' skills were obviously critical to the survival of people; however, women contributed an important element as well. Traces of more than 100 plant species have been found in campsites. They reflect the seasonality of a nomadic lifestyle—berries and fruits in spring and summer, roots and bulbs in summer, and grasses and seeds in late summer. Arrowroot, goosefoot, sego lily, yucca fruit, gooseberry, wild rye, ricegrass, saltbush seeds, and rosehips supplemented stores of meat. These plants added vitamins, fiber, and variety to the diet. Women prepared the food in earth ovens. They heated small stones that were placed in a clean pit with food wrapped in hide or fibers and covered with earth to bake.

PLAINS WOODLAND

The Plains hunter-gatherers made a successful living, and on the high Plains their culture continued unchanged into the historic period; however, developments changed the lifestyle on the eastern Plains. A new cultural period referred to by anthropologists as the Plains Woodland period began around A.D. 250. Some experts believe this reflects a movement onto the Plains by eastern farmers; others conjecture that locals developed woodland cultural aspects. Certainly the river systems of the eastern Plains allowed for more migration and transfer of ideas. In areas of Nebraska, northern Kansas, Oklahoma, and west to Colorado, we find evidence of pottery and mound burials, clearly eastern hallmarks. Pottery remains are thick, stone-tempered fragments with cord-marked surfaces and textured geometrical designs, which is similar to early Woodland types. Burials in circular mounds of earth and stone covering a chamber for human remains and offerings are found in the Plains

Woodland. Again, this is similar to the developments taking place to the east of the Mississippi River. The Plains, however, did not adopt increased reliance on horticulture, as we've seen in the Woodland tradition. Plains residents may have found that the sedimentary deposits of rivers in this region allowed for rudimentary agriculture, but they remained primarily hunter-gatherers. Particularly in the eastern Plains, hunters were able to exploit a wide variety of animals for food, in some places the count is as high as 45 species.

Hopewell traditions (Chapter 1) from the Ohio River valley entered the eastern Plains in the period A.D. 100–300. We see evidence of Hopewell trade and burial customs in the central Missouri River region from Kansas City north into central South Dakota. Hopewell peoples established villages near present-day Kansas City and were growing maize, although they had to rely heavily on hunting and gathering to survive. They hunted bison as well as elk, deer, antelope, bear, beaver, in addition to birds, small mammals, and occasionally fish. In many ways these Hopewellians were pioneers able to re-create only aspects of their lifestyles. They lived in small, semipermanent communities. Houses were shallow pit dwellings with simple roofs of wooden poles and hide coverings. People also might have used hide tipis when they were traveling to hunt. Like their relatives to the east, these people buried their dead in small mounds that often had stone-lined chambers. A mound might hold the remains of as many as 50 people. The bodies had been partially dismantled, with the bones arranged into bundles. This is often done so that the bodies can be easily carried from distant death sites such as out on a hunt. Some basic ornaments and artifacts accompany burials, but there is no status differentiation that makes these burials much simpler than the more elaborate mortuary customs practiced in the eastern Woodlands.

We can see Hopewell influences in pottery, copper, obsidian, and stone artifacts from archaeological sites. Pottery bears the distinctive rocker-stamping and design panels of eastern styles. They probably controlled an active trade route bringing raw materials from the Plains to the agriculturalists to the east. Obsidian from Wyoming and chalcedony from North Dakota were highly prized trade items. Marine shells such as conch, olivella, and dentalium traveled long distances to be used for decorative purposes. By the third century Plains Woodland people had pushed onto the high Plains, closer to these sources of exotic materials.

The eastern Plains shows evidence of a burial mound tradition that was a hallmark of the Woodland adaptation. The practice seems

to have spread from Minnesota into the eastern Dakotas. Lineal earthworks and well as conical mounds occur often with burial pits underneath. The ancestors of the historical Dakota and Assiniboine added their own Plains' aspect to the burial mound practice by including bison skeletons or skulls, reflecting the importance of the animal in their lives.

We see evidence of other Woodland settlements on the Plains, but there is no sense that Woodlands culture was a major cultural change as it was in the east. In most parts of the region the Archaic lifestyle persisted in a successful hunting-gathering lifestyle. One change in that hunting culture was the appearance of arrow points around A.D. 250. Delicately flaked arrow points began to replace atlatl points. Technique had to change with the new technology. Spear points had been used as javelins thrown from a moderate distance. Arrow points were effective at close range when bison were impounded in a corral. Hunters across the Plains readily adopted this new technology and hunting technique, which may have been introduced by Athabascan people migrating through the northwestern Plains, although there is no archaeological evidence to substantiate this theory.

PLAINS VILLAGE PERIOD

There was a second wave of eastern influence on the Plains. Around A.D. 950, Eastern Woodland ideas and technology entered the Great Plains. This new wave of ideas came from an expansion of the Mississippian culture to the east. It was not a mere carbon copy of the expansive Mississippians, but a blending of older Plains Woodland aspects with newer traits.

People began settling in more substantial settlements along the river valleys. villages were often constructed on the high ground above the river floodplain with the fields stretching out below. Dwellings became multifamily lodges that were more permanent and substantial than those seen before. A shallow depression cut into the earth was ringed with wooden posts and covered with earth for insulation. The entrance corridor was higher than the interior floor level, which helped air to circulate without a great loss of heat. A hearth at the entranceway kept the home warm, but smoky. These square or rectangle earth lodges were often 90 feet square and thus housed several families. Residents could now rely more heavily on maize agriculture because of the introduction of a tough strain of maize that withstood frosts and matured quickly for

shorter growing seasons. In addition, the great northern bean, still grown today, became a reliable crop for these early agricultural-ists to supplement their diet. They also raised squash, chenopods, and amaranth. They stored their harvests in deep pits sunk into the house floors. Agriculture was supplemented by hunting, par-ticularly for bison. Women used bison shoulder blades to hoe their fields, revealing the complementary dual nature of their economy.

Their proximity to the extensive bison range offered these prairie farmers a unique and valuable resource. Major bison hunts were annual or semiannual activities that provided most of the meat for the village for the entire year. Families packed up their belongings and streamed out of their villages in search of the herds. They used the ancient technique of forcing the bison into a confined area where they could be dispatched. Because these people were not nomads, they were not limited in the amount of meat they could keep. They took the time to butcher the animals and smoke and dry the meat. All the product of the bison would then be transported back to the villages for safekeeping in storage pits. The meat, hide, sinew, and bone would provide food, clothing, and tools for the coming year. Bison were an important complement to agriculture. Despite such balance, however, life must have been precarious. These south-central Plains villages were eventually abandoned, perhaps as a result of drought or raids, and the residents retreated to the Eastern Woodlands.

These farmer-hunters had expanded up the Missouri River all the way to North Dakota by A.D. 1200, and these villages contin-ued to thrive. As populations grew, groups split off and filled the stream valleys. This led to competition for arable land and resulted in increased warfare. We see that by A.D. 1400 the villages were larger with up to 100 tightly clustered homes. The earth lodges now tended to be round in the style of the central Plains rather than the rectangle style of the Missouri region. Most of these towns were fortified with stockades and ditches. Simple, smaller versions of the permanent round houses or hide tipis were used during the yearly treks onto the Plains for hunting.

The population of the upper Plains was thriving even outside of the Missouri River valley. Anthropologists debate whether the agricultural communities represent the reestablishment of eastern societies, or whether indigenous Plains groups adopted agriculture as the means to feed their growing population. One unusual group is the effigy mound culture in the Wisconsin-Iowa border area that we call Aztalan. This Middle Mississippian village and ceremonial

complex thrived between A.D. 1000 and 1300. Similar to the Adena and Hopewell people of the East, these people built low earthen effigy mounds. Bears, deer, turtles, and geometric shapes are represented. They even carved large animal shapes into the ground. A few burials are associated with the mounds and much of this culture remains a mystery to us. Aztalan was a palisaded town with both flat-topped and conical mounds in south-central Wisconsin. Shell-tempered pottery, which is rarely found outside the southeastern region, is the dominant ceramic type throughout this site, indicating a strong Mississippian tie. Most likely, this site represented a northernmost outpost of Mississippian culture, intended to anchor the end of the great river trade network. The people on the edges of the Mississippian network farmed corn, squash, tobacco, and sunflower and mined valuable minerals such as galena. That Mississippians must have fought hard to defend their valuable trade group is attested to by the existence of chopped human bone. As the great Mississippian center at Cahokia slipped into decline, however, so too did this northernmost outpost at Aztalan, but the descendants of these ancient people stayed in the region and eventually became the Winnebago tribe.

Oneota

A new culture, Oneota, began to expand across the Midwest in Illinois, Iowa, Minnesota, Wisconsin, as well as Manitoba, Missouri, and Nebraska. Some archaeologists have referred to this as a "bridging culture" that links the Plains to the eastern woodlands. It is characterized by dependence on maize agriculture and a reliance on a regular trade. The residents cultivated corn, beans, and squash in addition to local grasses. These early farmers cleared hundreds of acres of field, improving soil by mixing in ash and charcoal. Three thousand little hills of maize filled an acre and probably yielded about 23 bushels of corn. Even with that commitment to agriculture, the community still gathered seeds and nuts as a supplement and safety net. They hunted bison, elk, deer, small mammals, and fish. All these animals, in addition to the natural resources in the area, provided the people with tools. Remains have been found of ground stone mortars, mauls and celts, chipped-stone arrow points, drills and knives, and bone hoes, needles, and scrapers. Bones were also made into ornamental beads and pendants as was local shell and antler. The Oneota produced important pieces of art work both for their own use and for trade. They hammered copper, carved

catlinite, and wove baskets and clothing from plant fibers. They also produced attractive pottery tempered with clamshells. The Oneota potters showed a Mississippian influence favoring round or oval shapes decorated with geometric designs or stylized representations of birds and serpents.

The excavated sites connected with this culture are primarily villages alongside major rivers that date to the period between A.D. 1000 and 1650. House shapes varied from square oval individual dwellings to much larger rectangular houses intended for use by several families. They buried their dead in cemeteries next to the villages, and examination of the skeletal remains has yielded interesting information about the culture. Evidence of violence and physical trauma suggests that warfare was common. Add this to the evidence of fortifications and it seems likely that the Oneota had to defend their territory. The skeletons also reveal instances of anemia that is probably linked to increased consumption of maize. This was the negative side of the reliable food supply provided by agriculture. Around A.D. 1000, evidence of tuberculosis appeared in the region, causing a marked decline in life expectancy and population. The source of the disease has not been identified; however it is possible that it came to the Great Lakes from the Norwegian explorers who contacted the East Coast. It is also possible that a different epidemic disease may have caused the loss of population and abandonment of villages in the upper Midwest later around 1350. Eventually, the Oneota became the historic Iowa, Missouri, Oto, and Winnebago tribes.

The Plains had not finished drawing people to it, however. In the thirteenth century a migration, perhaps somewhat more of a drift, brought new people onto the Plains. Over the next several centuries before European arrival, dozens of different people would pass onto and through the Plains. The first groups were Caddoan speakers, now known as the Pawnee. These farmers of east Texas represented a western outpost of Mississippian culture. In the thirteenth century they began moving north, eventually traveling 300 miles to settle on the Platte River in southeastern Nebraska. There they found rich alluvial soil, lots of bison, and a few people. They brought with them their Mississippi farming skills complete with the new species of maize. Aspects of Mississippian culture and belief systems were also transported, such as the Morning Star ceremony, which involved the ritual of a captive girl. This rare example of ceremonial killing in the Plains region harkens back to the Pawnee's Mississippian influence.

The Pawnee built on the bluffs of the rivers much as Mississippians had done. The lodges were circular with heavy log frames and timber rafters covered by layers of dirt and grass. This provided a great deal of insulation to these large lodges, which held 40 people; however, it is also very heavy and after about a decade, the lodges collapsed. By this time the area timber had been exhausted so the Pawnee simply moved. They moved on a regular cycle of 10 years or so and followed an economic cycle throughout the year. In May, corn and other crops were planted, then in June the village packed up tipis on travois and headed out for a bison hunt. They returned in August to harvest the corn, which they shucked, shelled, and then stored. The women also gathered berries, nuts, and fruit; the men hunted deer and antelope. In October the whole group returned to the Plains for one last bison hunt to accumulate enough meat for winter.

This type of migration onto the Plains continued. In the fourteenth century another Caddoan speaking group, the Wichita, also left Texas. They went north, but only as far as the Arkansas River in Kansas. They had a similar lifestyle to the Pawnee, who were of the same language group. Their multifamily lodges looked different because they were covered with long reed grass thatch rather than heavy sod. It was one of these Wichita communities in Kansas that was encountered by the Spanish conquistador Francisco Coronado in 1541 on his quest for the "seven cities of gold." The Wichita and the Pawnee adjusted to a new life that exploited the incredible richness of the Plains. They kept their agricultural practices, but could not ignore the huge herds of bison that thundered across the land. They built a lifestyle that balanced hunting with horticulture, which was really the only way to farm on the Plains.

Siouan Speakers

Another group of tribes, unrelated to those who came before, began moving on to the edge of the Plains. These various Siouan speakers would eventually dominate the region, providing half of the population and many of the stereotypical images of Plains Indian life. Experts believe that Siouan speakers originated in the southeastern part of the country and around the fourteenth century moved north into the Ohio valley. There they would have encountered the end of the Hopewell culture and perhaps adopted some of their traits. The rich Ohio valley region became quite crowded and the Siouan speakers moved west.

One group that left early and established themselves across the Mississippi River were the Hidatsa. They eventually settled in the Red River valley of southern Manitoba. Here they developed a balanced existence combining farming and hunting. The successful adaptation continued for nearly 300 years until population pressure and aggression from neighbors once again forced the Hidatsa to move. This time they went south to the Missouri River in what is now North Dakota. Lewis and Clark found them here at the beginning of the nineteenth century still following this ancient pattern of agriculture supplemented by seasonal hunting. Parts of the tribe had split off over the centuries and migrated westward. As they moved west, agriculture became less viable and hunting took on greater importance. In southern Montana and northern Wyoming, these people who became primarily bison hunters referred to themselves as Absaroka or large bird, later known to Euro-Americans as the Crow tribe.

The Mandan also left the Ohio valley and crossed the Mississippi River. In the west they adopted a housing style much like the Pawnee—heavy earth lodges. Because they moved every decade on the collapse of their homes, the Mandan continued moving west. Eventually, they settled permanently in North Dakota, pursuing a lifestyle similar to the neighboring Hidatsa. They successfully blended agriculture and bison hunting into a prosperous, sustainable economy. Both these tribes, however, would be ravaged by disease before extensive white contact; thus only remnants of their great culture are known.

One of the most influential Siouan speaking groups to cross onto the Plains were those known today as the Sioux. The Oceti Sakowin or "Seven Council Fires" moved from the Midwest to the lake country of Wisconsin and Minnesota. In this region rectangular homes could be built of heavy timber cut from nearby forests. These forests included open meadows and small prairies, which were home to small herds of bison. Men continued the tradition of hunting deer, elk, and bear, as well as limited numbers of bison; however, the area would not support traditional maize agriculture. Instead, the women exploited a unique resource, a native grass referred to as wild rice. The local seed-bearing grass that grew in the abundant shallow muddy waters became the focus of intense horticulture. Women went out in canoes and bent the stalks of grass into the boat, then beat them to release the seeds. This provided an important food source both for consumption and trade.

Women also cultivated tobacco in their fields. Tobacco, a much harsher native variety than that used today, was considered a gift to

Indian people from the spirits. Offerings of tobacco showed grati-
tude to these powers and natives seldom went out without a small
pouch of dried tobacco for this purpose. The dried leaves could also
be smoked, a practice that had a ceremonial significance, particularly in establishing peaceful relations among people.

All the tribes of the Great Lakes region valued the ritual of smoking. They created special sacred pipes or calumets (from a French
word) for the purpose. The pipestems were carved from wood,
often quite elaborately, and then decorated with feathers, quills, or
paint. They fitted into a bowl carved from a special stone called
catlinite or pipe stone. It is metamorphic claystone, a soft reddish
rock that gains its reddish color from iron ore. It is thus perfectly
suited for carving and display, although it is fairly rare. This rock
occurs in outcroppings in the Midwest with by far the best known
at Pipestone in Minnesota. These ancient quarries have been in continuous use since at least A.D. 900. Many tribes valued catlinite, so
it became an important item of trade. Of more interest, the quarries
themselves became somewhat sacred so that no one would com-
mit violence there for fear of contaminating the sacredness of the
place. The usual territorial squabbles were put aside at the quarries
indicating that the acquisition of the stone served to honor peace
much as the smoking ritual did. An old Sioux story underscores the
importance of pipestone as a symbol of peace.

At an ancient time the Great Spirit, in the form of a large bird, stood upon
the wall of rock and called all the tribes around him, and breaking out
a piece of the red stone formed it into a pipe and smoked it, the smoke
rolling over the whole multitude. He then told his red children that this
red stone was their flesh, that they were made from it, that they must all
smoke to him through it, that they must use it for nothing but pipes: and
as it belonged alike to all tribes, the ground was sacred, and no weapons
must be used or brought upon it.[1]

In time, some of the Siouan-speaking Oceti Sakowin would be
pushed farther west out of the lakes area and onto the Plains proper.
Those who remained in Minnesota became the Dakota, or Eastern
Sioux; those that moved only as far as the edge of the Plains are the
Nakota or Middle Sioux. The seven bands that speak the Lakota dialect ranged all the way out to the western Plains. Here they were well
placed for the arrival of the horse and gun and with them the Lakota
became the classic bison hunting nomads of the American West.

Not all the power in the Plains came from the eastern portion. In
the northwest corner of the Plains lay the rich hunting territories of

Alberta. This region supported a powerful group later known as the Nitzitapi or "Blackfoot Confederacy." These Algonquian speakers organized in five bands that formed a loose affiliation. Although they spoke Algonquian, the language is so different from eastern Algonquians that anthropologists believe they must have separated thousands of years earlier. The bison jump at Head-Smashed-In is in Blackfoot territory, and it is likely that their ancestors used it more than 5,000 years ago. The Blackfoot formed an impressive coalition and their power likely kept other tribes from settling the region.

Many Siouan and Caddoan speakers pushed onto the Plains from the east, and other groups migrated to the region from the north. The Athapaskans had been in the Northwest since their migration from Asia. One group we know as the Apache began migrating southward in small groups in the early fourteenth century. From the northernmost portion of the Plains in Alberta, the Apache moved southeast through Montana, across the Platte River into Nebraska, and then to the Texas panhandle. They soon became dominant players in the southern Plains.

The Apache developed a unique adaptation to their new home. In a sense it was similar to that pursued by the Missouri River tribes such as the Mandan and Hidatsa. The Apache followed a nomadic pattern, hunting bison in spring, summer, and fall. They were quite successful and acquired all the meat and by-products they needed from the large southern herds. Like other groups, however, they also desired the fruits of a sedentary lifestyle. But rather than take up farming themselves, the Apache simply sought out others who already did so. In the winter the Apache moved west into New Mexico to trade with the Pueblo people. For several months they camped near towns and conducted a lively trade. The Apache brought the products of the hunt—dried meat, skins, and bone and horn tools—to people who had no access to roaming herds of bison. In turn, they received corn, squash, and other vegetables from Pueblo fields. They could also obtain pottery, weaving, and other artistic goods. Trade was not always peaceful and raiding could occur, but both groups valued the relationship and influenced one another. Over the centuries the Apache adopted some sedentary Puebloan ways.

The Apache were clearly an adaptable people. One of the many Apachean groups that migrated southward encountered the Pawnee. Dominant militarily, the Apache had no trouble pushing the Pawnee back into Nebraska; however, they must have taken some

of the women captive and then learned from them the skills of a sedentary lifestyle. Soon this Apache group was building earth lodges and growing corn along the Colorado-Kansas border. Another Apachean group when passing through Montana, allied with the Kiowa tribe and became the Kiowa-Apache, pursuing a typical nomadic bison hunting Plains lifestyle.

PLAINS CULTURE

In the period before the arrival of white men, the Plains was a dynamic region. Groups moved through the area, settling for a time in one location and then moving on to another. Many of these groups were the ancestors of the historic Plains tribes encountered by Americans. As we have seen there were some unique adaptations to the realities of life in a sea of grass before the arrival of the horse. Eastern residents, like the Hidatsa and Pawnee, blended aspects of eastern Woodlands with Plains culture, combining hunting and agriculture to achieve a well-rounded economy. These subsistence patterns were successful enough to continue the contact period. Arikara, Mandan, and Hidatsa are the survivors of that late prehistoric horticultural way of life.

Most Plains peoples, however, especially those in the central and western portions, maintained an Archaic style hunting and gathering life that revolved around the bison. Although their names and many details have been lost to us, we can still reconstruct their civilization based on the continued nomadic lifestyle into the historic period. The introduction of the horse intensified nomadic patterns on the Plains.

Although we routinely speak of tribes, nomadic bison hunters did not belong to anything similar to a nation or an organized political unit. Early residents lived in extended family groups. Their basic identification, and thus loyalty, would be to these relatives. Related family groups might travel together as a band. All the bands that were related to others with the same language and culture might come together a few times a year; however, they remained extremely independent. Political integration as we think of it was tenuous so the bands might choose to join a different group from year to year.

Seasonal Patterns

The size of a group of people was essentially dictated by ecological factors. They would travel in the largest group practical

for exploitation of a resource—usually bison. So the people's band size basically mimicked the bison herd size. Most of the year bison live in small groups with the mothers and calves together and the bulls off in their own herds. The hunters also then stayed in small groups that provided enough people to successfully hunt a small bison group, but not too many to feed with the produce of the kill, that is, about 20 to 30 families. The band traveled from camp to camp following the bison. Without horses almost everyone walked the five or six daily miles of travel. Mothers carried infants on their backs; the very ill and elderly lay on a litter between two travois. Dog travois bore the heaviest burdens, up to about 75 pounds, but dogs made for erratic and somewhat unreliable pack animals. Such a group would be vulnerable to attack, so scouts watched ahead for danger and for signs of game while the rest of the men protected the sides and rear of the moving band. If anyone spotted a herd, the group stopped and made camp. In July and August bison go into the mating season and congregate in large herds into the fall. At this time all the related bands came together in a group of perhaps several thousand people, which provided them the human power necessary to hunt a bison herd of 10,000+ animals.

Hunters relied on similar technique no matter the size of the herds. Cliff jumps and blind canyons remained popular kill sites. If none of those were available hunters would create a temporary corral. On the open Plains a flimsy corral could be constructed of dog travois poles standing upright. The women and dogs would hide behind the travois screaming and barking to confuse the animals that the men had driven toward the corral. In the ensuing panic the animals could be shot. In the winter the bison divided again into small groups, which were better able to find forage. Humans also struggled to find food and would hunt deer, elk, mountain sheep, or anything that would feed their families. Bison often took refuge in wooded areas and valleys. Here hunters could fell trees to create a corral of sharpened stakes to contain the bison for killing.

Such hunting techniques, although successful, were neither easy nor safe. It is not surprising that people relied on spiritual help and protection in hunting these massive animals. The hunters honored the spirit of the animal they sought. It is likely that these Archaic people believed, as did later hunters, that appeasing the spirit of the bison with proper ritual and respect would ensure successful hunting in the future.

Importance of Bison

It was absolutely critical that these early Plains dwellers kill bison. Their entire economy and culture centered around this one species that predominated on the Plains. Plains residents were primarily hunters supplementing their meat diet with limited gathering. People could eat up to three pounds of meat per day. After a kill the people ate liver, kidneys, and the best meat immediately, enjoying these delicacies, which would not keep. In a typical band the hides of the animals would go to those who did the killing and the meat was shared among the group. Women dried the lean meat and packed it with layers of fat and berries into pouches made of skin. When the meat was pounded with marrow grease and berries, it created pemmican, which was placed in bags of unborn calfskin for storage. After the meat was prepared, the rest of the animal was dismembered and put to use. Once seasoned with a mixture of fat, brains, and liver, the bison skin became pliable. With the fur left on, it served as a warm, waterproof robe; if the hair were removed it could become a tipi cover. Old tipi covers softened by smoke and grease from cooking fires could be recycled into clothing. Seasoned rawhide was pliable enough to make rope; untanned rawhide dried into an incredibly tough material that lashed tools together. Bison sinews could be separated to create strong, thin lines for thread or bow strings. Horns became spoons, hooves boiled down to glue, and bones formed all kind of useful tools. The bison even provided tools for the artistic expression of Plains people. Artists used porous bones or tufts of hair for brushes to apply yellow paint made of bison gallstones.

Family Structure

Much like the animal on which their life depended, Plains residents followed a communal social structure. Life on the Plains would have been impossible without the support of others. An individual could not have successfully exploited the available resources, so people naturally relied on the group for success. Most communal societies value harmony. If the harmonious flow of the community is disrupted, everyone suffers. Rules existed to encourage and preserve harmony. Each person had their place in the group, no one was seen as dispensable. As each child entered the community, he or she received a special name in a ceremony marking inclusion in the group.

The bison skull and catlinite pipe figured prominently in Plains spirituality. Library of Congress.

Children were highly valued and were generally raised by the community of relatives rather than just by two people. Important events later in life might require the bestowal of a new, more appropriate name, especially for boys. The idea that individuals could change names during their life reflects this society's belief that power and respect were based on individual acts rather than on inheritance. What a person did in life mattered for the person as well as the group. A great person would always have the band's welfare at heart. Warrior skills, artistic talent, or healing power used to benefit the people could make someone great. Similarly, prestige could be gained through generosity rather than accumulating wealth.

Spirituality

Because life was precarious in this harsh environment, people often turned to spiritual help. Most groups believed in sacred powers that could affect humans' daily life. Spirits came in the form of

Young girls played with miniature versions of the items they would use as adults. Library of Congress.

familiar animals and birds or they could be rocks, thunder, or even an event. The existence and plans of these powers often came to people in dreams or visions. Men often sought these visions on a multiday quest of fasting and offerings. Not everyone received a vision from the spirits, but individuals who did tended to carry its representation with them through life. Some people might be given healing powers with which they could benefit their people. It is likely that such spiritual understanding has continued unchanged for centuries. We have some evidence of ancient ritual sites. Scattered throughout the West are medicine wheels. These are piles of rocks placed in a pattern of concentric circles or ovals. Spokes radiate out from the central cairn to intersect the outer circles. Although, these are clearly important sacred sites, their exact use is unknown. The Majorville Medicine Wheel in Alberta contains *iniskims*, which are stones used by the Blackfoot "bison calling society," suggesting a ritual use of the wheel. Another use might have been as a calendar. The outer cairns could have supported poles that would align with the sun, moon, or stars. The location of most of these medicine wheels on high points with expansive views has led to the suggestion that they were a sort

of map. People might have traveled to these spots to look over their territory. The lines could have pointed to important natural landmarks so that members of the group could become familiar with their region. The sites appear to have been respected by all groups and were not destroyed or vandalized in ancient times.

The idea of a map drawn on the ground with stones reminds us that these cultures did not have the written word. Everything they knew and passed on to others had to be remembered. Oral cultures such as these tend to have devices to aid in remembering important events or ideas. On the Plains it appears that the people turned to the ever useful bison to provide this mechanism. Using mineral paints and bison brushes men recorded significant events onto a tanned bison hide. The symbols served as pneumonic devices for the storytelling that would have preserved the group's history and culture. It is likely that one member of the group who excelled at this was charged with remembering and retelling the important past events. On a more individual basis, men decorated their tipi covers with representations of their accomplishments that identified them and marked their place within the group.

There were aspects of both individualism and communalism within Plains society. Men sought to achieve and display the results of brave, powerful actions. Everyone within a band knew who were the strongest warriors, best hunters, and most powerful spiritual leaders. Much of the activity both men and women engaged in centered on communalism. Men fought to protect the people; they divided their kills with those in need. Women also shared childrearing duties and other skilled work. Despite an aspect of solitude in a nomadic lifestyle, the Plains people also enjoyed large communal gatherings.

When the main prey came together in large numbers, so did their predators, primarily in an attempt to efficiently exploit large bison herds, but it also served many other purposes. Like other nomadic peoples who dwelled mainly in family groups during the year, Plains societies welcomed an opportunity to see others, forge and renew social ties, establish new families, and share common cultural elements. Large summer camps were the best time for young people to meet and flirt with others their own age. Leisure time, feasts, and dances offered opportunities to get to know one another, and relationships forged here often led to marriage.

Adults also welcomed the opportunity to socialize with kin. Most Plains groups had societies whose membership cut across clan lines. Societies usually focused on gender-specific activities so men joined warrior societies while women met to quill or decorate tipis. Plains

women developed stunning techniques for decorating everyday items with dyed porcupine quills. The meetings of societies allowed people to share new ideas and reinforce cultural similarities across a widespread group. Some warrior societies also performed a public service by policing the large summer camps. Keeping peace, organizing hunts, and restricting unauthorized raids fell to those recognized as the elite warriors. Young boys saw the honor that skill could bring and thus strove to become worthy of membership upon maturity. Joining a warrior society could actually be quite competitive in some tribes, especially those with a reputation for prowess in battle.

Another highlight of the summer gathering was communal ceremony. At this time rituals were held with the widest possible participation and audience. All manner of passages were marked—births, puberty, first hunts, adulthood, society initiation, marriage. Many involved dancing and celebrating with feasts. Some were strictly religious, meant to honor the spirits with praise and sacrifice. A common theme was the pledge dance held after a warrior vowed to stage a ceremony in exchange for spiritual protection. It took many forms among the diverse Plains people, but its essence was a ritual of sacrifice to the spirits. The offering could be physical suffering or mental anguish at many levels, but all were intended to repay the powers of the world for their protection and intervention on their behalf. One of the most famous was the Sun Dance, which persisted into modern times among the Lakota and Cheyenne tribes.

Much of the lifestyle of the Plains persisted for thousands of years. European altered, but did not end, the unique nomadic culture of the lords of the grasslands. Horses and firearms magnified rather than destroyed most aspects of that lifestyle. The basic adaptation to living in the central grasslands of America remained the same. Males hunted bison and fought to defend their territories while women prepared the bounty from the prey and gathered plant materials. This economy required a nomadic existence that Plains groups honed to a near perfect system. The tribes that best mastered the requisite Plains survival skills dominated the region for centuries, undone only by diseases imported by European in the seventeenth century.

NOTE

1. George Catlin, "Sioux account of the origin of the pipestone, as recorded by 1836," in *Letters and Notes on the Manners, Customs, and Conditions of North American Indians*, London, 1941, http://www.xmission.com/~drudy/mtman/html/catlin/letter54.html.

FURTHER READING

Fresno, George. *Prehistoric Hunters of the Great Plains.* New York: Academic Press, 1978.

Head-Smashed-In Buffalo Jump. Head-Smashed-In Buffalo Jump is a UNESCO World Heritage site with an informative website. http://www.head-smashed-in.com/ (accessed September 1, 2007).

Lakota Winter Counts: An Online Exhibit. The National Anthropological Archives of the Smithsonian Institution provided the information for this site documenting the Lakota practice of making winter counts to record important events. http://wintercounts.si.edu/ (accessed September 1, 2007).

Taylor, Colin F. *The Plains Indians.* London: Salamander Books, 1994.

Wishart, David J., ed. *Encyclopedia of the Great Plains Indians.* Lincoln: University of Nebraska Press, 2007.

Wood, W. Raymond, ed. *Archaeology on the Great Plains.* Lawrence: University Press of Kansas, 1998.

4

The Southwest

The southwestern portion of America is often considered harsh and desolate, an area in which humans are not welcomed by nature and, in fact, struggle to survive. Because it is one of the last regions to be heavily settled by modern American populations, it often surprises people to learn that the desert and mountain region of the Southwest is in some ways the cradle of civilization in the United States. Humans inhabited this area for many thousands of years. These early residents did far more than merely occupy the Southwest, far more than simply struggle to survive. They understood how to live in a demanding environment and thrived there. They became intricately adapted to the environment that could easily have killed them.

The arid Southwest gave rise to complex and extensive populations of Native Americans who regarded the area with the utmost respect. Native residents of the Southwest formed close bonds to the physical settings they inhabited. Their ties to the land go far beyond merely territorial claims. Mountains and mesas, cliffs and canyons, springs and rivers have spiritual importance. Sacred sites are woven throughout the Southwest; many have been regarded in this way for thousands of years by many cultures. Descendants of the original inhabitants still live in this ancient homeland and are known to us as Yuma, Pima, Papago, Pueblos, and others. Their

lives are shaped by the traditions of their culture and the certainty of their place in the Southwest.

The whole Southwest was a house made of dawn. It was made of pollen and of rain. The land was old and everlasting. There were many colors on the hills and the plain, and there was a dark wilderness on the mountains beyond. The land was tilled and strong and it was beautiful all around.[1]

Southwest Indian Song

CONNECTION TO THE LAND

The attachment of southwestern natives to their homelands is revealed by their creation stories. Zuni tradition holds that humans began life in a dark underworld that gradually filled with people and creatures. Seeking room to grow, the ancestors emerged from that underworld into the world of light and earth carrying seeds from below. They encountered others who claimed the region into which the Zuni had just emerged. To impress the others, the Zuni planted the seven seeds they had brought, which quickly sprouted but did not bear fruit. The strangers offered to help perfect the beginnings of agriculture that the Zuni had brought to the New World. They chose seven holy maidens who danced with a sacred man chosen by the Zuni. As the young people danced around the seven plants all night, they coaxed each one to grow tall. When the day dawned the seven plants put forth multicolored kernels covered in silk. The two groups of humans joined together to live on the bounty of the corn brought from the other world.

The Hopi, the Zuni's neighbors, also explain the world and their place in it through a creation story. According to the Hopi tribe, this world is the fourth way of life that the Hopi have lived. Different Hopi clans and animals emerged from the third into this fourth way of life. Hopis tell how the people of the world were offered ears of corn by *Ma'saw*. Many jumped in ahead of the Hopi and picked large ears of corn and left Hopis the smallest ear. This symbolizes the difficult but enduring life the Hopi live in the arid Southwest. Along with each ear of corn, the various peoples of the world inherited homelands, cultures, and responsibilities from the rest of creation. The Hopi fulfill their responsibilities through their daily life and ceremonies. Hopi life revolves around agriculture, in particular, corn. The Hopi way of life is the corn—humility, cooperation, respect, and universal earth stewardship.

Such creation stories are a major part of the lives of southwestern native people. They do more than just tie the people to the land and give them an understanding of their identity. The stories also explain the world and the beings that natives might encounter. For example, the Pima of southern Arizona trace their past to a story about the Magician who made the world, and then finding himself lonely, set out to create other beings like himself. He molded clay figures of himself and set them in an oven to bake. Coyote, often the trickster character in Native American stories, could not resist meddling with the figures. First he made one to look like himself, thus creating the dog, a long-time companion to indigenous people. Then he bothered the Magician while he baked the rest of the figures. The first came out too early and were underdone and thus too light. The Magician said the light figures did not belong in the Southwest, but rather across the water someplace. Another batch stayed in too long and came out too dark and likewise would have to be placed across the water. Finally, the Magician ignored Coyote's advice and took out two figures who were just right and belonged in the Southwest. He breathed life into them and they became the ancestors of the Pima. Besides placing the Pima as the perfect people in the proper place, the story also explains the existence of other humans who did not belong, but would eventually come to the region.

In the view of anthropologists, humans migrated to the American Southwest as the glaciers retreated with the changing global climate. When the earliest Americans reached the Southwest, they found a land quite different from today's conceptions of the region. Indeed, the very ancient Southwest of 10000 B.C. was tropical. Instead of a dry, desert region in Nevada, there were juniper-covered plains. In the western reaches of the plains in Texas and New Mexico, pine and spruce trees grew among small lakes. Small rivers and streams flowed through the area, providing critical water resources to animals and humans. The large megafauna found elsewhere in America—mastodon, mammoth, bison—were also the prey of early southwestern hunters, with their stone spearheads and organized hunting techniques. The major archaeological finds that give rise to our understanding of these big game hunters are in the Southwest.

Clovis, Sandia, and Folsom are the New Mexico sites that yielded tantalizing indications of stone tool making on which much of our knowledge of Paleo-Indians is based. Other southwestern sites have generated similarly remarkable evidence. Greenbush Creek

near Naco, Arizona, harbored a mammoth skeleton containing eight stone spear points. At Lehner Ranch along the San Pedro River, nine elephants, a primitive horse, bison, and tapir apparently provided food for the hunters whose nearby fire pits date to around 9000 B.C. An important window into early life in the Southwest was found at Ventana Cave on the modern Papago reservation in Arizona, which shows signs of continuous human habitation in the area from the end of the Ice Age up to the present.

As the major climate shifts of the waning Ice Age occurred, they affected the Southwest. Beginning around 8000 B.C., the region began to dry up. Several fewer inches of rainfall each year combined with increased mean temperatures changed the vegetation and thus the animals that could inhabit the area. As elsewhere, the loss of large game animals required a corresponding shift in the food supplies of the human hunters. No longer able to obtain vast quantities of meat and hide from one kill of a huge animal, men had to diversify their prey animals. The new prey was considerably smaller and thus required many more kills to provide enough sustenance for a family. The smaller animals, however, did not require as much manpower for a successful kill, so individual hunting became more common.

ARCHAIC INDIANS

The lifestyles of people that developed after the big game hunters in America are generally referred to as Archaic cultures. In the Southwest the Archaic culture is termed the desert culture, reflecting the region's changed climate and the corresponding adaptations of humans to it. Four distinct groups can be identified within the larger designation of desert culture, basically divided by region: western or Pinto, southern or Cochise, northern or Oshara, and southeastern or Fresnal and Hueco.

The Pinto culture existed in western Arizona and southern Nevada from 7000–5000 B.C. As might be expected from an early, transitional culture, this lifestyle differed little from the earlier Clovis people to their east. They hunted with projectile points, used sharpened stones for knives, and fashioned bone scrapers to clean animal hides. Not specialists in any one area, these Archaic peoples survived by hunting and gathering the resources they could find in the area.

The Cochise culture bears the name of a nineteenth-century Apache leader. As with most ancient groups, we have no idea what they called themselves. In this case, the Apache chief's name was

given to a modern day county in Arizona where physical evidence dating to 7000–6000 B.C. was found by Euro-Americans and dubbed the Cochise culture. The nature of archaeology means that we may never discover the name, religion, or political system of these early inhabitants. We do know that Cochise hunters had to diversify their hunting to feed their families. The drier environment did not support large mammals, so many smaller animals had to be taken to fulfill protein needs. Wild vegetation, such as nuts, roots, seeds, and berries, helped to supplement the diet of these desert people.

In the northern section of the Southwest, a group known as the Oshara appeared slightly later than the cultures of the west and south. Material found in this region date from 5500–4800 B.C. The tools and evidence of settlement found here differ markedly from those associated with earlier paleo-Indians. These Archaic Indians exploited a wide variety of resources. They hunted bighorn sheep that lived in the mountains, and the local deer. Smaller animals like rodents, squirrels, rabbits, and birds added welcome variety to their meat intake. Different prey types encouraged variety in hunting techniques as well, so that hunters used spear and dart throwers and snares. Exploitation of insects and reptiles required even more diversity in hunting techniques.

As these Archaic people developed their cultures, they came to use more of the natural resources to create a stable lifestyle. This required them to adapt new techniques, tools, and ideas to food collection and preparation. Many plant parts can provide nutrition to humans, but many also need to be altered before being ingested. Humans had to grind the hard coverings off many types of seeds to render them digestible. Stones may have been an obvious choice for a grinding surface, but the southwestern Indians cleverly created a reservoir in the bottom stone to hold the seed and used a smooth top stone fitted to the human hand to apply the necessary pressure. In this way the seeds could be crushed to a powder, similar to flour, to be used as food. Other gathered plant materials had to be sifted or beaten to separate them from the seeds. Baskets and trays helped Indians to gather, transport, and store plant materials. Such lightweight, flexible containers made of plant material were a natural choice for nomadic people concerned about carrying items.

AGRICULTURE

All the early cultures of North America were nomadic. Reliance on a variety of food sources required mobility. The only reason to

remain in one area for extended periods is for proximity to the food supply. Development of agriculture provided that condition in early America. Agriculture is the deliberate planting and harvesting of domesticated plants. Its adoption by a group signaled revolutionary changes in their lifestyle; however, of itself the process of agriculture is not a radical invention, nor do a people embrace it swiftly. Rather, the production of plants for human use is a gradual process that evolved over years of people interacting with the native plants in their region.

It begins with human selection of certain wild vegetation based on preferences, such as larger fruit or thinner seed coverings, and continues with accidental or intentional scattering of preferred seeds in new areas. This was clearly a supplemental aspect of the natives' diet, so if the plants produced it would be a good season, but if not the failure did not doom the people to starvation. Gatherers might manipulate the environment; some frequently used fire as a tool to encourage favored species or discourage competitors to desirable plants. The process moved forward with cultivation: weeding, pruning, tilling, transplanting, and sowing. Agriculture is finally achieved when humans domesticate plants for their own use, some of which could not survive without human intervention.

The times at which distinct human groups engaged in agriculture is a continuing source of debate. We know that domestication of corn, beans, and squash took place in Mesoamerica before appearing in North America. Corn, or maize (*Zea mays*), was fully domesticated there by 5000 B.C. The practice then slowly spread northward to the American Southwest. The reliance on agriculture that came to characterize the Southwest developed only gradually. The investment of time in planting particular seeds meant that the people would return to that site for a period each year. The certainty of return allowed for a greater commitment to housing and other improvements at the site such as dug wells and, over the long term, resulted in semipermanent villages. This new idea of planting desirable seeds to make them more readily available and abundant did not immediately change the Archaic way of life. All these southwestern people remained primarily hunters and gatherers for thousands of years after first aiding nature to encourage their favorite plants.

The dry southwestern climate has preserved more artifacts than other regions of the country. Bone, stone, clay, seeds, and some fibers can be found at various archaeological sites. Anthropologists generally characterize cultures on the basis of the tools, vessels, weapons,

and other material objects found in an area. Yet it is clear that fairly extensive trade moved such items between cultural groups, which often confuses our picture of distinct regional cultures.

Weapons are a critical tool for hunters. Early southwesterners initially relied on sharpened sticks to kill or wound animals. The advent of stone projectile points attached to spears obviously improved hunting efficiency. Hunters continued to adapt their technique by making the spear points detachable so they remained in the animal's body after the spear fell away, causing further damage. Stone workers refined their projectile points to increase effectiveness and to reflect the peculiarities of different prey animals. Such developments as the atlatl drastically increased hunters' effectiveness. The atlatl remained the weapon of choice until a revolution in weaponry came to the Southwest—the bow and arrow. The bow and arrow, prized for its accuracy and effectiveness at long range, was widely adopted for hunting and warfare after A.D. 500. It could be adapted by changing the size, shape, and design of the arrow shaft and point for any type of prey. The bow and arrow remained the weapon of native America until the introduction of guns by Europeans in the seventeenth century.

Although humans develop similar adaptations to life in certain regions, there was also a clear diversity in development. Distinct cultural traditions emerged in the Southwest that we can identify through artifacts and other indicators of culture. As with most ancient groups, their original names are lost, and the ones in current use reflect a choice made by modern peoples.

HOHOKAM

One of the unique areas of the Southwest is the Sonoran Desert. This vast ecological region of more than 100,000 square miles extends from southeastern Arizona to southern California and into northern Mexico. It does have some typical desert characteristics such as high heat and extended dry periods, but it is also a diverse place with more than 2,000 plant species supported by the seasonal rainfall. The people known as Hohokam inhabited this area 2,300 years ago. Their homeland stretched from the low desert country of southern Arizona northward to the Mogollon Rim escarpment and onto the Colorado Plateau's southwestern edge. Not simply a flat desert, this region includes elevations reaching 10,000 feet and low valleys of only 500 feet. The elevation changes support distinct plant communities, ranging from spruce, fir, pine, and oak trees to

mesquite bushes and chollo and saguaro cacti. Rainfall varies from 4 inches in low areas to 30 inches at higher elevations and usually arrives in mid-winter and mid-summer.

From about 7000 B.C. to about A.D. 300, the desert Archaic culture flourished in this area. These people lived in small groups or bands traveling around the region to use the natural resources. As they moved frequently, permanent housing would not have served their needs, but temporary shelters must have existed seasonally. Like most other hunter gatherers, the seasons dictated the peoples' migration pattern. When the acorn and pine nuts fell from trees in the higher elevations, people went there and when the many cacti varieties produced fruit, humans moved down onto the valley floor. Certain areas that were known to produce many favored plants became traditional gathering areas each year. To supplement this fairly varied plant diet, desert dwellers hunted mammals and reptiles, particularly in the winter when vegetation dwindled.

After several centuries of this lifestyle, a change occurred. A different type of lifestyle emerged in the region, one we have come to call the Hohokam. Although the Hohokam are relatively well studied, scholars do not agree on their origins. A University of Arizona archaeologist, Emil Haury, conducted the major excavations of Hohokam villages in the mid-twentieth century. He believed that the ancestors of these people migrated from Mexico and established themselves in the northern Sonoran. They would naturally have brought aspects of their culture with them when they moved northward around 300 B.C. Not all scholars agree with Haury's thesis, positing either a later arrival for the migrants or rejecting the migration theory altogether. If the Hohokam ancestors did not migrate, then the culture must have developed from earlier local peoples already occupying the region. The debate over Hohokam origins will likely continue until more conclusive evidence is found; however, scholars chose a name suggesting a continuous connection to the area. It is a Pima word referring to "the vanished ones" derived from the word "hokam" or "a thing used up." Whether or not the Pima are descended from the Hohokam, the modern-day natives live in the same region and surely use many of the same resources as these ancient people.

Snaketown

The reason we know anything about the "vanished" people of the Sonoran region is the discovery of remains of their towns or

villages. The best known of these sites is Snaketown (from the Pima name *Skoaquik* for "place of snakes"), which sits along side the Gila River, near today's Phoenix, Arizona. The remnant mounds at the site attracted the attention of newcomers to the area in the nineteenth century, and major excavations led by Emil Haury yielded much of our understanding of the Hohokam culture. Haury and his colleagues dug at the site in the 1930s, covered the remains to protect them, then returned for further excavations in the 1960s and re-covered the area. This intense study allows scholars to paint pictures of Hohokam life. Future exactions using new technology may tell us yet more about the lives of these vanished people. As the Phoenix area grows rapidly in the twenty-first century, many more Hohokam sites are being exposed and excavated. Each year brings new insights into this ancient culture.

Snaketown covered almost 400 acres of land and was occupied from A.D. 550 to 1450 by up to 1,000 people. It consisted of hundreds of homes, fairly spread out from one another. From this site, it is known that the Hohokam did not seek city-style, close quartered dwellings as later pueblo people would. The earliest Hohokam houses were unique in that they were wattle and daub structures built inside shallow pits. These small structures must have been cramped with probably four people sharing less than 300 square feet. Within 200 years, the Hohokam were building more traditional pit houses by excavating down about four feet and then constructing a frame of saplings covered with grasses over the pit. The earth excavation had the advantage of retaining warmth in the winter and coolness in the summer as a result of the earth's insulating properties. Fires in the middle of the homes served for heat and cooking but would also have created a smoky interior. Because these homes faced the threat of fire and then of flooding during strong storms, they probably had to be rebuilt periodically. Generations of people rebuilt on the same site, leaving layers of evidence of human habitation. As the Hohokam remained in the region, their house styles continued to evolve until after A.D. 1000 when they began building multistory, aboveground houses of adobe material.

Villages such as Snaketown contained more than just homes. A central plaza created a focus for community life. Here work, socialization, and probably religious and political events could be held in the open. Recreation had to have been a priority for the people of the Sonoran region, as a major feature of their towns was a ballcourt. Archaeologists have excavated numerous elliptical structures with floors almost two feet below the surface. Earth was piled along the

edges to form a low sloping wall, presumably to keep the ball inside. Initially, these structures puzzled anthropologists, but excavations revealed stone markers, entryways, figurines resembling ball players, and even natural rubber balls. Similar ballcourts are well known from Mesoamerican sites, but nothing is known of the connection between the two occurrences. Another familiar structure from farther south—the mound—also occurs in Hohokam villages. Villages often had raised platform mounds capped with clay scattered throughout. These seemingly Mexican culture traits led early anthropologists to regard the Hohokam as immigrants from the south, but now their indigenous development is relatively well accepted.

Even if they were not immigrants, the Hohokam would certainly have had contacts with other culture groups. An extensive trade network tied the Sonoran region to a vastly larger world. Exotic items such as marine shells, copper bells, and brightly colored macaw feathers made their way to Snaketown. Many trade items became part of Hohokam arts. Initially artists carved the shells that came in trade and then began etching them using a technique of applying acidic, fermented cactus juice to eat away the surface. Beads, bracelets, and pendants could be created from shell and bore elaborate designs of frogs, birds, snakes, or even humans. The work of Hohokam shell artists became prized by other cultures as collectible goods. Hohokam women created pots by a technique referred to as "anvil and paddle," which used stones and wooden paddles to draw the pot walls upward. The buff-colored base was decorated with red paint applied with yucca fiber brushes. Typical designs included lines and scrolls, turtles, quails, and snakes, and dancing human figures.

Many of these artistic creations played important roles in the ritual life of the people. Several motifs suggests that water was a focus of Hohokam sacredness and ritual. Water truly was the key to human survival. Fine pottery, shell jewelry, pyrite mirrors, and other worthy objects were placed with deceased bodies on funeral pyres, which were then cremated. (The Hokokam are the only early southwestern culture known to have practiced cremation.) The remaining ash and unburned objects went into cemetery areas in the village. In other cases artistic or ritual objects have been found buried in caches in house floors.

Irrigation

The Hohokam had a varied and well-developed artistic tradition, which indicates that individual community members had the

luxury of time, provided by a stable economic system, to create nonessential items. In the Sonoran region, the stability rested on the Hohokam's most impressive achievement—an irrigation network. They designed, built, and maintained an elaborate irrigation system that would not be equaled until the nineteenth century and the age of machines. In fact, nineteenth-century Phoenix's main canals lay on top of the Hohokam's. The Gila and Salt Rivers provided the only reliable water source in the valley, so the ancient irrigators dug main canals from the river to an ever-widening system of distribution canals that took water to fields up to 10 miles from the rivers.

Merely constructing the canals was not the end of the Hohokam commitment. They also built intake structures, headgates and diversion gates, and constantly maintained and improved the system. Nearly 300 miles of major canals and almost 1,000 miles of smaller structures have been recorded just in the Salt River valley. All this was built with human labor without the aid even of draft animals, which obviously required a group effort. This represents an incredible commitment to community success and clearly reveals the existence of a planning authority in the Hohokam culture.

The extensive irrigation system required a great deal of labor but allowed the Hohokam a measure of prosperity in a harsh region. They probably put in two separate crops each year since they could rely on the delivery of water. They grew at least 16 different species including maize, beans, agaves, cotton, tobacco, and squash. In addition to agriculture, men would have hunted bighorn sheep, elk, mule deer, white-tailed deer, antelope, rabbits, rodents, turkeys, quail, and reptiles. Women gathered wild fruits, seeds, nuts, and roots. For several centuries the Hohokam carved out a successful and thriving lifestyle in the desert. This naturally attracted migrants from all over the region. It appears that seven different languages were spoken in Phoenix during this period. Newcomers brought new skills, traditions, and labor supply and it seemed the system could support them all. The Hohokam people, however, remained at the mercy of changing natural conditions, despite their seeming abundance. Both droughts and extensive wet periods threatened agriculture. Flooding required continual rebuilding of canals and drought withered crops even with a controlled water supply.

The Hohokam experienced both of these extremes and that may be what finally drove them to leave the area by the fifteenth century. After four centuries of successful adaptation to the environment, climate change finally proved too much for the population to bear. Beginning in the twelfth century, the weather became erratic,

and rivers started flooding and dwindling; sometimes blowing out canals and other times leaving them dry. As this occurred throughout the Southwest, people began moving to find new opportunities, and masses of people flooded in to the Phoenix area. Communities had to reorganize and quickly absorb the migrants. This put tremendous stress on Hohokam society. Multistory dwellings were constructed, characteristic red pottery gave away to styles brought by migrants, and more canals were built closer to the headwaters of streams in an attempt to capture yet more water. The combination of overpopulation and inadequate food supply spread disease and malnutrition. Women and children were the first to succumb, but the devastation eventually hit the male population as well. Burial excavations show that 66 of every 1,000 people died each year. As mortality rates climbed, the space under homes and courtyards was pressed into service for burial sites. As the collapse progressed, trade faltered and outmigration began.

By the end, only a few people were left living among the grand ruins of the fourteenth century. The most striking of those ruins remains near Phoenix, Arizona, and has been named *Casa Grande.* This three-story adobe towers rises imposingly from the flat landscape and may have been a religious structure, a chiefly abode, or an observation platform. Begun in 1352, at the height of Hohokam culture, Casa Grande stands as a mute testimony to the remarkable civilization who, in the end, could not sustain themselves in the harsh environment of the Southwest.

MOGOLLON

When the Hohokam left the area, human occupation in the Southwest did not end. One of the remarkable aspects of the ancient Southwest is the continuity and diversity of human habitation over the centuries. Various groups made the region home in overlapping and distinct periods. The people we call Mogollon are an example of desert region inhabitants who adapted differently to their environment than the Hohokam who had done much to control nature with their elaborate irrigation systems.

The Mogollon chose to reside at the source of the precious commodity of the region—water. They lived in the mountainous area straddling the Arizona–New Mexico border. Their territory was large, extending south from the Little Colorado River in Arizona all the way through Chihuahua, Mexico, and eastward from the Verde River in Arizona to the Pecos River in New Mexico. Despite this

huge homeland, the Mogollon remained a small population, living lightly on the land and leaving few traces of their culture, including their name. Archaeologists named their culture for the Mogollon mountains, which had themselves been named in honor of Juan Ignacio Flores Mogollon, Spanish governor in the eighteenth century.

These people we call Mogollon descended from longtime inhabitants of the area. Their culture probably developed out of the much earlier Cochise group, which lived as hunter gatherers in the seventh century B.C. Unlike the Hohokam, the Mogollon did not change the old culture radically by building large towns and complex irrigation systems. Instead, they remained close to their hunting and gathering patterns. The rugged terrain, with its tall peaks and steep valleys, suited hunting far better than agriculture. They killed and ate large mammals, such as mule deer, bighorn sheep, and pronghorn, as well as smaller species such as jackrabbits, gophers, prairie dogs, and badgers. The area yielded rich resources for gathers who collected nuts: walnut, acorn, pinyon; fruits: juniper, chokecherry, prickly pear; and grasses: ricegrass, peppergrass, tansy mustard. In addition to a successful hunting and gathering strategy, the Mogollon added limited agriculture. They inherited maize from their Cochise ancestors and cultivated it along with varieties of beans and squash. As strains of these crops improved, the people could rely more heavily on them. Corn became a major plant food, despite the challenges to its production. The Mogollon homeland had few flat, rich valleys suited for large fields, so in many areas crops struggled in steep terrain, surviving with only 100 frost-free days and widely varying rainfall.

The Mogollon lived in pit houses. The use of basic subterranean housing is widespread, but there are often regional adaptations. In an effort to insulate themselves from the cold in the mountains, the Mogollon excavated their pits 5 feet deep and at least 10 to 15 feet in diameter. A ramp provided access to the interior after a frame of saplings and mud created the roof. This natural insulation worked to keep out the extremes of heat and cold that are characteristic of high elevations in the Southwest. Location could also be used to make dwellings more comfortable. The Mogollon often built on mesas or ridges that would have been warmed at night as the cool air drained into the valleys. Mogollon, however, primarily chose high ground for the good view of the surroundings that it afforded to inhabitants. At a site known as the Bluff in the White Mountains of New Mexico, archaeologists found that the Mogollon excavated pit homes around immovable boulders, giving the walls a wavy

appearance. In other small ways housing differed as some families chose to build crude fire pits in the home, but most appear to have cooked outside.

Pit houses served the basic need for shelter and storage. A Mogollon family's possessions would not have taken up much room. Women had pottery vessels, woven baskets, and grinding tools to prepare daily meals. The tools of a hunting life such as knives, axes, bone, and projectile points would have been men's items. The food supplies like seed and grain were stored in pits in the house floor or just outside. Family members might possess fur, hide, woven fiber clothing, and shell, bone or semiprecious stone adornments.

The Mogollon continued to adapt and change as life progressed in the Southwest. They changed the pit house plan from circular to rectangular. After about A.D. 700 the Mogollon developed more reliance on corn agriculture. These people never built the elaborate irrigation systems that the Hohokam relied on, so they lived at the mercy of natural rainfall. The greater importance of crops prompted a movement of settlements to the valley floors. Here the Mogollon had more room to expand as well as more constant sources of water such as the Mimbres River.

The Mimbres River has given the name to a flourishing of Mogollon culture occurring along the valley after A.D. 1000. At this time several notable changes occurred in the lifestyle of the Mogollon. In a departure from the traditional pit houses of their ancestors, Mogollon of the eleventh century began building above-ground masonry structures. This new construction style, perhaps borrowed from neighbors, offered distinct advantages. Made entirely of stone and mud, the homes contained no wood and thus would last virtually forever. Furthermore, now a growing Mogollon family did not need to cram into their original small pit house, but could easily add rooms to their rectangular adobe structure. Dwellings with more than a dozen rooms could house a small cooperative of labor for various tasks. In a few instances, like the grasshopper site in Arizona, they constructed very large complexes. These expansive structures would have include ceremonial "kivas" rooms, as well a family dwelling space.

As these Mogollon developed more complex lifestyles, they also made attempts to ensure a reliable water supply for their cops. This effort yielded check dams that paled in comparison to the Hohokam's extensive network but did provide steadier water delivery. In turn, the predictable harvest of crops supported population growth to about 3,000 people in the Mimbres valley.

A successful agricultural economy usually produces enough surplus to allow the pursuit of other occupations by some members.
Among the Mimbres, some individuals became potters. The pots
they produced have become some of the most evocative and
famous ceramics from Native America.

Art and Ceremony

This coil-constructed pottery began with locally gathered clay.
After the walls had a smooth finish from shaping and scraping, a
slip or thin wash of clay made a smooth surface for decoration. Part
of the allure of Mimbres pottery is the stark contrast between the
white slip and the dark painting. This striking white background
came from *kaolin,* a white clay found in the area. The true artistry of
Mimbres pottery is apparent in their painting techniques. Chewed
yucca fiber made a soft brush for applying dark red or black paint.
Native artists often depicted elements observable in their world and
the Mimbres were no exception. They are best known for a style that
matched geometric shapes, which may have represented lightning,
mountains, or other natural features, with stylized representations
of animals. Animals, including game species, clearly figured impor-
tantly in Mogollon life. Turtles, fish, turkeys, and mountain sheep
grace Mimbres bowls and pots. Mimbres' artistic skill apparently was
as admired when it was new as it is today and thus was often traded
outside the Mogollon homeland and collected by other groups. The
Mimbres kept their best work at home where pots might be used
daily. They also placed beautiful pottery vessels over the head of a
deceased relative buried under the floor of the house. These pots had
holes in them, presumably to allow the deceased's soul to escape.

The Mogollon apparently honored their dead by keeping them
close to their families. Such a burial practice may seem be strange
to us, but it simply reflects one approach to dealing with the dead.
A change in burial practices often signals to anthropologists a
change in cultural influences such as the interjection of outside
ideas. When the Mimbres began using cremation, it may have
reflected their absorption into the sphere of a larger culture. In the
twelfth century, Casas Grandes, a Mexican town, exerted a strong
pull on its northern neighbors. The Mimbres seem to have served
as middle men in a vibrant trade route stretching from Chihuahua
to northern New Mexico. It appears to anthropologists that Casas
Grandes absorbed the Mogollon after a period of intense stress
linked to drought.

A woman building a pot by the coil method. Library of Congress.

Those Mogollon residing in more inaccessible mountainous regions maintained a distinct cultural identity at sites such as that protected by Gila Cliff Dwellings National Park. Here Mogollon constructed more than 40 stone rooms in alcoves on the cliff face. These are generally called cliff dwellings and may represent an attempt to find more secure dwelling sites. These were only inhabited for a short time, from A.D. 1280 to 1300. By A.D. 1400, the Mogollon people had abandoned their mountain homeland in the face of extensive drought that disrupted cultural patterns in the Southwest. Some of them may have joined their northern neighbors, the Anasazi.

ANASAZI

In some sense the Anasazi are the premiere ancient culture of North America. This is the culture whose ruins are visited by millions each year at Mesa Verde National Park, and whose images of the god Kokopelli have become an icon of the Southwest. The cliff dwellers left grand statements behind to tantalize modern people with glimpses of the complexity of the past. Yet little in their origins

would suggest that these people would have the largest preindustrial dwellings in the continental United States.

America's fascination with this ancient culture started when amateur archaeologist Richard Wetherhill began digging and collecting the remains that survived in the dry western climate. The arid air had preserved many forms of plant materials, including beautifully woven baskets, prompting Wetherhill to refer to their makers as the "basket people." The currently used name, Anasazi, is a Navajo word meaning either "ancient people" or "enemy ancestors," which reflects the fact that the Navajo are not descended from this group, but perhaps the Navajo's traditional enemies, the Hopi, are the descendants. It is from the practices of these historic pueblo people that we must infer much about the culture of the ancient people the Hopi call the Hisatsinom.

The Anasazi inhabited the Four Corners region: the high plateau and canyon area of northern Arizona and New Mexico and southern Utah and Colorado. They probably descend from earlier desert culture, Archaic-era nomadic hunters and gatherers. The adoption of maize agriculture marked the shift to a sedentary lifestyle, although that would have to wait for the development of cold tolerant varieties. As in other areas, types of squash provided another important crop. As their Hopi descendents do today, the Anasazi relied mostly on the natural rainfall of summer and snowmelt in the spring to bring moisture to the seeds. Seeds were placed in holes that had been poked in the earth with a digging stick. A few check dams and copious prayers to the gods aided these ancient farmers. Of course, in such a harsh environment agriculture could not be the sole source of nutrition, so the Anasazi continued to gather and hunt, adding pinyon nuts, yucca, and prickly pear fruit, as well as rabbit, deer, and prairie dog meat to their diet.

Around A.D. 500, the Anasazi lifestyle began to change. The addition of beans complemented corn and squash to yield a stable nutritious base that led the Anasazi to a more sedentary existence. Now tied more closely to the land, the people switched from portable baskets to more fragile pottery for storage and cooking. Not surprisingly, this sedentary shift was also reflected in housing styles. Initially, the Anasazi lived in pit houses, much as their neighbors did. They constructed a variety of shapes—round, rectangular, square, or D-shaped. These appeared clustered around reliable water sources and usable agricultural land. The pit houses served their purpose of basic shelter, although they must have been cramped, smoky, and dark.

Pueblos

The movement to above-ground dwellings must have been a welcome change for residents. The Anasazi began building rooms of wattle and daub or stone structures around A.D. 700. Those made of stone blocks laid up to form straight walls resulted in rectangular or square rooms that could be connected to each other. Additional stories could be added on top of sturdily built walls and thus the iconic southwestern *pueblo* style of architecture emerged. One reason this style has become so well known is that the dwellings have lasted so long, a clear testament to excellent workmanship. Unlike pit houses, which generally had a useful life of about 15 years, these pueblo structures served people for many decades. The builders must have spent countless hours shaping stones with stone tools, mixing mortar, and fitting it all into a beautiful wall. As was common in other cultures, the masons' painstaking work was often covered by a plaster of mud and perhaps a coat of whitewash. Anasazi homes can be distinguished by their characteristic T-shaped doors. Despite speculation, modern observers still do not know the reason for this odd design.

Anasazi pueblo structures generally followed a common pattern. Dwelling units, often stacked several stories high, clustered around a central plaza. This plaza served as an open air community center. With small, dark living quarters, people chose to perform many daily tasks outside. Women could gather to grind corn, prepare food, make and repair clothing while socializing and watching the children play. Men met to repair tools and weapons, and discuss community issues. Men might also gather in the underground kivas located at the center of the plaza. Even after puebloans moved their dwellings above ground, their sacred space remained subterranean. Kivas were pit houses dedicated to use for religious societies. This special form of pit house embodied the peoples' belief that humans had come to this world from another. The old world represented by the kivas was dark; the next world above on the plaza was suffused with light. This usually circular structure contained benches, a firepit, niches for sacred objects, and the *sipapu*—a hole in the floor that represented the connection between the worlds. Kivas and the religious societies who used them were the domain of men. Here they met to plan the elaborate dances and celebrations the community held to honor the gods. Because the gods controlled critical powers like the sun, wind and rain, corn, animals, and fertility, it was important to maintain harmony with them by showing

proper respect. The ceremonial dances often occurred in the winter when the pace of village life had slowed. Eagerly awaited by young and old alike, the dances featured costumed, masked dancers representing the gods familiar to onlookers. These dances must have served to both renew faith in the spiritual system and provide vivid and much anticipated entertainment on long winter nights.

CHACO CANYON

The Anasazi are best known for the different ruins still evident at two major sites: Chaco Canyon, New Mexico, and Mesa Verde, Arizona. These ancient people built more than a dozen large communities along a nine-mile stretch of Chaco Canyon. The scale of planning and building at this remote site still takes visitors' breath away. Pueblo Bonito, which covers three acres, is the largest and best excavated of the ruins. In fact, it stood as the largest building in America until it was finally surpassed in 1882. Such a complex had to be built and occupied over a long period: A.D. 800–1150. About

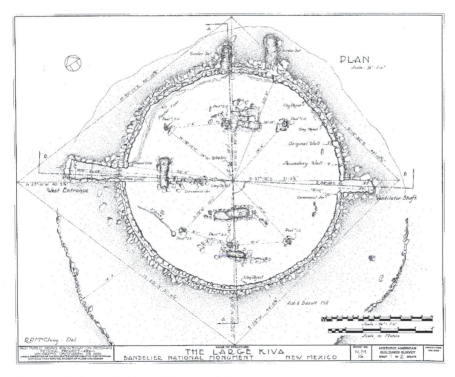

A general plan of a kiva. Library of Congress.

145 rooms laid out in a D-shape had been constructed by A.D. 880. The central plaza included six kivas to service the numerous religious societies supported by the growing population at Chaco. It appears that the ongoing construction spurts coincided with periods of increased precipitation in the region. Perhaps the extra rainfall produced surplus crops that could feed additional residents or be stored for future use. Archaeologists have found corn preserved in storerooms for thousands of years, so additional storerooms would have served the people well. As construction continued, the rear walls of the town rose up to five stories and contained 800 rooms.

This scale of construction clearly required considerable labor as well as adequate materials. The limiting factor had to have been wood. The communities of Chaco required an estimated quarter-million trees for posts and beams. This meant the builders had to venture to distant mountains for their timber and carry the felled trees up to 40 miles. They apparently shepherded this critical resource carefully by thinning selectively to preserve the integrity of the forests.

The structures of Chaco Canyon are definitely amazing; however, the Anasazi left other remarkable evidence of their culture. Chaco Canyon contains an extensive network of ancient roads. Aerial surveys reveal a road system of nearly 1,500 miles. The roads are 25 to 35 feet wide and generally very straight, changing direction with sharp angles. The existence of this ancient roadway system is even more remarkable when we remember that the builders had neither wheels nor draft animals. The question recurs to modern observers: What was the purpose of this straight, connected, purposefully built road system? The roads must have served to unite the early pueblo people in the region. The longest roads reached 50 miles outward from Chaco. They provided an obvious and impressive link between the great pueblos of Chaco and smaller outlying settlements. People would have used the roads to come to the core of the canyon area for a variety of purposes. Religious observances could have been one such motivation. With its two great kivas, each more than 50 feet in diameter, Pueblo Bonito could have been the focus of major ceremonial observances. If the great houses served as political centers as well, then officials would have been able to move efficiently around their territory.

It may seem that early pueblo people at Chaco had it all: extensive dwellings, an elaborate road system, a far-reaching trade network. And yet 300 years after this great building boom began, it was over. Nothing new was built in Chaco Canyon after A.D. 1140,

An interior view of a reconstructed kiva.
BigStockPhoto.com

and it was probably abandoned by this time. The power of the great ceremonial, political, or religious center was over. Experts continue to debate the reason for this apparent collapse of a thriving system. It is easy to imagine the combined pressure of drought in a harsh environment and an expanding population simply overtaxing the resources such as trees, water, and crops. The three-century trend of higher than average rainfall seems to have ended. We can imagine a loss of leadership and social chaos under such an economic collapse. But other theories emphasize factors that could have pulled the ancient peoples from their homes to a new life elsewhere, rather than having them forced from their homes.

Chaco was reinhabited in the early thirteenth century, but never returned to its former power. A half-century of drought sealed the fate of Chaco, depopulating the area until the Navajo arrived in the eighteenth century. We do know that the Chaco residents left on their own terms in an orderly fashion, taking their valued possession with them. No signs of destruction, fire, or violence mar the impressive ruins at Chaco Canyon.

The record of the ancient puebloan people does not end after the abandonment of Chaco Canyon. The twelfth century, with its limited rainfall, clearly taxed populations throughout the Southwest. The pressure on limited water resources may have prompted conflict among the humans in the region. Some may have become more concerned with defense than comfort. How else can we explain the Anasazi's move to cliff dwellings after the dawn of the thirteenth century.

CLIFF DWELLINGS

Modern Americans remain fascinated with the cliff dwellings of Mesa Verde, rediscovered by Richard Wetherill in 1888. What was described as *a little city of stone, asleep . . . in a great cavern in a cliff* has become a major American treasure known as Cliff Palace. This large, well-preserved dwelling provides us with a unique window into a remarkable period of Anasazi life.

At the turn of the twelfth century, Four Corners residents chose to move from their mesa top homes to the natural alcoves in the cliff face below. This entailed a tremendous amount of labor. The residents of Sun Point Pueblo, the last to be built on the mesa top, actually took their town apart and rebuilt it in a cliff opening by reusing the precious timbers and stones. Throughout the region villagers made the decision to relocate to the cliff faces. It is hard for us to imagine the forces that drove people to this difficult lifestyle. It would seem that only the threat of violence and an overwhelming interest in defense would justify this arduous new settlement pattern.

Not only the building phase—hauling timbers and stones to the cliffs—was difficult. Daily life became more challenging. The Anasazi people continued to farm so they had to move up or down the cliff faces each day to tend their fields on the valley floors or mesa tops. Similarly, food, fuel, and probably water had to be carried up or down to the cliff dwellings. Handholds and footholds carved into the rock remain as mute testament to the arduous daily journey. The Anasazi who moved to the cliff sides re-created traditional villages as well as they could. Space constraints may have prevented the geometric perfection seen at Chaco, but otherwise the building style is similar. Sandstone blocks formed rectangular rooms and timbers held up roofs, often in multiple stories. Wooden ladders facilitated access to upper levels.

At Cliff Palace the rooms grew to more than 200, which could have accommodated several hundred residents. There are other

The Anasazi ruins at Cliff Palace, Mesa Verde
National Park. BigStockPhoto.com

large dwellings like Long House with 150 rooms, but most of the
National Park's 600 ruins contain less than five rooms. Most of the
rooms served as residences, but others tucked against the cliff wall
held food supplies like corn. Perhaps the strongest mark of Anasazi culture shows in the existence of kivas. With level ground at a
premium, residents of Cliff Palace still dedicated space for 23 kivas.
Religious rites could be held in the subterranean kiva while daily
life went on overhead on the communal plaza.

The challenges of living on the side of a cliff did not last long for
the Anasazi. Within 100 years from their inception, the cliff dwellings were empty. Spruce Tree House, the last active site in Mesa
Verde, contains timbers cut in A.D. 1282. This thirteenth-century
abandonment has perplexed scholars for a century. The conditions
that caused the Anasazi to leave these spectacular but difficult residences are not known. Most modern analysts refer to a cycle of
drought that caused a precarious agricultural system to fail, but
there may have been other factors as well. For example, a female
skull found fractured by a spear point lends credence to theories of

conflict, perhaps exacerbated by the hardship of drought. Cultural practices may have contributed to the fall of Mesa Verde. Inhabitants discarded waste over the edge of the cliffs, creating huge garbage piles. These middens are a boon to archaeologists in search of clues about Anasazi daily life, but probably posed a health threat to the community. It appears that half of all Mesa Verde children died by the age of four.

Residents moved away from Mesa Verde, probably in large groups. If conflict in the region was a concern, then individuals could not safely have stayed behind. People simply packed up and left, taking valued possessions and leaving the rest. Five hundred years later, Richard Wetherill found broken stone axes, pottery, and water jugs sitting where they had been left by those who chose not to carry them on a long journey. The migration of the Anasazi seems to have taken them south and east toward the Rio Grande River region with its more reliable rainfall. Evidence of the remarkable Anasazi culture has been protected and can be visited at numerous national sites including Hovenweep, Navajo, Canyon de Chelly, Bandelier National Monuments, and Grand Canyon, Zion, and Canyonlands National Parks.

SINAGUA

The rich cultural traditions of the Hohokam, Mogollon, and Anasazi blended in some areas to produce distinct cultures after about A.D. 1100. The Sinagua culture (literally "without water" in Spanish) left remains of large settlements in the oddly named Tuzigoot and Montezuma's Castle National Monuments. The naming confusion reflects the fact that archaeologists are still unclear about the Sinagua's origins. We do know that they lived successfully in the desert region north of Phoenix, Arizona, from the seventh to the fifteenth centuries. During the height of their success in the twelfth and thirteenth centuries, the Sinagua dominated the San Francisco Mountains and Verde River Valley region. They built large, multiroom pueblos that could house hundreds of people. The ruins at Tuzigoot had 110 rooms. The residents combined hunting, gathering, and farming to survive in the arid landscape. They were very adaptable and took whatever measures they could to produce enough foodstuffs. In some areas they built irrigation ditches while elsewhere they dry-farmed maize, beans, and squash. Sometimes they created shallow ponds and scooped the water out with clay pots. Sinagua pottery was a unique style of

mostly undecorated brown, red, and buff pottery made from local clay with a paddle-and-anvil technique.

In addition to growing enough to feed themselves, the Sinagua also traded extensively with others, especially with the peoples of Mexico. They may have been the most successful traders of the prehistoric Southwest. Among the items exchanged were decorated pottery, shell jewelry, copper bells, live macaws, salt, pigments, cotton cloth, and argillite. Their successful adaptation, however, finally ended by the middle of the thirteenth century. Like many other ancestral puebloan groups, the Sinagua abandoned most of their settlements and concentrated in a few and then left those by the mid-1400s. At this point they drop from the archaeological record, probably merging with ancestral Hopi groups.

SALADO

To the southeast of the Sinagua lived the culture we call Salado after the Spanish name for the Salt River, *Rio Salado.* It is a fitting name, for in the desert Southwest such a river was important to humans of every period. The people we know as Salado depended on the river as a critical water source. The Salt River comes out of the White Mountains of eastern Arizona. In some places and at certain times of the year, it runs as a powerful river while near its end, in the dry season, it dwindles to a trickle. The Salt River would have historically carried more water in a steadier flow rate before human diversion of the water in recent centuries. It would have been even more impressive a resource in ancient times. A major tributary, Tonto Creek, gave its name to the area called the Tonto Basin, which was the heartland of the Salado culture.

These people blended aspects of other cultures as they came into contact with them. Originally dwelling in pit house compounds similar to the Mogollon, they later switched to Anasazi-style pueblo structures. They maintained their own tradition of walled compounds despite the dwelling style change. In some places along the riverbanks, they carved out homes in the cliff alcoves. Along the river the Salado tended fields of corn, beans, pumpkins, amaranth, and cotton. They also supplemented agriculture with hunting and gathering. Any surplus productions could be traded along the network that reached from Colorado to Mexico to the Gulf of California. The Salado's distinctive black-on-white and later polychromatic pottery style became a hallmark of their existence. Like other desert dwellers, however, the Salado

left their homes after A.D. 1450 and disappeared; we have no evidence of their fate.

When the various ancient cultures of the American Southwest dispersed and faded from the archaeological record, the land was not empty. Human habitation continued undeterred in the challenging climate and landscape. When Europeans arrived in the early sixteenth century, they found thriving cultures so comfortable in their place that they could conceive of no other homeland.

The valleys of the Gila and Salt Rivers, once home to the Hohokam culture, later supported people who were their likely descendants. The O'odham people continue to inhabit the region today. The name given to them by the Spanish—Pima—derives from the "pi-nyi-match" or "I don't know" answer they repeatedly gave to the Europeans' endless questions. Another group became the "Papago" from "papebotas" or bean eaters. The peoples' traditional name, meaning "river people," reflects the close relationship these southwestern farmers had to the large water sources. Like the Hohokam before them, the O'odham harnessed the power of the river by creating irrigation devices. They built dams of stones and branches to divert water to ditches that, although not as elaborate as the Hohokam's, did effectively water the fields. The fields yielded maize, beans, pumpkins, and other crops. This agricultural harvest usually provided about 60 percent of the O'odham diet; the other 40 percent came from hunting and gathering. One important wild plant was the large saguaro cactus. The ripened fruit of the saguaro prompted a community-wide gathering festival among the Akimle O'odham and their Tohono O'odham (desert Pima or Papago) relatives who lived farther south. When the red fruit ripened in early summer, women knocked it from the tops of the high cactus. The fruit could be eaten fresh, dried for later use, or crushed and boiled into a syrup. After the multiday harvest finished, this syrup fermented into *nawait*. Male leaders drank the fermented juice for days with the goal of purging and thus symbolically returning moisture to the earth. The cyclical rainy season began at this time and marked the beginning of the O'odham new year.

Life dependent on agriculture in a dry region was always precarious. Any individual or group could face failure; however, cultural tradition buffered hardship. A destitute village could perform a begging dance after which they would receive gifts of food from others. Other reciprocal gift giving also ameliorated hardship. Trade for items valued by others, like salt, brought in much needed items.

EASTERN PUEBLOS

Major migrations usually have both "push" and "pull" factors. If drought and worsening conditions for agriculture pushed ancient puebloans from their canyon dwellings, then the availability of water and success of groups to the east pulled them toward new settlement areas. For example, people moved to Kuana Pueblo, north of Albuquerque, New Mexico, because the irrigated fields produced enough corn, beans, cotton, and melons to support a 1,000 room town.

Many puebloan groups resided in the Southwest before European arrival. They shared many cultural traits, but did not recognize themselves as one people in a political or kinship sense. Non-natives have grouped them together from contact to the present based on perceived similarities, particularly dwelling style, from which the Anglo term *puebloan* derives. The Spanish recognized residents' adobe structures as grouped houses in a way that tipis or wickiups in other regions would not have been familiar, and they quickly declared them "pueblos."

Two of the best known puebloan cultures are the Zuni and Hopi, although *known* is a relative term, as these people have been protective of outsider's knowledge of their society. They share many cultural traits and adaptations with others living in the region. Their lifestyle, including politics, economy, religion, and social organization, revolve around the expediency of surviving in the harsh semi-arid climate.

Hopi

The Hopi, like their Anasazi ancestors, live in the northern reaches of the Southwest. Three mesas along Black Mesa in northern Arizona have always been home to the Hopi. This long tenure gives the tribe claim to the title of oldest continuously inhabited town in North America. Old Oraibi was settled around A.D. 1100. In the manner of Hopi towns, Oraibi perches high on the barren mesa, offering a commanding view of the surrounding countryside. Like the Anasazi cliff dwellings, the mesa sites offer the Hopi protection from raiders both indigenous and later European, although at a distinct cost in convenience.

Following southwestern tradition, the Hopi were farmers. Because this western area had few permanent rivers, the people had to rely on rainfall to support their crops. Unfortunately, this valuable rainfall often comes in the form of violent storms that can destroy

planted fields. Centuries of knowledge taught the Hopi the best strategies for dealing with the uncertainties of the weather. The Hopi scattered their fields widely around their lands, thus ensuring that localized storms would not destroy all the crops at once. Another adaptation for successful harvests was to stagger their planting throughout the season so that different plots reached various stages of maturity to offer protection from calamity.

Unlike most other Native American cultures, the Hopi men did all the farming, drawing on generations of accumulated experience. They planted varieties of corn, beans, squash, tobacco, and cotton. Each plant was important and was nurtured by the attention and prayers of the farmer. Maize held the premier position in the world of southwestern farming. The Hopi grew two dozen varieties of various colors that yielded remarkable bounty under harsh conditions. To supplement the agricultural harvest, women gathered more than 100 different wild plants. Additional protein came into the diet via wild game such as rabbits, which men hunted.

The power of farming in daily life is revealed in the Hopi ceremony celebrating a new life in the tribe.

When a child was born his Corn Mother was placed beside him, where it was kept for twenty days, and during this period he was kept in darkness. . . . Early on the morning of the twentieth day, the mother, holding the child in her arms and the Corn Mother in her right hand, and accompanied by her own mother—the child's grandmother—left the house and walked to the east. They stopped, facing east, and prayed silently, casting pinches of cornmeal to the rising sun. When the sun cleared the horizon the mother stepped forward, held up the child to the sun, and said, "Father Sun, this is your child."[2]

Just as their economic roles were divided along gender lines, so, too, were other daily tasks. Hopi men engaged in weaving. They wove cotton fibers on large looms to produce clothing: breechcloths, belts, skirts, and one-shouldered dresses. These items were enough cover for most of the year, but turkey feather or rabbit skin robes could be added for warmth. The whole ensemble was often enlivened by decorative pieces of shell or turquoise. Individuals could further enhance their appearance by crafting elaborate hairstyles, specifically those for unmarried women whose long hair was wrapped on stick frames to make huge loops. Less complicated styles served married women and men. While men produced clothing, Hopi women made the beautiful and practical pottery so iconic of the Southwest. Vessels began as indigenous clay and, under the

guidance of skilled hands, emerged in the shape of a jug or pot to be decorated in the local fashion and fired in a pit. Hopi pottery could be distinguished from other pueblos by distinct color and design styles. The skill and artistry of potters passed from mother to daughter, representing generations of achievement.

Corn was clearly the most important commodity in Hopi life. Even their religion recognized this critical crop. Religious practices centered around the goal of maintaining harmony and honoring the gods so they would favor the Hopi people. In the harsh environment it would surely have seemed as though divine intervention was necessary for success. Religion was a communal activity for the Hopi. Men and women joined different societies whose initiation marked a person's full membership into the tribe. Societies held responsibility for performing the proper rituals to ensure the gods' favor for the entire community so that it was a serious undertaking. Like their ancestors, the Hopi used kivas as both sacred and secular spaces. Different societies owned kivas, which were open only to men. Men might gather in these square chambers to weave on large looms, to discuss village issues, or just to socialize. The kivas, however, also served as sacred centers where men offered altars, tobacco smoke, songs, dances, and prayers to honor their gods.

The Hopi referred to the good gods or spirits as *katcinas*. These beings controlled powerful forces in life such as rain, lightning, wind, and clouds. The province and power of the katcinas are clear evidence of the critical importance of the weather to these desert farmers. They literally lived and died by the coming of rain, so ensuring its arrival was paramount. The katcinas spent part of their year with the Hopi people. Male members of the katcina society dressed to impersonate the gods and community members honored them with ritual and gifts. The katcinas appeared at the Soyal ceremony on the winter solstice and stayed with the people until summer solstice. In the village the spirits could be counted on to exercise social control by visiting children to check on their behavior and reprimanding or rewarding accordingly. Parents gave their children carved images of the katcinas to teach them about these important spirits. Other ceremonies and ritual observances filled the Hopi calendar. These festivities emphasized and maintained community identity.

Hopi could never forget they were a part of a dynamic community. All aspects of their lives centered on the village. Every person was a member of one of several clans. Membership passed through the female line; a person shared a clan with his or her mother and siblings, but not father. Clans governed daily life from regulating

behavior and ceremonial roles to planting and harvesting crops. Clans controlled the fields, which were owned by the women. Clan elders decided which plots would be planted at what time after consultation with the religious calendar. A religious official, the Sun Watcher, tracked the sun's progress from winter to summer solstice and announced important dates based on the Hopi calendar. The responsibility for each of the many ceremonies in Hopi life fell to different ones among the more than two dozen clans. Clan membership also governed appropriate choices for spouses and proved an important level of identity for Hopi people.

All of this connectedness affected Hopi life and brought advantages and disadvantages. The communal, kinship ethos created an important barrier against the hardships of desert life. Individuals without a safety network of relatives and friends would have faced setbacks, disasters, and dangers alone and could well have failed the survival test. Family, kin, and town commitments meant assistance would be available in time of need. This is an important strategy for success in a challenging region; however, the fairly structured society left little room for individualism. Behavior outside the norm could threaten the whole group and thus was poorly tolerated. Strict rules for marrying outside the clan, although important for long-term success of the people, could thwart individual desire. With a government that was a form of theocracy, tying religion to every aspect of life, there was no room for unbelievers or challenges to the Hopi way. Overall, however, the Hopi way of life proved remarkably successful, adapting to threats from nomadic raiders and later Europeans while perpetuating the traditional culture.

ATHABASKANS

One of the challenges to puebloan harmony in the Southwest surfaced before the devastating European invasion. The ancestors of the people known today as the Navajo and Apache, linguistically Athabaskan speakers, represented a distinctly different culture from the puebloan people. The traditional culture of these groups and Anglo scientific thought differ sharply as to the origins of the people. Both versions of ancient Athabaskan history are offered here.

Navajo

The Navajo (Dine) believe that they as a people were created and placed in the Southwest by powerful forces. No idea of migration

during human times would make sense to a traditional Navajo. The process of placing the Dine in the Southwest was through the emergence of four previous worlds into this, the fifth world. Each time the Holy People found harmony in a world, it eventually fell apart as a result of poor, antisocial behavior so they had to leave for another world. The first world was that of insect people, usually depicted as a red world. Leaving that place, they emerged into a blue, bird-inhabited world where they learned agriculture. Poor behavior pushed the Holy People out and into the third yellow world of grasshoppers. Valued skills learned in this world included hunting and use of cloth, as well as the cultural practices of languages, marriages, and exogamy. Creating disharmony once again pushed the Holy People into the fourth world, and finally they climbed a tree to escape a flood and emerge into the present or fifth world.

The fifth world is the world where the sun, moon, and stars were created. It is also where Changing Woman created the Navajo people as well as the Monster Slayer and Child of the Water to combat the disharmony in the world. These Hero Twins left a few powerful forces that shape Navajo life, such as old age, winter, poverty, and hunger. Much of what Navajos see in their world is explained in the creation beliefs, including the landscape. The Dinetah, or land of the people, is embraced by four sacred mountains created by the Holy People: Tsisnaasjini, Dawn or White Shell Mountain; Tsoodzil, Blue Bead or Turquoise Mountain; Doko'oosliid, Abalone Shell Mountain; and Dibé Nitsaa, Obsidian Mountain. So the Navajo world makes little sense to them without their sacred origin stories.[3]

Anthropologists believe that they can distinguish Navajo and Apache origins by a study of their language. In this theory, a wave of migration later than the first contact between Asia and America, perhaps around 1000 B.C., brought a new group of humans to the New World. These more recent migrants, identified as *Nadene*, included culture groups who stayed in the Pacific Northwest, Tlingit and Haida, as well as the Athabaskans who continued to push inward into the continent. Some small groups dropped out of the general movement to remain scattered through the West; others moved all the way to the Southwest. This group can be identified as linguistically distinct by about A.D. 1000 and are termed the *Dine*. By the time of European arrival, two separate groupings of Navajo and Apache had been established. Scientists regard these "newcomers" as the most recent and last indigenous people to populate the Southwest.

Whether emerging from a previous world or walking from Asia, the Dine continued to follow nomadic lifestyle patterns. They moved out through the mountainous regions following game, constructing temporary housing, and surviving as hunter-gatherers in a harsh landscape. In time they had moved all around the sedentary puebloan people. Some conflict would be inevitable as the wealth of an agricultural people attracted the attention of those who subsisted by hunting and raiding. But the ensuing contact developed into a cultural exchange that altered the lifestyle of the Navajo people who have persisted in the Southwest to the present day and are now the largest tribe in the United States.

The Navajo witnessed aspects of sedentary agricultural life among the puebloans and adopted and adapted those elements that fit their needs and desires. The cultural exchange was not a wholesale adoption of pueblo ways, but rather a selective choice of attributes. For example, from the Hopi the Navajo learned the art of loom weaving. The ability to make cloth and thus fiber clothing was an important skill to borrow, but the Navajo adapted it to their own needs. Among the Hopi, the men are exclusively weavers, whereas as Navajo men ranged far in search of game, the women became the weavers. The designs Navajo women incorporated into their weaving further distinguished their work as Navajo, learned from others but soon distinctly their own. The art of weaving became so thoroughly part of the Navajo people that their traditional beliefs trace the knowledge of weaving to a gift from the spirit Spider Woman who continues to guide the work of weavers.

The security of planted crops that sustained the puebloans appealed to the nomadic Navajo. They were not going to give up their mobile lifestyle, but did begin using some techniques. Planting things that did not have to be tended and nurtured a great deal, like certain wild plants and later fruit trees, allowed the Navajo to travel seasonally and then return to specific areas to harvest. The postcontact Navajo would become well known for their extensive orchards. They also proved adaptable to the European introduction of livestock, basing their lives around extensive herds of sheep and goats.

Navajo housing also adapted to the people's changing needs. They did not adopt the pueblo's stone architecture that lasted for generations, but did develop a fairly substantial dwelling called the hogan. Hogans typically began with a frame of sapling poles to which mud was applied. Early forms followed a conical shape that later evolved to an octagonal form. These hogans were sturdy

A weaver with the large floor loom characteristic of the Southwest. Library of Congress.

enough to be reused season after season but could be easily repaired and replaced after years of wear. This seemingly simple structure is sacred to the Navajo people. It is an ideal form transmitted to them by the Holy People, or Navajo spirits who originally constructed them from precious materials of abalone, obsidian, and turquoise. The door of a hogan must face east toward the rising sun, be blessed by corn pollen at construction, and usually be destroyed upon the death of its owner.

Spirituality and Ceremonialism

The religious practices of the Navajo also reflect their seminomadic lifestyle. They did not adopt the elaborate ceremonial calendar of community-wide ceremonies of their puebloan neighbors; however, the gods or spirits of the Navajo helped them in many of the ways that katcina spirits helped the Hopi. Like most native peoples, the Navajo and linguistically related Apaches believed

that life and all the good things in it came from spirits, often animals. The White Mountain Apache tell how the staple of life, corn, came to the people.

In olden times when animals could talk, a turkey overheard a hungry child begging his sister for food. The turkey shook himself all over and many types of fruit and wild food dropped off his body. The hungry children quickly ate these up. Then Turkey shook himself again and a large ear of corn dropped out. Another shake and yellow corn fell to the ground. The fourth time he shook white corn dropped out.[4]

This story shows the sustenance of life as a gift from helpful spirits, and both the gift and the giver must be properly respected.

Navajo also strove for harmony in life by maintaining the proper relationship with the earth and other creatures. This required both correct behavior from each individual every day and the observation of important rituals designed to perpetuate harmony. All Navajos tried to walk a path laid out by supernatural beings along which steady, straight progress yielded harmony in the form of health and some measure of success, whereas deviation brought sickness, death, and grief. According to Navajo belief, the earth's creatures came to this world of harmony and happiness after ascending from a place of error and uncertainty. The Holy People came here through the Hole of Emergence and then made the mountains, deserts, springs, and animals of this world.

The earliest people who struggled to this place were First Man and First Woman. It was they who provided the sun from a turquoise disk and the moon from rock crystal. They also cared for the infant who was born of the first dawn. Raised on pollen and dew, the child grew to become Changing Woman who created the Navajo people. She also gave birth to the Hero Twins—Monster Slayer and Child Born of Water—who created the harmony the Navajo people enjoy by ridding the world of monsters and dangers. The twins slew most of the threatening evils in the world, but spared a few such as Hunger, Old Age, and Dirt. They then created the Earth Surface People and taught them critical survival skills like exactly how to build houses, find food, and marry. Later, Spider Woman taught the art of weaving and Spider Man warned the people of coming danger. Naturally, these early ancestors are revered by the Navajo who feel a strong connection to the region where they believe the Holy People created them.

Four sacred mountains—Blanca Peak in Colorado, Mount Taylor in New Mexico, the San Francisco Peaks in Arizona, and Hesperus Peak in Colorado—define the area of the Dine, one at each cardinal

point of the compass. Although nomadic, early Navajo moved within a defined world that they knew intimately. This world was inhabited by other powers than humans. Holy People had considerable power and were not always benign toward the Navajo, so they must be propitiated by rituals and offerings. The Sun, Gila Monster, Thunder People, Cloud People, Wind People, and Coyote the Trickster all had power they could use for good or evil, so it certainly was important to stay on their good side.

Other negative powers existed in the Navajo world. The most common was *chinde* or ghosts of humans. When people died they left only the bad part of themselves behind as ghosts. These *chinde* were wholly evil and could not be cajoled by ritual or offering. The only hope to avoid ghost sickness was to conscientiously avoid any contact with ghosts. This required a strict avoidance of anything connected with death. Navajos abhorred dead bodies, places of death, and the names of the dead, and they would often destroy a structure if it had been associated with death. Ghosts were bad and frightening, but witches were perhaps even more horrible. These were living humans who practiced evil intentionally, usually for personal gain. This association reveals the Navajo focus on community and rejection of the acquisition of personal wealth and pride, for these are the very qualities associated with evil witches. The worst aspect of witches was that they looked like normal people during the day so they were hard to distinguish. At night they donned animal skins as they traveled around doing evil to others. They then engaged in other socially unacceptable behavior such as incest and cannibalism, embracing the most powerful Navajo taboos. As witches fed on greed, envy, and hatred of people, they worked their power by means of spells that could induce illness. Spells could be directed at individuals by incorporating a hair, fingernail, or even piece of clothing of the intended victim. Thus the Navajo world was full of challenges to harmony.

If the Navajo world operated on a conception of harmony, then any problem—illness, pain, loss—must be caused by an imbalance. Elaborate ceremonies were held to restore the balance, to bring individuals back into a state of harmony or *ho'zho'*. They were designed to remove the cause of the disease or disharmony, which could stem from the ill-intentions of witches or Holy People, or the influence of ghost or contact with outsiders. These rituals follow a prescribed format, often over several days. Men studied for years to become sacred singers, *h'athali*, able to perform the chants and create the accompanying dry paintings.

Singers created complex and beautiful designs from fine sand, powdered minerals, pollen, and charcoal. The healing power of the work was transferred to the patient who often sat in the midst of the finished design. These sings were generally performed to cure an individual of a problem caused by a perceived rupture of harmony. Many were quite problem-specific. For example, a Shootingway was appropriate for problems stemming from thunder or lightning, and a Beautyway addressed problems brought on by snakes. Other sings like the Blessingway would be held to ensure future harmony and to mark important events like marriages and births. Families usually sponsored these curing sings for their relatives; however, the entire community might participate in more public ceremonies like the Enemy Way held to remove the evil influences men had been exposed to in battle. This multiday ceremony included social dances that often served as courtship ritual, thus celebrating the future while expunging the disharmony of the past. Another long ritual was held over nine days in the winter. This *Yeibeichai* included masked, costumed dancers and dancing with fire, and was one of the most complex Navajo ceremonies.

A wickiup could be quickly constructed to provide adequate shelter for seminomadic people. Library of Congress.

The ceremonial culture of the Athabaskan people was suited to a nomadic or seminomadic lifestyle. The chants and rituals could be carried in the minds and hearts of those with spiritual knowledge to be performed anywhere. It is just one example of the remarkable adaptation that nonsedentary peoples made to life in the Southwest. The Athabaskan speakers who migrated here developed a successful culture that continued nearly unbroken from their first arrival to their near destruction by Euro-American violence and disease.

The American Southwest has always been a beautiful but harsh landscape. The environment is quite challenging for those without modern technology. We might not expect to find rich human cultures here and yet we do. The southwestern prehistoric Indians left evidence of a remarkable mastery of their environment. The Hohokam and others after them used ingenuity to harness the scant moisture for their own purposes. Many southwestern cultures supported large, dense settlements in an arid land. In a region stalked

A child in a cradleboard was safe and near his mother at all times. Library of Congress.

by drought and other environmental extremes, puebloan people developed unique religious, artistic, and social cultures. In turn, their life was precarious and the disappearance of groups like the Anasazi continues to puzzle anthropologists.

NOTES

1. Alvin M. Josephy, Jr., *The Native Americans: An Illustrated History* (Atlanta, GA: Turner Publishing, 1993), 66.

2. Josephy, Jr., *The Native Americans: An Illustrated History*, 59.

3. Mount Blanca is called Tsisnaasjini' meaning Dawn or White Shell Mountain, the Sacred Mountain of the East. It is located near Alamosa in San Luis Valley, Colorado. Mount Taylor is called Tsoodzil meaning Blue Bead or Turquoise Mountain, the Sacred Mountain of the South. It's located north of Laguna, New Mexico. The San Francisco Peaks is called Doko'oosliid meaning Abalone Shell Mountain, the Sacred Mountain of the West and in located near Flagstaff, Arizona. Mount Hesperus is called Dibé Nitsaa meaning Big Mountain Sheep, Obsidian Mountain, the Sacred Mountain of the North, and is located in the La Plata Mountains, Colorado.

4. Josephy, Jr., *The Native Americans: An Illustrated History*, 63.

FURTHER READING

Bahr, Donald. *The Short, Swift Time of Gods on Earth.* Berkeley: University of California Press, 1994.

Bartlett, Michael H., Thomas Kolaz, and David Gregory. *Archaeology in the City: A Hohokam Village in Phoenix, Arizona.* Tucson: University of Arizona Press, 1986.

Castle Rock Pueblo: A Trip through Time. Crow Canyon Archaeological Center interprets the same site throughout several historic periods. http://www.crowcanyon.org/EducationProducts/ElecFieldTrip_CRP/index.html (accessed September 1, 2007).

Mesa Verde Museum Association. The Mesa Verde Museum Association page has many images of Ansazi pottery. http://www.mesaverde.org/ (accessed September 1, 2007).

Plog, Stephen. *Ancient Peoples of the American Southwest.* London: Thames & Hudson, 1998.

Roberts, David. *In Search of the Old Ones: Exploring the Anasazi World of the Southwest.* New York: Simon & Schuster, 1997.

Sipapu: The Anasazi Emergence into the Cyber World. This is an interactive site that explains concepts like the symbolism of kivas. http://sipapu.gsu.edu/ (accessed September 1, 2007).

Warren, Scott. *Cities in the Sand.* San Francisco: Chronicle Books, 1992.

5

The Far West: Great Basin and California

GREAT BASIN AND PLATEAU AREA

One of the most desolate landscapes in North America is in the intermontane West. It is generally referred to as the Great Basin and Plateau region. The word basin roughly reflects its topography. The area lies between two important mountain ranges. Along the eastern border run the Rocky Mountains and to the west the mighty Sierras. The presence of these high peaks gives the region its characteristic dryness. Moisture-laden winds from the Pacific do not cross the Sierras, and the Rockies form a similar barrier to precipitation from the east. The region generally runs south to the Mojave Desert and north to the Snake River watershed.

The basin itself covers 200,000 square miles. Within that vast territory there is a great deal of topography. Ancient, eroded mountain ridges run north and south, so there are a series of high ridges often dropping a mile down to the valleys. This elevation change affects climate and moisture and thus plant, animal, and human life. There are variations within the area. There are some flat valleys, and some high peaks in addition to lava plains in the northeast, along with streams and grassy meadows, sagebrush deserts, and pine-covered hillsides; however, it does not look particularly attractive for human life.

When early indigenous peoples first encountered this region, it looked quite different. In 8000 B.C., everything was much wetter. The

melting glaciers created two great lakes, Lahontan and Bonneville. Numerous streams, lakes, and marshes collected the glacial runoff. The additional moisture meant that different plants and animals inhabited the region. Conifers grew rather than sagebrush. Perennial streams provided water and shade in what is now a dry basin range. It is not that hard to imagine humans thriving there. Men hunted big and medium game species rather than megafauna as in other parts of the country. They also exploited fish and waterfowl to add protein to their diets. They gathered vegetable materials and nuts. This was a hunting and gathering lifestyle, which meant the people traveled between the valleys seeking food supplies. We find evidence that they camped in the valley meadows and used rock shelters where they found them. This would have been a fairly stable, if not particularly prosperous, lifestyle.

At Danger Cave, Utah, evidence exists of human habitation stretching back for 11,000 years. The archaeologist Jesse Jennings summarized the harshness of the life at Danger Cave. He said life in this primitive culture was "directly and continuously focused on sheer survival. In such situations, there is little leisure, and almost no certainty about the morrow. No long-term building projects, no complicated rituals, no extensive amassing of personal property, nor any long-range plans can be undertaken in such circumstances."

This site yielded more than 2,500 stone tools, 1,000 grinding stones, and 65 types of plants. Even more remarkable is the preservation of wooden artifacts like arrow shafts, traps, animal stick figures, as well as basketry and hide moccasins. All these objects reveal something of the lifestyles of the nomadic peoples using this cave over the millennia. The location was used for so long that we can see the introduction of bow and arrow into the toolkit of the local hunters. Over the life of the cave, however, humans would have seen a profound change in the climate. Around 4000 B.C., a drying and warming trend affected the area. Plants, animals, and humans all had to adapt. Drier and warmer was not necessarily better, and many species struggled to survive. As lakes disappeared and streams dried up because of greater evaporation, less rainfall, and loss of snowmelt, the resources humans relied on vanished. The two enormous glacial period lakes shrank and exist only in reduced form today: Lahontan as Pyramid Lake, Nevada, and Bonneville as Great Salt Lake, Utah. Fish, waterfowl, and larger mammals could not survive in the newly arid climate. Thus the people who used those species could not continue in the same patterns. We find that people left the lower elevations in the east,

perhaps moving to the uplands where they could more easily find prey such as mountain sheep.

ARCHAIC INDIANS

Human habitation in the Great Basin and Plateau settled into an Archaic lifestyle that continued until the mid-nineteenth century. There are many similarities in culture throughout the region seen in basketry, building technology, puberty rites, and other character-istics. Some experts point to this as evidence of shared, common, ancient traditions; others argue that these commonalities could reflect recent adaptations to stimuli such as European contact. In the Archaic period, the region's climate offered few choices for human survival. In difficult dry years, they were really more foragers and gatherers than hunters and farmers. In lean times they relied more on small animals and wild seeds, which required a great deal of effort to obtain enough food for life. Such a lifestyle required almost constant movement to exploit limited resources. These nomadic people left almost no record of their lives, and so anthropologists know frustratingly little about them. Theirs is mostly a story of sur-vival with little cultural development. Basin inhabitants have long been regarded as poor and primitive, barely surviving in a harsh landscape. They have never attracted the attention or admiration of non-Indians. Without a legacy of highly developed art, complex religion, or complex political system, these desert dwellers have been disregarded.

The northern portion of this region is referred to as the Plateau, and it shared many similarities with Great Basin culture. People hunted deer, antelope, rabbit, and beaver and collected and ground wild seeds. The major difference is that the Plateau had two major rivers, the Columbia and the Fraser. These great river systems pro-vided seasonal salmon runs that proved critical to the subsistence patterns. Early Indians caught salmon with hooks, dip nets, weirs, gill nets, seines, harpoons, snares, traps, and poison. Although they fished only seasonally, the salmon was dried and stored and may have provided half of the annual diet. Excellent fishing spots along the rivers were highly valued, and such areas as the Dalles in Oregon remained important resource and intercultural meeting areas for centuries.

As archaeological sites come to light, we begin to learn more and more about the peoples who called this unique landscape home. In Utah and some adjacent areas of Colorado, Idaho, and Nevada,

archaeologists have found evidence of a highly flexible culture. Because many of the first sites were found along the Fremont River and its valley, that is the working name for this culture. Once considered to be a poor branch of the famous Anasazi, the Fremont are now recognized as a unique prehistoric culture. They may have traded and even intermarried with the Anasazi at their southern extent, but they are a distinct group. As the Anasazi flourished in the desert Southwest, the hunter-gatherers of the Great Basin coalesced into a widely varying culture defined by several distinct characteristics.

Fremont

Despite ongoing research, experts can agree on only the bare outlines of the Fremont story. The beginning dates vary widely but generally hover around A.D. 700. The Fremont began as scattered groups of hunters and farmers who used diverse survival strategies depending on their immediate environment. The difficulties of the region forced people to be flexible. A group might shift between complete nomadism and settled farming, even switching seasonally or over a lifetime. Hunting required frequent movement. There were no large herds of bison or other major game animals to exploit. Bighorn sheep were never particularly abundant, nor were deer nearly as prevalent as they were in the eastern woodlands. Fremont hunters often relied more on small mammals such as rabbits and rodents. They used atlatl and bow and arrows for larger animals and snares and nets for smaller ones. They fished with spears, nets, and hooks, and shot and netted birds as well. As gatherers, these people collected pinion nuts, rice grass, berries, nuts, bolts, and tubers. Locally they might be able to find wild onion, cherries, sego lily bulbs, rosehips, prickly pear cactus pads, and seeds of sunflower, goosefoot, and sedge.

Around A.D. 400, corn arrived in trade with the Mogollon to the South. The species that had originated in Mesoamerica is resistant to drought and environmental extremes and has a short growing season. Now called Fremont Dent, it was particularly well suited for the Plateau region. The groups of Fremont who embraced agriculture often used flood irrigation to improve their chances for a successful crop. They used river bottom soil and dug ditches still visible in places today. The corn grew alongside beans and squash, which added to their diet of gathered native plants. Much of this vegetable material would be ground between two stones

and stored in pottery jars or baskets inside small masonry structures called granaries.

Unlike many farmers in America, the Fremont did not come to rely more heavily on agriculture or increase their population extensively. They continued to collect wild seeds even as they grew more maize. Only about 10,000 Indians populated this region, which has an annual rainfall of just five to seven inches. Their exploitation strategy, still based heavily on hunting-gathering, required frequent movement. They maintained a fairly simple organization of small bands of a few families. Their housing style varied from natural rock shelters, to temporary wickiups (simple brush covered pole structures) to slightly more permanent pit houses. Most excavated sites reveal only up to a dozen pit houses, which were not all occupied at the same time. The Fremont, however, have more exceptions than rules, so there are villages of more permanent settlement some of which housed up to 60 people at a time.

The Fremont have several unique characteristics that set them apart from other Western cultures. We find evidence of a singular style of basketry, called one-rod-and-bundle, which used willow, yucca, milkweed, and other native fibers. They also made a distinct style of pottery. It was a gray pottery with either a smooth, polished surface or corrugated designs pinched into the clay. Another indication that they were distinct from the Anasazi who wove yucca fiber sandals are the Fremont's hide sandals. They made moccasins from large mammal skins, such as a deer leg, with the dew claw intact to provide traction or a bighorn sheep leg. They also left somewhat mysterious clay figurines. The figures generally look like people and include intricate details. They often depict the torso of women wearing bead necklaces and short fiber skirts. Although we do not know their intended use, it is likely ritual or religious. The figures might also offer us a reflection of the Fremont people.

The Fremont are best known for their unique contributions to American art. They lived in one of the most visually stunning areas of the country. Their homeland now includes five national parks created to protect the spectacular beauty of the canyon country (Zion, Capitol Reef, Canyonlands, Bryce, and Arches). These parks and others also preserved examples of Fremont rock art. Rock art included pictographs, which are painted onto rocks, and petroglyphs, which are carved or pecked into the surface. Many areas of Fremont habitation contain amazing examples of rock art. Often they depict human-like figures with trapezoidal-shaped bodies with

arms, legs, and fingers. The portrayals are elaborately decorated with headdresses, earrings, necklaces, clothing, and facial expressions. The human-like figures often appear with animal-like depictions of bighorn sheep, deer, dogs, birds, snakes, and lizards. In addition to the recognizable figures, there are geometric designs and handprints. Entire panels of rock along a protected face might be decorated. This obviously was not idle doodling, although we do not know its exact significance. The pictures appear to be a record of something, perhaps of migrations, of hunting trips, of major events. They might be reminders of travel routes, resource locations, or other critical knowledge that could be left for others to use. Of course, they might be religious depictions meant to influence the spirits in some ways.

The remarkable rock art of the Fremont culture is almost all that is left of their way of life. By A.D. 1300, the Fremont had abandoned their villages. This was around the same time that the Anasazi farther to the south experienced dislocation. One probable explanation is changing weather patterns that plunged the Southwest into drought conditions. The Fremont would have been unable to maintain their tenuous agriculture and would have returned to nomadism, which, perhaps combined with disease, wiped them

Petroglyphs are often all that remains to reveal a people's culture. BigStockPhoto.com

out. The weakened Fremont may have been easily displaced by or absorbed into the arriving Numic-speaking peoples.

The speakers of a language we classify as *Numic* include the Mono, Northern Pauite, Shoshoni, Ute, Chemehuevi, and Kawaiisu people. These groups probably originated in southeast California and southern Nevada. Around A.D. 1000, they seem to have expanded to the north and east, bringing them into the Great Basin and Plateau area. They did not find the arid climate and rugged landscape any easier to deal with than the people who came before them. The Great Basin and Plateau region was still a difficult place to make a living and still demanded a flexible, mobile lifestyle.

GREAT BASIN CULTURE

We can get some idea of the pattern of life by examining adaptations of the Paiute people. The Paiutes lived in small kinship groups or bands. This was still the only viable group size that could be supported in such a precarious area. Because their food supply was very seasonal, they moved nearly constantly. They could always get food to sustain life, but it was never guaranteed and rarely easy. Much of the culture reflected this precarious, nomadic existence. For example, the housing of the Paiutes was somewhat disposable. When at a camp area they built a quick, useful shelter. They simply took willow shoots and pressed them into the ground to make a frame in a cone shape. Tule reed bundles were stood on end, leaned against the frame, and bound to it. This quickly formed a conical shape with an open top. It was fairly crude looking and reflected the minor effort that would be expected of a short stay. When the people moved on, the shelter was left for others to use as long as it lasted. The Paiutes built these disposable dwellings, not because they lacked the skills to do better; in fact, they wove beautiful baskets. Rather, it reflects the practical decisions that nomads made; it was not wise to waste energy or resources on a temporary object.

Human life followed a seasonal trend following the cycle of plants and animals. Winter was a difficult time. It was hard to find game, as all the burrowing animals were hibernating. Men might hunt a long time for a mere bird or rabbit. In this season the people relied on dried food gathered in previous seasons, which could be as meager as fish heads stewed with seeds and nuts. People might try to camp near a marsh so they would find a few plants surviving a harsh season. It could be a cold, long winter for everyone. On the

A tule reed house. Library of Congress.

positive side, the long winter nights could be spent companionably telling stories, weaving baskets, and sewing clothing.

As spring arrived, the prospects for hunting and gathering improved. Ground squirrels emerged from hibernation and provided sorely needed fresh meat. As waterfowl began migrating, men might bring home geese, mallards, and pin tails. They hunted these ducks with cleverly made decoys of feathers over tule reed bodies, which floated. When the hunters startled the birds off the water, they flew into nets where they could be retrieved. Reed rafts floated well enough to allow people to paddle along a marsh collecting eggs from nests. In early spring women collected tender cattail shoots for immediate consumption. Later in the year the thick mature reeds became construction materials. Spawning fish provided an important protein resource. As trout, suckers, and shiners moved up the local streams, the men speared, hooked, and netted them. On the shore women quickly gutted, split, and smoked or dried the fish. As spring moved up in elevation, so too did the people. A ridge could be a mile higher than the valley

floor, so things ripened successively, allowing people to continue the harvest.

As summer turned dry and hot, the food resources changed again. The hosts of insects that may have plagued future generations became a food resource for early Indians. They ate raw and roasted grasshoppers, locusts, and crickets. Roasted ants could be ground with seeds into a flour. And if a plague of grasshoppers came, the people drove them into the fire pits where they were roasted and then ground into flour. Nothing was wasted. As rice grass and cattail grew larger, they too were used. Women gathered the seeds and pollen and threshed them in a winnowing basket before grinding them between stones. Women also dug roots and bulbs, especially camas, sago lily, bitterroot, and yampas and then dried and stored them for winter use. They picked elder berries, choke berries, buffalo berries, and currants. The more food they could put up for the future, the less precarious life would be. Men shot or trapped rabbits, robins, and flickers. Magpies were collected, but only for their iridescent feathers. In a rare year (about one in eight) there would be enough antelope to warrant a drive hunt. The time for this communal hunt was set by the antelope shaman, a man thought to have a special relationship with the animals. This is a fast species and thus difficult to hunt on foot, but they are also curious and could be lured to stop and look at something.

An antelope drive required cooperative action. So too did a massive drive of rabbits. Bands of families would come together to exploit the abundance of a resource like rabbits. This might require some organization and thus temporary, specific leadership roles. The rest of the year there was no hierarchy or rank in Basin society. A rabbit boss, a man with experience, would assign people tasks for the drive to ensure a successful hunt that would benefit everyone. Beaters droved the animals toward nets where clubbers stood ready. The rabbit nets were woven of dogbane into a loose mesh that could be several feet long. Creating a net was a great investment of time and nets were carefully tended and passed down through generations. Rabbits were an important resource. They immediately provided fresh meat, but the dried meat would be cached in grass-lined pits against the shortcoming of later months. The stripped bones were pulverized for soup.

Rabbit skin was the only abundant hide/fur these people had. The rabbits were skinned in a spiral, then the pelts were sewn into lightweight robes. It took more than 100 pelts for a man's cloak and 40 for a child's. Although better than nothing, rabbit fur was not

that warm during a bitter winter wind. To make a cloak more insulating, the women sometimes wrapped the skin around a fiber core of yucca, cedar, or nettles. Because they had no other hide, nothing very tough, the people usually went without shoes. They occasionally wove tree bark into a type of shoe. Other fibers, like sagebrush and cedar bark, were pounded into shreds then woven into men's sleeveless pullovers and pants or women's blouses and skirts. Infants rode on cradleboards of chokeberry wood wrapped in rare antelope skin that was passed down through the generations.

New babies might be introduced to the larger family at the one time a year when everyone came together: the pinyon harvest. In the fall the pines were loaded with cones. The abundance of the year's seeds cycled so everyone hoped for a bountiful year. Scouts found the best trees and sent word to the family groups who traveled to the area and set up camps. The first night of the harvest was dedicated to thanksgiving. Basin dwellers saw themselves as sharing the land, water, and sky with the spirits so they offered back for everything they took. They prayed to the spirits of the trees asking them to share the nuts. The first day's harvest went to the evening's ritual dance. Nuts were scattered on the ground as a tribute and the people danced and sang. This was an important time both for food collection and socialization. This was an annual opportunity to mingle with other people from the larger group. It provided a time to renew relationships that held the group together, however loosely. For young men and women it was a critical time to court and marry those from outside their family. Generally, the desert people practiced monogamous marriages, but as women were both scarce and integral to economic survival; some men shared a wife rather than be alone.

In the midst of the reacquaintance of friends and the forging of new relationships, serious economic production went on. The second day, after the thanksgiving ritual was over, the people settled into serious pinyon gathering. Men lashed several lengths of willow together to create a 15-foot pole with a side bar to slap the high branches and shake the cones loose. Young boys contributed by shimmying up the trunks and knocking down cones on lower branches. The younger women gathered the cones, separated them from the twigs, and carried them in baskets called *kawans* to camp. There the older women got the nuts out of the cones and roasted them. Hot coals were placed on a flat winnowing tray with the nuts, which had to be tossed and shaken and roasted twice. This took considerable skill and attention so the wooden tray did not burn.

The roasted pinyon nuts were ground into paste and boiled for soup. The harvest went on for months as families worked to secure a food supply for the coming winter. At the first snow the groups left the slopes and headed down to the desert floor. They might get in another rabbit hunt before winter. As winter set in, the family groups split up again to hunt and gather on their own until they came together to communally exploit a resource the next year.

The environment in the Great Basin and Plateau region dictated human lifestyle. The climate was demanding and harsh and remains so to this day. People could survive, but perhaps not thrive. They achieved success through careful regional adaptations, seasonal migration patterns, and low population density. Although people in this region shared similar subsistence strategies, they never coalesced into any overarching political unity. Their cultural adaptation could be found anywhere with a similar climate, including into the western regions we identify as California.

CALIFORNIA

The culture area of California essentially mirrors the political region of the modern state. The northern section, which is about three-quarters of the area, is a long narrow valley with mountains on three sides. The Cascade and Sierra ranges form a distinct eastern border; the Coastal Range in the west and the Klamath in the northwest separate much of the interior from the sea. At the far south of the main valley, the Mojave Desert forms an important border for the region. The entire area encompasses extremes of elevation and precipitation. For example, in the Mojave annual rainfall is only 15 inches, but 40 inches of precipitation might fall in the north and an amazing 70 inches in extreme northwestern elevations. It is an environmentally diverse region that supported a wide variety of human cultures. It was a biologically rich and densely populated region in both ancient and modern times. By the time of European contact, the more than 300,000 natives spoke nearly 100 languages drawn from seven language stocks and divided into hundreds of dialects.

The diversity of language tells anthropologists that the region was settled in waves. The earliest language group seems to be the Hokan speakers who settled in the far south of California. Around the same time, Yukian speakers made their homes in northern redwood forests. The Penutian language appeared later and dominated the central valley. Language families seen elsewhere also arrived in

California such as Algonquian, which was in the north, and Uto-Aztexcan in the south. The last migrants to bring California another language group were the Athabaskans who migrated into the northwest region. The various regions of this large culture area also had links to neighboring regions. Northwestern California shared climate and cultural traits with the Northwest Coast groups, and southern Californian's pottery and sand painting traditions linked them to the Pueblos of the Southwest.

California encompassed a variety of environments. The diversity varied widely depending on latitude and elevation. The Desert Shrub consisted primarily of sagebrush and creosote bushes with additional local grasses growing after a rain. This environment was a carryover from the Great Basin area, and the human culture dependent on it would be similar to that in the Basin region. Much of California is the central valley, which was a large grassland. The abundance of bunch grasses provided forage for both humans and pronghorn antelope. Bordering the grasslands in most areas were oak woodlands. Oak were the dominant trees here, although the species of oak varied depending on the climate. People and animals such as deer depended heavily on the bounty of the oaks. Gatherers might travel considerable distances to obtain nuts from a preferred species while bypassing an abundant but less desirable group of trees. The top five oak species choices for early residents' use were tan, black, blue, valley, and coast live oaks. The dominant oak woodland gave way to pine-fir forests at higher elevations. Again, the prevailing species of pine depended on local environment. One of the unique features of the California culture region is the juxtaposition of coastal environments alongside oaks and grasslands. The western portions of the region bordered an extensive coastline that played an important role in human habitation.

Each of these subregions provided a microenvironment that created small territories for people and animals. Humans used all of these environments. Some were clearly richer than others and people adapted accordingly. Along the coasts early Indians learned to exploit marine resources. They fished the anadromous species of salmon—king, coho, and steelhead trout—in addition to pelagic fish. Mollusks such as clams, oysters, and abalone were harvested off shore. The three most commonly hunted sea mammals were sea lion, sea otter, and harbor seals, all of which provided valuable fur and skin in addition to meat. Land mammals could be important game species depending on the region. Deer were hunted nearly everywhere, Roosevelt elk in the coast range, Tule elk in the

marshes, and antelope on the grasslands. Gathering rounded out the human diet, with sage seed and yampas root preferred, while buckeye served as an emergency provision.

There is so little archaeological evidence available for ancient California that much of our knowledge is well-informed deduction. Theories might change if new materials come to light. So far, the earliest finds in the region have been proved to be unreliable. The resulting lack of information, combined with the diversity of California natives in terms of habitats and languages, has resulted in a lot of confusion. In attempting to write about early California, one author described the archaeological record as "often obscure, frequently virtually unintelligible and always incomplete." What follows is a discussion of the general outline of early habitation in the region.

PALEO-INDIANS

It appears that paleo-Indians had migrated to California from the north or east by about 12000–11000 B.C. They would have found a climate wetter and colder than the one modern people know. The summers were short and dry, creating food shortages for most animals. Vast sections of the interior burned after lightning strikes ignited the parched vegetation. Cool, long winters could be harsh in the interior and milder on the coast except when fierce storms bore down from the north. The great central valley froze under a blanket of snow each winter. The snow levels in the Sierras dropped to lower elevations, thick pine forests grew up to the coast, and shallow lakes lay across much of the interior.

The coast looked quite different as well. With sea levels up to 300 feet lower, much more of the coast and the western continental shelves were exposed. The rivers ran into the sea through narrow valleys where San Diego and San Francisco Bays are today. This changed the way people could access and use the land. For example, the four northern Channel Islands were one island that lay only six miles from the mainland. It also means that many resource extraction and perhaps settlement sites along the coast are now underwater and thus lost to modern researchers. If early humans made it to California by 12000 B.C., they would have shared the land with Ice Age animals such as wild horses and camelids before the animals went extinct about 11000 B.C.

As did paleo-Indians across the continent, early Californians hunted for a living. In the interior they left behind fluted or Clovis-

style projectile points, associated with a big game hunting subsistence strategy. Sites also contain characteristic stone crescent knives, scrapers, and other stone tools. It is likely, however, that these early hunters supplemented big game with smaller animals and extensive plant food gathering. They located their camps at permanent water sources such as estuaries, streams, and lakes, which were more prevalent in this early period. Such areas had more high yield food sources to support a group of people. Some groups might even have been nearly sedentary if they found all they needed at one location.

Tulare Lake in central California was quite large in 11000 B.C., and here people left points, scrapers, and other tools. There are bison, horse, and ground sloth bones here as well, but they cannot be conclusively tied to the human artifacts. People occupied the Mostin site along Clear Lake in northern California for 3,000 years beginning in 9250 B.C. Over time they exploited fresh water mollusks, waterfowl, and a wide variety of plant foods. These early hunter-gatherers built the earliest cemetery found in California. They apparently traveled nine miles east from this area to Borax Lake specifically to collect obsidian.

The Clovis hunters succeeded in California and slowly increased their population. In fact, the indigenous population of California continued to increase until the arrival of Europeans after which it took a precipitous and irrevocable fall. The climate, however, was changing around the later generations of Clovis hunters and they would have to adapt. The characteristic fluted points disappear around 10900 B.C. and do not reappear. The megafauna and other Ice Age remnants died out by 10000 B.C., but the humans who had preyed on them had diversified their subsistence enough that the loss of one group of game animals did not threaten their existence.

The climate of the region changed soon after humans arrived. Temperatures warmed up and rainfall decreased. People had to be much more conscious of available water supplies as the shallow lakes of the interior shrank or dried up completely. Always mobile in order to exploit a variety of resources, early Californians had to be anchored to reliable water supplies. The coast saw some of the greatest change. After 13000 B.C., the sea level continued rising as 95 percent of the glacier water melted into the oceans. Sea level continued to rise until 5000 B.C. when it slowed while still about 50 feet lower than today. The dramatic influx of water quickly flooded shallow coastal shelves and estuaries. In northern California where deeper water extends up to the coast, the shoreline merely moved

inland without seriously affecting food resources. In southern California, however, where shallow shelves lay just offshore, the rising sea covered a great deal of land. At San Francisco Bay, the coastline moved from 12 to 16 miles eastward. Along the southern coast, the Pacific Ocean flowed into river valleys and created productive estuaries. This rapid a change in the environment had to be noticed by the people of the area. The disappearance of coastline was so extreme that it would change a great deal in one generation. People could lose a vital food resource area in their lifetimes.

ARCHAIC INDIANS

As the coastline evolved, early Californians learned to exploit its resources. In the earliest period they did not live on the water, but rather traveled to the shoreline from more stable interior camps anchored to water sources. At the ocean they hunted sea mammals, which were in rookeries or hauled out of the water on sunning rocks. Numerous mollusks could be easily gathered from tide pools and rocky shores. Any resource site drew people to it. Fairly early in this period people crossed the short stretch of water from the mainland to the large island called Santarosae (now the northern Channel Islands). Here they harvested mollusks on the shore but camped in the deep canyons of the interior near water supplies. The evidence points to seasonal camps, suggesting that people continued to live on the mainland and travel to the coast and islands to gather food. Of course, any coastal sites would be underwater now. Not until after sea levels stabilized did people begin settling along the southern coasts.

On the mainland, indigenous Californians had to adjust to the changing climate. At the most basic level their adaptations remained the same. People survived by being conservative, flexible, mobile, opportunistic, and willing to adjust quickly to new conditions. The region may have offered considerable bounty, but it also had a number of perils such as drought, fire, heavy rains, and earthquakes. Life was unpredictable for hunter-gatherers living close to the land. At the end of the Ice Age, California Indians lived mainly by hunting. Then gradually over the course of time they changed their subsistence patterns. This change took place from 9000 B.C. until 2000 B.C. when distinct culture areas are identified. As the earth warmed, the land supported a richer assortment of plants despite the increased aridity. California Indians now had a wide choice of food items to add to their diet. Slowly, seed

collecting replaced hunting, which then developed into specialized exploitation of local resources.

We know little of the several thousand years of native life during the warming trend. The lack of physical evidence suggests that people moved frequently and stayed in temporary shelters. The existence of many more seed-grinding tools shows the new importance of vegetative material. Milling stones are flat rocks that have been worn smooth by countless hours of nut and seed cracking and pulverizing. More stable settlements and bigger refuse piles indicate a permanence of territory. Sites reveal burials that range from flexed position to extended position interments, as well as bone reburials. Few grave goods accompanied the deceased, but the presence of milling stones with some bodies reinforces the importance of seed preparation. One site, Skyrocket, in northern California has yielded a record of continuous settlement from 7200 B.C. to mid-A.D. 1800s. The presence of springs explains why generation after generation remained at Skyrocket. The inhabitants relied heavily on plant foods for subsistence, which is evident from the number of milling stones they left behind.

Stones show wear from years of repetitive grinding. BigStockPhoto.com

During this period, some regional adaptations developed. In the south of California around 5500 B.C., the Encinitas tradition arose. They left behind evidence of their subsistence patterns in the form of grinding stones and shellfish remains. Like many other regional groups, they harvested and used native grasses. They also went to the shoreline where they collected locally available shellfish. This must have been a stable way of life, as it lasted until A.D. 1000 in the San Diego area. Around Santa Barbara, however, this lifestyle ended by 3000 B.C., when it was replaced by the Campbell culture. This group used tools such as points, knives, and scrapers, indicating a hunting economy. They hunted deer, rabbits, bear, seals, and fish. This successful exploitation strategy evolved into the Chumash culture, which lasted until the contact period.

The Northeast was home to indigenous people dating to 6000–4000 B.C. These mostly sedentary Indians lived in semi-subterranean pit houses. They ground acorns with mortars and pestles and made bone and antler tools. The central region in 3000 B.C. was home to a people who resided in waterside villages. They may have summered along the region's rivers and wintered in the foothills. Their artifacts include a wide range of sea and land resources including coyote teeth, bear claws, and abalone beads. Some of these objects were buried with the dead in large cemeteries. None of these early cultures had much pottery, but they relied heavily on baskets for containers. Woven materials also made up some of the scant clothing they wore. Women usually just wore aprons; men had a thong at the waist to carry their tools. Cooler weather brought out shirts for both sexes.

By 3000 B.C., broad changes are evident in Indian lifestyles. This marks the beginning of people's adjustment to specific regions. They began relying on a wider exploitation of available food resources. From 2000 to 1000 B.C., residents of the coastal areas began using marine resources, which materially altered their culture. The bow and arrow entered California in the first few centuries A.D. and offered another hunting method to exploit locally available animals. Acorns, sea mammals, and fish each became critical subsistence sources for different groups. This specialization is part of the general trend of the late Archaic in America. By A.D. 500, the movement toward specialization was reflected by 500 different tribes in California, which varied widely in speech, subsistence, technology, religion, and social organization. Because the area defined as California covers a wide variety of natural settings,

it supported a wide variety of human cultural adaptations. People lived as they could, surviving by exploiting local resources. Culture became more a product of subsistence adaptation than shared heritage or language. Indeed, a group had more in common with those in their region who may have spoken a different language than with fellow language speakers dwelling in another resource zone. For example, the Pomo, who spoke a Hokan language, were spread from the Pacific across the mountains to the central valley. They harvested and prepared distinct foods and each of the 34 bands spoke a mutually unintelligible dialect. Even their names for themselves would have been distinct, and they are referred to as tribal groups only as a result of historians' sense of organization.

LOCALIZED CULTURES

After the subsistence changes of the late Archaic in California, the culture can be characterized as very localized. This applied to the economy, political system, and social structure. Some experts refer to this period as a sort of flowering like that in the east during the Woodland tradition. Each area focused on a few local foods. In the desert it was mesquite and screw beans; in the central valley acorns, deer, and seeds; on the coast sea mammals, fish, shellfish, seeds and acorns; and in the mountains deer and pine nuts. Some groups may have even cultivated plants such as acorn oaks or prickly pear cactus. In most places the economic adoption was successful. It often led to larger communities that could be supported by the bounty. At times this expertise resulted in surplus production, which then led to redistribution. Food stuffs intended for redistribution had to be transported by foot or by canoe, the only available methods. The environmental diversity of California allowed for this type of local surplus and then distribution. Often in cultures that develop redistribution networks, a form of political control emerges concurrently. This did not occur in California, perhaps because there was no horticulture with corresponding ownership of fields and probable water control.

California indigenous people had numerous levels of political and social organization. They ranged from a tiny collection of a few families existing in one spot to a permanent settlement in which strict social ranking was based on kinship ties. In ancient California, small nomadic bands coexisted with elaborate village societies. The situation was so unusual that anthropologists feel that the term *tribe* could not even be applied, as it was in the rest of America.

The 500 to 1,000 estimated small living groups have been referred to as *tribelets* in an effort to convey their distinct size. In a favorable resource area a tribelet might support many people in a fairly small area, and more impoverished regions like the desert would require thousands of acres for just a small group. Each tribelet had a central base or camp that served as the focus of any resource distribution and storage.

Much like their neighbors in the Great Basin, California Indians lived in small family groups. A few adult couples along with their children and elderly relatives made up a band. Band members were often related by blood and marriage because two sisters might marry one man. Families might contain two women so that one women could weave, process food, and watch the children while the other worked at collecting. Women dug roots, picked berries, and cut grasses. They used the resources seasonally, digging camas bulbs in late spring for example. Women prepared and stored these foodstuffs, often in their own baskets. The men of the family fished with spears or nets, hunted mammals and waterfowl, and helped with major gathering events such as acorn harvests. Daily life operated on a mostly egalitarian basis. They maintained ties both within the group and with neighbors through shared trade, ceremony, and ritual.

There is always an exception, and in California it occurred in the north. Here groups along the Klamath River followed patterns more typical of residents of the Pacific Northwest. Individualism reigned supreme, as the focus on status, prestige, and wealth led to competition for resources. Other groups like the Chumash and the Yokut also varied from the basic egalitarian band structure because they lived under the leadership of wealthy, hereditary chiefs. Here, however, inheritance was not the only measure of a leader and personal qualities did matter. A local Big Man would have relied on his personality to rise to power. If he were wealthy, he could have built loyalty through his own redistribution system in the form of bribes, feasts, and charity. He might exert a measure of power by conducting the trade in the area. A Big Man's power, however, did not extend beyond his local area. The groups in California were either organized in an egalitarian system where only a local headman stood out from the community or in a ranked society, which recognized a chief, his privileged family, and various elites, all of whom held a position above the commoners. To make matters more confusing, most of California society was in a constant state of flux with changing allegiances, rituals, and economic networks.

One way that indigenous Californians stayed in contact with disparate groups was through trade. Obsidian was a major trade resource found in the mountainous regions. It is not a particularly common mineral, and some of the finest deposits occur in California and the western Great Basin. In northeastern California, people exploited the obsidian deposits for 11,000 years. Obsidian is a black volcanic glass. It is both striking to look at and very useful. This substance can be chipped into an incredibly sharp cutting surface; thus it was highly valued by nonmetal working cultures. In earliest times hunters preferred to travel to the rock outcroppings to obtain their own supplies of raw material. But as California filled up with people, it became more difficult to maintain access to deposits and trade became the more common means to get obsidian. The desirability of obsidian spawned a system of trade and interconnectedness that linked disparate people from distant areas.

In addition to obsidian, the peoples of California traded all manner of other objects, a brief list of which would include food, bow wood, basketry, canoes, pestles and mortars, ceremonial regalia, and stone and shell beads. Although all these items were traded across the length and breadth of California, as well as into neighboring regions, people did not travel far from their home territories. Rather, the items passed through many hands as they wound their way over hundreds of miles of interconnected trade routes. The continuing relationship forged between distant peoples helped to create aspects of common culture. For example, shell beads of standardized size were traded in measured strands, thus becoming a widely recognized validation of social status. As California became a more densely populated region of interconnected groups, other social aspects also became more complex.

Ritual and spiritual beliefs were a facet of indigenous life that most groups shared. Like oral, subsistence cultures across the continent, early Californians had an intimate relationship with their environment that was passed between generations. They felt closely connected to the world around them and their beliefs reflected that understanding. The Modoc Indians explained the natural phenomena they saw in their creation story.

Before there were people on the earth the Chief of the Sky Spirits became tired of his home in the Above World. It was always sharply cold up there. So he carved a hole in the sky with a stone and pushed all the snow and ice down below. It piled up until it made a mound that reached from the earth almost to the sky, we call it Mount Shasta. The Chief stepped from the clouds onto Mount Shasta's peak and walked down the slope. Half-way

Beautiful and practical, high-quality baskets
might be traded over long distances. Library
of Congress.

down he put his finger in the snow here and there. Wherever his finger
touched the snow a tree grew. The snow melted in the Chief's footsteps
and the water ran down the rivers.[1]

Thus the mountains, forests, and rivers that the Modoc relied on
were gifts from the creator and not to be disrespected or taken for
granted.

Most groups had similar understandings of the earth that usually placed the highest peak at the center of the creation of the current world. Gods or supernatural beings created animals, rocks,
trees, and other physical items as well as humans. All the known
objects around an indigenous Californian had value. The Nomlaki
people said that everything in the world talked—trees, rocks,
everything—but humans could not understand them. With so
many spirits inhabiting one space, it is not surprising that people
invested a great deal of time in ritual intended to ensure harmony
and stability.

Ceremonialism served many purposes. Besides placating powerful forces, it reinforced group relationships, stimulated production and exchange, and bolstered political authority. As in many indigenous groups, shamans who understood and interacted with the supernatural served as Californians' conduit to the spirit world. Most shamans used their special powers to heal, although some would intentionally inflict disease and had to be guarded against. Shamans contacted the spirit world by entering a trance sometimes aided by hallucinogens like jimsonweed or tobacco. They usually received the aid of an animal as a spirit helper. Fasting produced visions or dreams in which the shaman interacted with spiritual forces. He then interpreted his experiences to explain and manipulate the connection between the physical and supernatural worlds. Specialized regalia often incorporating bird feathers added to the shamans' mystique. Their obvious influence within the community led to shaman's courtship by political leaders who tried to form alliances with these magical men in order to gain standing.

Much of the world of California ritual and ceremony has been lost. One feature that remains is rock art. No explanation of this artwork survived, so anthropologists have to make educated guesses as to its significance. It seems clear that paintings in caves and rock faces were intentionally created. They could have been made for initiation, rainmaking, or other ceremonies; as records of unusual events or astronomical observations; or as celebrations of powerful spirit beings. Much of the rock art in California is found in the arid western region of rock outcrops and shelters. It has been pecked onto the rock in the shape of humans, animals, especially bighorn sheep, and geometric designs. It often depicts humans in ritual regalia and is thought to be mostly the work of shamans while in trances, who often used rock shelters to perform rituals, store paraphernalia, and connect to the spirit world.

REGIONAL ADAPTATIONS

We have seen that indigenous Californians shared similar ritual beliefs and were generally linked to neighbors through trade networks. Adaptations to local variations, however, created some fairly unique regional cultures. The great diversity of California, from desert to coast, bay to mountain, and snow to cactus ensured a wide range of subsistence techniques.

In the far north of California the climate is cool and moist, supporting lush forests, and the topography is shaped by mountains

sending rushing rivers to the coast. Although this setting bears little resemblance to the desert of southern California, it shares much with the Pacific Northwest Coast. The people of northern California developed a culture that paralleled the highly developed Northwest Coast culture in many ways. One of the most notable similarities was the use of forest resources. No where else in California did people have access to giant trees. They used the huge redwoods as the more northern coastal people used giant cedars. Groups such as the Yurok along the Klamath River crafted large dugout canoes for sea travel. Smaller vessels for river use could be made fairly easily, but the large style required considerable effort from a team of builders. They had to fell the tree, use fire and tools to hollow it, and carve the ends and sides. Such an undertaking could be supported only by a wealthy individual.

Wealthy, powerful individuals thrived in northern California. Individual social status and wealth mattered in this culture. This could be displayed by ownership of valuable items such as obsidian blades and dentalium shells both in life and in burials. Wealth was usually a result of control of abundant food resources. Family rights to oak groves, offshore rookeries, and salmon run sites ensured continued success in resource gathering and the concurrent status that they brought. Salmon returning to spawn in freshwater streams in predictable patterns provided much of the stability and success of northern California's economy. The abundant fish were netted, harpooned, and trapped. Weirs trapped so many fish that control of a critical spot on the river could nearly stop the upward movement of salmon. The Indians recognized the incredible bounty of the salmon migration and always performed a First Salmon ritual, which acknowledged the people's reliance on the spirits for the harvest. All this salmon was dried in the reliable California sunshine and eaten throughout the year. Other food sources like sea and land mammals would also be harvested, but the salmon remained the dominant food supply in the north.

Other Californians also lived close to the sea but did not enjoy the bounty of migrating salmon. San Francisco Bay has apparently been a popular place to live for millennia. The people who lived there in ancient times left little record of themselves except for shell mounds. These accumulations of shells dotted the marshy landscape, providing useful high ground in an area of changing water levels. Mounds supported villages strategically located to take advantage of local resources such as oysters, clams, and fish. Lightweight watercraft made of reeds took hunters into the shallows

The easily constructed trap helped to increase fish harvests. Library of Congress.

where waterfowl, fish, and mollusks could be taken. Mounds were used for settlements, burials, and ritual centers. Food was readily available and the population of the mounds in San Francisco Bay swelled until A.D. 700, when they were suddenly abandoned, perhaps as a result of drought or the lure of more stable food supplies to the east.

To the east lay the great Central valley at the foothills of the Sierras. This extensive lowland stretches for hundreds of miles. It is fertile and well watered by the Sacramento and San Joaquin Rivers. The watered areas—streams, lakes, and marshes—attracted the densest human settlement in ancient times. Over the years several different groups of migrants moved into the valley, perhaps fleeing droughts in their homelands. They pursued a varied subsistence strategy that used a wide range of resources. Streams yielded salmon, perch, suckers, minnows, and other freshwater fish. Ducks, geese, and turtles could been found on lakes and ponds. Men hunted Tule elk and Pronghorn Antelope on nearby plains. And the oak trees produced vast aquantities of acorns that became a staple of valley diets. Inhabitants also harvested a wide supply of plant materials.

The rivers and corresponding marshes were the lifeblood of this hunting gathering existence, so groups such as the Yurok based their homelands along the river.

At the southern end of California, the land bears little resemblance to the redwood forests of the north, the foggy coasts, or the well-watered valley. Here is a desert created after the Ice Age gave way to a serious drying and warming trend. The desert is not flat, comprised instead of low mountains and valleys, but it is dry. Water courses run only after heavy runoff from infrequent rains. The area is bitterly cold in winter and scorching hot in summer, and can receive less than three inches of rainfall a year. Despite this seeming desolation, humans lived in the region. They had to know the landscape intimately, for here a miscalculation meant certain death. Water sources were critical to survival. Desert dwellers such as the Mohave and Yuma had to be mobile. There were many types of food, but never much in one place, so gatherers moved constantly from forage site to forage site to catch foods when they ripened. The Cahuilla people harvested six varieties of oak, two types of mesquite, pinyons, edible cacti and fan palm, as well as many other plants.

Desert groups' whole lifestyle was predicated on the availability of food and water. They could gather together only when enough food could be found to support a larger group. When resources became scarce, survival dictated dispersal. Trade in foodstuffs helped create a buffer against extreme want. Along the Colorado River, maize farming, which made up half the diet of the Mojave and Quechan people, could fail, forcing the people into the desert to gather wild plants. Their constant movements, combined with intense trading and warfare, exposed the southern groups to diverse beliefs. They received the bow and arrow from the Great Basin around A.D. 500 and were influenced by Ancestral Puebloans who settled to the east.

It is hard for anthropologists to discuss the region of California and the Great Basin. A wide variety of peoples made their homes in the diverse ecosystems of the desert, basin, mountains, and shorelines of California and the Great Basin. With the exception of the most northern coastal areas, which were blessed by massive salmon runs, the region could be a difficult homeland. Droughts, storms, earthquakes, and intense seasonal variations made subsistence challenging. Most early inhabitants did not have agriculture, living instead on a constantly changing array of seasonal resources. This led to small, impermanent settlements linked by an extensive

trade network. More than any other region of America, California and the Great Basin were characterized by local adaptations to the environment.

NOTE

1. Editors of Time-Life Books, *The Indians of California* (Richmond, VA: Time-Life, 1994), 7.

FURTHER READING

Chartkoff, Joseph, and Kerry Kona Chartkoff. *The Archaeology of California.* Stanford, CA: Stanford University Press, 1984.

Elsasser, Alfred. *The Natural World of the California Indian.* Berkeley: University of California Press, 1980.

Forbes, Jack D. *Native Americans of California and Nevada.* Happy Camp, CA: Naturegraph Publishers, 1982.

Petroglyphs San Rafael Swell. This home page posts numerous pictures of important archaeological sites in the west, including pictographs. http://www.geocities.com/Baja/Dunes/2319/glyphs.html (accessed September 1, 2007).

Powers, Stephen. *Tribes of California.* Berkeley: University of California Press, 1976.

Western Artifacts. This site offers reproduction artifacts for sale and has pictures of numerous ancient-style points from the Great Basin area. http://www.westernartifacts.com/greatbasin.htm (accessed September 1, 2007).

6

The Pacific Northwest Coast

The Pacific Northwest is a unique region in America. It is a place of great abundance in both the environment and indigenous culture. The Northwest Coast defies long-held assumptions about human societies. It was generally felt that only agricultural societies would develop cultural complexity, for example, stratified social groups, complex artwork, and political elites. All of these characteristics, however, were evident on the Pacific Coast and the indigenous peoples there were hunter-gatherers, not farmers. Part of the explanation lies in the incredible richness of the natural world in this region. The sheer abundance of resources that can be obtained by an industrious people allow a great deal of flexibility in their lifestyle, and these early Indians maximized the possibilities. The Northwest Coast developed one of the greatest art styles in the world by supporting a talented group of artists with the surplus production of others. The monumental and intricate carving, ceremonial dances, and stratified society of this culture area rivaled any contemporary European court.

The Northwest Coast culture area can roughly be defined as a region stretching from the mouth of the Columbia River north to the Alaskan panhandle, encompasses 1,500 miles of coastline. It is the most westerly portion of Washington state, British Columbia, and the Alaskan coast up to Juneau. Most topographic features in

this area run from north to south, the rivers run east to west, and the weather moves west to east. This is an area that has experienced major volcanic upheavals that have produced impressive topographic features. Off shore lies the continental shelf, where shallow nutrient-rich waters support fish, sea mammals, and seabirds. Major mountains include the coast ranges that stretch from northern California up to the Olympic Mountains of Washington, across Vancouver Island and the Queen Charlotte Islands, and ending with the St. Elias Range in Alaska. Another set of mountains, including the Cascades and the Coast Range of British Columbia, flank the region on the east. There is a low area between these mountain chains that is underwater north of Seattle, creating the "Inside Passage," but to the south it forms a 500-mile long lowland.

The climate of the region is generally maritime. This means cool summers and wet mild winters that result in long growing seasons. The coast is generally mild year-round and seasons are distinguished only by the amount of rainfall. The coastal mountains catch the moisture-laden winds from the Pacific and cause them to dump their moisture. The heaviest rainfall is on the outer mountain ranges, where the upper slopes can get 120 inches annually and extreme places may get 400 inches. The highest areas of mountains cause rain shadows, so some regions such as the south coast of British Columbia and the San Juan Islands receive relatively little precipitation. The interior mountains perform a similar function, making their western slopes moist and the area to the east dry with a continental climate.

As a result of the abundant moisture, much of the region is covered by temperate zone rain forests of western hemlock, Sitka spruce, Douglas fir and red cedar. These are magnificent forests with giant specimens reaching hundreds of feet into the sky. They are damp, dark wet woods with little underbrush. In contrast to these mighty forests, the coastal lowlands are more open with grasslands and prairies. The Willamette valley of Oregon, for example, is an important oak savanna habitat. Indigenous people kept the small prairies open by deliberate burning. From these areas they collected a wide variety of plant materials, so it was important to keep those renewable resources available. The importance of plant materials declined farther north in the region where plant productivity also declined.

Experts still know little about the earliest people of this region. Archaeological work has not revealed evidence of early human occupation; however, this may reflect a rise in sea level that destroyed

the sites, rather than pointing to nonexistence. We know that people would have chosen coastal locations, and these could easily have been inundated by rising seas. The Washington and Oregon coastlines experienced large sea level changes, as well as tectonic movements over the centuries. Habitation sites also could have been swallowed up by the verdant rainforest of the area. This maritime climate quickly deteriorates most artifacts, especially those of wood, which would have been people's preferred resource for structures and material objects.

By 8000 B.C., people had migrated to the Northwest either by coast or through an interior corridor. They used land and ocean resources to sustain themselves. The Haida Gwaii (Queen Charlotte Islands) in British Columbia experienced less ocean fluctuation than the mainland and so provide a few sites that have been excavated. It is clear that these early inhabitants had to be excellent mariners to survive in the area they chose, which is still noted for rough waters. Ancient hunters used sea mammals, land mammals, and fish while living in small settlements tucked along stark coastlines.

ARCHAIC INDIANS

By 3000 B.C., the sea levels in the Pacific had stabilized. This is an important change that allowed for the nearly constant occupation of the region up to the present day. Although anthropologists still debate the origins of Northwest Coast people, they generally agree that there were no major population influxes for the past several thousand years. By the third millennia B.C., early Indians were building the unique lifestyle referred to as Northwest Coast. Initially, they hunted coastal caribou, which later became extinct. They also maintained contact with the interior where they hunted land mammals and quarried stone that they carried to the coast to make projectile points.

The stabilization of sea levels established the annual spawning runs of anadromous fish species that would become an important part of the Northwest culture. Once the supply of salmon and eulachon fish was proved to be reliable, people began to winter on the coast, staying in sedentary villages and subsisting on dried salmon. By 1500 B.C. in the United States section of the Northwest culture area, people built pit houses like those in the plateau area. Gradually, they began to focus on accumulating wealth, which would be a strong characteristic of the northwestern cultural pattern. Some aspects of earlier adaptations, however, remained in this southern

region of the Northwest. For example, they continued to excavate the floors of their houses even after switching to a plank style structure.

Around 1000 B.C., a truly distinct Northwest Coast pattern began to flower. Villages supported themselves by catching salmon, halibut, eulachon, and herring with nets, lines, traps, and weirs. They hunted sea mammals as well as mountain sheep, mountain goats, and deer and collected shellfish, berries, and roots. Competition must have existed for these resources because there is evidence of wooden slat armor of the Chinese Shang Dynasty style, war clubs, trophy heads, and burials of bodies killed by blows. By A.D. 500, the historic Northwest Coast culture was established and groups generally remained in the same territories practicing the same lifestyle for many centuries.

Asian Influence

The Northwest Coast occupies a position unlike any other on the North American continent. It is closer to another continent with a distinct culture than all the other culture areas in the United States. It lies between two very different worlds—Eurasia and America—and to some extent it is cut off from the interior of America by rugged mountain ranges. Anthropologists used to view the region as an anomaly, a primitive outpost of American society; however, the Northwest Coast should rightfully be viewed as a crossroads between two worlds. Ideas and materials traveled that crossroad. One of the most obvious interchanges was iron. Northwest coast peoples had iron before the arrival of western Europeans, which set them apart from the rest of the pre-Columbian Indians. The source was apparently Japanese fishing boats, which wrecked in the stormy Pacific and occasionally washed ashore in the Northwest. Later European traders were shocked when their offer of iron was rebuffed because a tribe already had enough.

Only some of the contact between the coast and Asia can be documented, but the influences are clear. Trading chains circled the Pacific Rim and allowed for a flow of ideas. The technology and design of Asian fishing villages clearly reached the North American Coast. Some aspects like wooden-slat armor, hat styles, and tattoo styles clearly reflect an Asian influence. Many aspects of Northwest art appear connected to Asian styles. There are also generalized cultural traits of the North Pacific such as feasts of merit where claims to rank and the honoring of the deceased are important, as well

as elaborate masked dance ceremonies that were incorporated into Northwest Coast life.

The region defined as Northwest Coast is fairly small and homogenous. It is long but narrow, stuck between the mountains and the sea. It has none of the vast expanses of land that characterize the Plains or Southwest. Dense forests, rocky divided coasts, and precipitous mountains served to keep the inhabitants fairly isolated. They could therefore develop a unique adaptation and set of cultural traits. Although several groups were divided by language and fiercely independent, they did share a relatively similar lifestyle. There is some evidence that the typical Northwest Coast pattern may have been forged by Wakashan and Salish speakers in the central region who appear to have been in their territory the longest.

NORTHWESTERN TRIBES

Many of the groups in the Northwest retained their lands and tribal identifies from ancient to historical times. Although they were not truly nations in any political sense of the word, we can identify many of them who shared similar cultural adaptations and kinship. Beginning in the northern section of the Northwest Coast culture region, we find the Tlingit culture. They lived in Southeast Alaska along the coast from Juneau south to Ketchikan. Although beautiful, this is not a particularly hospitable place. Winter storms come off the ocean and severely pound the coastline. The steep and rugged mountains to the east kept these people fairly isolated. Obviously, the sea was a major resource for them; however, strong tides and floating ice made sea hunting a distinct challenge. The Tlingit apparently did have some contact with other groups because they were formidable warriors who wore wooden helmets and masks.

To the south of the Tlingit lived the Tsimshian. They controlled both the coast and considerable inland territory using both the Skeena and Nass River systems as waterways to the interior. They traded the bounty of the sea with inland tribes. Across the water from the Tsimshian lived the Haida on the Queen Charlotte Islands. The sea surrounding this island group is particularly treacherous. Because the Haida had to brave rough waters to contact any other group, they developed an independent culture. They were well known as master carvers of argillite stone, canoes, and totem poles. The Kwakiutl (*Kwakwaka'wakw*) lived on northern Vancouver Island and the British Columbian coast. Their position allowed them to dominate the narrow straight between the island and mainland.

The west side of Vancouver Island was home to the Nootka (*Nuucha-nulth*) people. These master canoe builders expertly navigated the rough waters of the Pacific just outside their sheltered harbors. One of their groups, the Makah, lived across the water on the edge of the Olympic Peninsula. They engaged in whale hunting as well as the traditional subsistence patterns of the region.

Below the Kwakiutl on the mainland stretching south to Puget Sound was Coast Salish territory. These were really a series of small tribes linked by language. Actually a distinct tribe inhabited each inlet. The Chinook people lived in the Columbia River valley. They maintained an extensive trade network. They served as middle men for both the shore to interior trade and the northern to central Pacific Coast network. They controlled the Dalles, a critical fishing spot on the river as a result of its waterfalls, which blocked the progress of salmon.

There were certainly differences between tribes, particularly related to northern or southern subregions, but it is possible to examine a generalized picture of Northwest Coast culture. The subsistence pattern of the coastal groups is the key to their development. With few exceptions, the territory close to their villages provided everything they needed and they cleverly adapted many resources to meet their needs. The success of the Northwest Coast is due to fish, more specifically salmon. The inhabitants of this region literally lived on it. Anadromous fish reach maturity in the sea and then return to the freshwater stream where they hatched in order to spawn and restart the life cycle. Until their decimation in the twentieth century from habitat loss, pollution, and dam construction, the fish could be counted in the millions. Each species undertakes its long journey at a slightly different time so that runs would come in successively. A salmon spawning run would clog a stream with writhing fish bodies intent only on upstream progress. With one goal in mind, the fish neither eat nor take much account of their surroundings and are thus relatively easy to catch. The Northwest Coast people relied on this incredible bounty of returning salmon in the spring and summer.

As each species began its long journey upstream, people would flock to the riverbanks. Mindful of the incredible importance of the salmon to their survival, the Northwest Coast cultures treated the fish with respect. The first fish caught was part of a thanksgiving ritual designed to ensure a successful fishing season. The salmon was shown reverence, given a speech of welcome, roasted, and shared among many. Its bones were returned to the stream in

a symbolic completion of the cycle of life that intertwined fish and humans. After proper respect was paid to the spirit of the salmon, the real work began. Men built weirs, which were a system of latticework that held the fish in place in the stream; they could not swim past the barriers. Fishermen then had several choices of how to catch the fish. They could harpoon them with a 16-foot spear with a barbed bone point. A dip net made of woven netting hanging from a round frame scooped up many fish. Traps captured fish as they were swept into these funnel-shaped boxes by the current. By using many different methods, the men caught thousands and thousands of fish. The women immediately took them from the riverbanks and began to prepare them. Women split, beheaded, and gutted each fish in preparation for hanging on the drying racks spread out behind the houses in each village. Generally, the salmon were dried for storage at inland sites where sun and wind could accomplish the task. At the damp fishing camps, women kept a fire going in a plank smokehouse, which dried the fish into a tough, pliable substance suitable for storage. The smoked pieces could be dipped in oil or steamed to replace the moisture. Fish heads went into a stew to add flavor. Most salmon was dried or smoked, but other fish required different preparation.

The eulachon, a type of smelt, is a small, oily fish that earned the nickname candlefish because when dried and fitted with a wick, it burns like a candle. Women let thousands of these fish rot for days, then mashed them and put the mess into a canoe buried in the sand and filled with water. When heated stones were dropped in, the oil rose to the surface and could be ladled off, then cooled and ladled again in preparation for storage. This was a smelly but critical task to ensure an adequate oil supply for winter.

Herring was another fish species whose spawning season was exploited by humans. Herring lay their eggs on submersed vegetation. People set out hemlock branches that were weighted down and tied in place. After the herring deposited their eggs on the branches, the fishermen could just pull them in and harvest the roe. Much of the catch from the spring and summer fishing season would be eaten dried during the winter. Such a steady diet could be monotonous, so often men fished in the winter to supplement the stored supplies. They took their canoes to the ocean to catch halibut or cod on hooked lines. They also hunted sea mammals with harpoons with detachable heads that required great strength and skill. Seals and sea otters provided meat, fur, and blubber, an important source of grease and oil. Similarly, land mammals provided more

than just meat as people used their skin, bones, and fur for tools and clothing. The most northern groups particularly valued mountain goat hair, which went into elaborately woven Chilkat blankets.

To augment their primarily fish-based diet, women gathered locally available berries, roots, and tubers. Salmonberries added color and flavor to their diet. They might take steps to improve the yield of native plants such as transplanting or seeding. They did plant small quantities of tobacco, but the Northwest Coast did not engage in agriculture. Their entire successful, wealthy lifestyle was supported by hunting, fishing, and gathering.

Housing and Settlement

Most of the resource extraction of the spring and summer months was intended to sustain the people through the winter. Families enjoyed fresh salmon at the riverside, but most of the catch was dried for storage. Family groups worked hard all summer to ensure that the area's bounty would take them through the less productive winters. Northwest Coast culture essentially fished, hunted, and gathered from May to September, which brought in enough food to allow them to pursue other interests in the winter. Their lives were divided into two seasons: the spring and summer secular season where everyone migrated to the resource locations to work, and the winter ceremonial season, when only daily chores would be allowed. During the winter season other activities such as art, ceremony, trade, and social status were the focus of the people. People even had two names, one for each season, to reflect the dichotomous nature of their year.

Families spent their year together and were the primary unit of a person's identity. In the spring, family members traveled to various resource locations, usually fishing camps, where they spent the summer. These were literally camps with temporary shelters. Some tribes in the central region actually dismantled their winter homes and carried the material to their fishing spots. Most groups, however, simply constructed temporary camps with available material. In the winter the Northwest Coast people moved to their permanent villages. These were located on the coasts, usually in a protected bay or inlet, which offered some respite from the Pacific winter weather. A village might stretch several miles along the coastline. It would consist of one or two rows of houses facing the water with canoes drawn up on the beach in front and covered from the elements. Behind the house stretched drying racks, storage sheds,

smokehouses, and huts for childbirth, menstruation and puberty rituals. There were also shelters for the ashes of cremations.

The Northwest Coast plank houses are as characteristic of the culture area as tipis are in the Plains. The usual size varied between regions with southern houses being much larger than northern, but the general design and construction remained the same. House construction was a long, formalized process involving many ceremonies and feasts. It was such an important ritual event that slaves might be sacrificed and their bodies placed under the house posts. The nearby forest provided all the building materials. Large cedar trees were felled, debarked, and moved to the village site, but only after their spirits had been thanked for giving of themselves. Because building was a quasi-spiritual activity, only highly regarded master craftsmen could work with the wood. Adzes, wedges, mauls, and stone hammers helped men split the wood into planks. Huge support posts and long ridge beams were erected to serve as the frame of the house, and then the planks were sewn and pegged on, usually vertically but in some areas horizontally. Roofs might be pitched, gabled, or shed-style, depending on the local custom. The resulting structure was rectangular, longer than it was wide. It had no windows and no ventilation except for a hole in the roof, which could be covered by a sliding panel in poor weather. The small door was in the wall facing the beach and was often incorporated into paintings on the house as the gaping a mouth of a creature. In the north the houses were typically 30 by 45 feet, but in the south they might be twice that size. Evidence exists for houses as large as 1,000 feet, which would have housed a whole village.

In most regions the houses were designed to shelter several related families. A chief presided over the kinship group and derived some of his status from his house. Each chief wanted to build or rebuild a house in his lifetime. The ownership of the house would be declared by the carvings on the house posts and the decorations on the front. Each nuclear family had a section of its own in the large room. In an attempt at privacy, wooden screens partitioned the space. They generally constructed two tiers of shelves around the outside walls and stored belongings on the upper one and slept on the lower bench. Cooking fires were placed in the middle and dried food hung from the ceiling or sat in boxes and baskets on the shelves.

The house was well organized and structured. Each group of items and people had its proper place. An individual's position in the house was based on his or her position within the kinship group. The most important families resided at the back wall, which

Northwest plank houses featured heraldic poles in their structures. Library of Congress.

was a place of honor. If the house was large enough, two ranking families would live side by side in the back. The rest of the families occupied the exterior walls in descending rank toward the entrance door. The last people sleeping closest to the door, and thus most vulnerable to attacks, were slaves.

Social Organization

Northwest Coast housing reflected a unique aspect of the culture—the existence of a highly stratified, hierarchical social system. There were two basic classes of people, free and slave, who essentially did not interact socially. Slaves did not have the right to disobey masters or to follow their own will. Periodic raiding produced war captives and although those of high rank were ransomed, the rest became slaves. An individual also could sink to that status through gambling debt. Slaves obviously had a low status and thus performed the worst, most onerous tasks in daily life. They chopped

wood, hauled water, and tended fires all year no matter their gender. Masters denigrated them by calling them only by the name of their tribe, not acknowledging their individuality with a personal name. A master could hurt or kill a slave to show his power, but it was not common. A slave might be killed in order to accompany a deceased person on his journey. Despite their loss of freedom, however, most slaves had similar living conditions to others in the tribe. A free man could marry a slave woman and their offspring would be free; however, the children born to two slave parents inherited their slave status. Although possible, it was hard to move out of slavery through marriage because a slave would debase the family of his or her spouse. The class of slaves was well established in Northwest Coast society; for example, one-fifth to one-fourth of the Kwakwaka'wakw tribe may have been slaves.

Among the free class there were also distinctions among chiefs, nobles, and commoners. Each maintained a specific rank within society, and although it was possible to move between ranks, particularly by marriage, it was not that common. Commoners had their freedom, but little else, as they had no rights in a household. They were required to give tribute to the nobles, the elite who enjoyed all the privileges in the society. The houses were the political entities of the Northwest Coast. Chiefs ran the houses, supported by the elite within their lineages. Chiefs wielded power through their control of resources, wealth and maintenance of prestige. Each chief claimed ancestry to a mythical or quasi-historical figure, which was the basis of his claim to leadership. He frequently recounted his genealogy to remind everyone of his status, and many of his actions went toward maintaining that prominence.

The chief of a household not only owned the house but also the rights to images, songs, and ceremonials connected to that house and lineage. On behalf of the house he owned and protected the rights to specific resource sites. A house would "own" a certain section of a salmon spawning stream where they fished each year. Ownership was taken very seriously and a trespasser could be rightfully killed without warning. This approach to natural resources seemed quite different from other indigenous groups who practiced a more communal distribution of subsistence sites. A lineage or household group worked together to obtain resources. Their exploitation patterns were planned by elders to ensure sufficient production for winter food storage. If a lineage produced excess, the chief could participate in exchange networks and thereby gain greater prestige.

A chief's power rested on his continued prestige. To make the best possible impression at the many public events he attended, the chief relied on a professional public speaker. These excellent orators could spend hours recounting the great deeds of the ancestors. Chiefs also often had a close connection to doctors or shamans who wielded considerable power in Northwest Coast society. Those with privilege formed a fairly tight circle, which they jealously guarded.

Most marriages in Northwest Coast society were arranged to ensure the continued prestige of the family. Young adults generally married outside of their villages to secure a wider base of influence. The structure of lineages varied among tribes. The Tlingit divided all their people into two lineages—Wolf or Raven—and then those each had subclans. Each clan was exogamous, meaning that no intermarriage was allowed. Much of the purpose of marriage was to achieve greater wealth and status and to consolidate relationships within clans. After parents selected a suitable mate, the boy's family generally offered the girl's family gifts, which reflected their wealth. If the match was acceptable, then the girl's family sent gifts in exchange. The marriage ceremony was held in the bride's house and included elaborate songs and dances and a wedding feast at which the couple was not allowed to eat. If the groom's family had enough wealth, they would give another feast a few weeks later. The bride generally moved into her husband's family house, but a noble woman would stay with her house where her husband would assert the privileges of rank until their sons were old enough to accept them.

A young woman would be expected to bear healthy children. A pregnant mother was secluded in a hut attended only by women. She remained there for eight days during which the father could see neither her nor the infant. A name was chosen for the baby that was associated with the lineage, as it was believed he had previously been one of the ancestors. Young children grew up in their parents' house surrounded by relatives. Older children, particularly those of noble rank, were expected to learn by watching adults. They needed to understand the behavioral code and complicated social hierarchy of their people. By the time they were 10, boys were sent to live with their maternal uncle who would be responsible for their upbringing, as most Northwest Coast peoples practiced matrilineal descent. The chief of the lineage would often take the boys to teach them the stories connected with their family and its position in society. It was critical that a noble son learn his clan's ceremonies,

songs, dances, legends, and symbols, as well as its territorial rights for hunting, fishing, and trade routes. Boys also had to learn to be worthy hunters and warriors. A strict pattern of discipline that involved daybreak dunks in the frigid ocean helped to strengthen and harden the boys. They learned to hunt, fish, work with wood, and care for a fire through daily chores.

Girls similarly had to learn their position in the group. They learned gathering, food preparation, and often artistic skill. Noble women might become accomplished artistic specialists. The graduation to adulthood was not easy for girls. Their first menses initiated a long, hard indoctrination, which might last as long as two years for noble girls. They spent the time in a special hut built at the back of the village. For the first eight days the girls were to sit immobile, maintaining a fast that could be broken only briefly on the fourth day. During this period they were to run a stone over their face and lips at least eight times a day to prevent a future tendency to gossip. The ritual had to be strictly followed to ensure a successful adulthood. After this, the young girls learned skills such as basketry and sewing during their isolation. On completion of their puberty ritual, women received a tattoo of the family crest on their hand and the labret for their lower lip, which marked their entrance into society.

The labret and the tattoo were marks of status. The labrets were elliptical plugs of bones with grooved edges that were inserted in perforations in the lower lip. Ear pendants and nose pins were also common forms of personal adornment. Although often decried by outsiders as deforming, labrets were considered attractive by the people. Some tribes in the central and southern parts of the Northwest practiced head-flattening, or intentional deflecting of an infant's skull. Different tribes sought distinct skull shapes that they found desirable. People of high rank would likely be tattooed with family crests on their hands, arms, chest, thighs, lower legs, and tops of feet. Tattoos showed well on men who rarely wore clothing in warm weather. Women generally wore skirts or sarongs woven of goat or dog hair and shredded cedar bark. Neither sex wore shoes, but they both donned watertight conical hats and cedar bark ponchos during the frequent rainy weather. Chiefs might have Chilkat robes or sea otter cloaks to show their status.

At the end of the lifecycle, death was marked by ritual. A deceased noble person's body would be dressed in ceremonial robes and placed in a sitting position at the back wall of the house. The body remained there for several days surrounded by grieving relatives.

Relatives cut their hair and blackened their faces while clansmen chanted ritual dirges. Because ghosts faced a long journey, the bodies were provided with food and dressed for travel. Among the Tlingit, the body was then cremated on a funeral pyre and the ashes transferred to special structures behind the village. The one exception to this practice was for shamans whose bodies were too powerful to cremate and instead lay intact on a platform that was forever treated with respect. Other tribes placed chiefs' bodies directly onto mortuary poles or elevated boxes without cremation.

Spirituality and Ceremonialism

The Northwest Coast had a rich belief system and shamans played an important role. Shamans or doctors were highly trained men or women who often assisted or allied with chiefs, which increased their prestige. They did not accept payment for their services, but were given gifts and thus could become quite wealthy. Many shamans inherited their positions, but usually served an apprenticeship to learn the local medicinal plants and their uses. They fasted, purged, and abstained from sex to make themselves acceptable to the spirits and thus receive a personal relationship. This spirit connection made a doctor a powerful person who was respected in both life and death. Drawing their supernatural powers from personal guardian spirits, shamans could both heal disease and send disease. A shaman could be called on to heal disease, bring good or bad weather, or ensure a heavy salmon run or success in war. They could also neutralize the power of witches who sent evil to people by obtaining a personal item and then burying it near a grave house so the victim would fall ill.

Shamans made quite an impressive spectacle as they worked. They never cut or combed their hair, which made a wild tangle around their heads. They often wore a crown of mountain goat horns inlayed with abalone. Their ritual paraphernalia included animal claws, teeth, and horns, rattles, masks, and amulets. Their necklaces of animal parts and carved charms clattered when they danced.

Much of the shaman's cure was performance. It took place in a dim house where the patient lay and involved drumming, chanting, and sleight of hand. The doctor danced in his various masks to commune with the spirits. The spirit informed him of the cause of the patient's evil and he set about to remedy it. For example, the spirit might tell him that a witch had embedded a cursed object in a patient. The shaman could then "suck" out the offending object

with his lips or a special bone whistle. A person would become ill if their spirit was stolen by a ghost or if it simply strayed away. The shaman would swing an elaborately carved "soul catcher" to snatch the wandering soul of the patient and restore it with health. Even more impressive feats made up his advertising performances, including swallowing sticks and knives, walking on hot coals, and fainting to appear dead.

In addition to shamans, southern groups participated in religious societies. This was especially evident among the Kwakwaka'wakw who had three secret societies each with subgroups consisting of people of similar rank and wealth. Membership was usually limited to men and women of the elite ranks for whom the societies served to reinforce their bonds and status. The *Dog Eaters* followed the spirit of the wolf; the group *those who descended from the heavens* celebrated the spirits of the sky like the stars and birds; and the most famous, the *Shamans' Society*, could only be joined by shamans. People usually inherited membership, although the privilege could be purchased from a member who needed money or in the worst case a member might be murdered for the right. This, of course, was quite dangerous and care had to be taken not to kill someone of higher rank, as the consequences would be terrible. The societies held complex ceremonials primarily focused on initiating new members. They staged elaborate dramas of initiation that followed a pattern where the initiate was kidnapped, possessed by spirits, and finally reclaimed by his fellow members. Magic tricks abounded with staged beheadings and dismemberment intended to shock the crowd.

In addition to religious societies, each person sought out relationships with the spirits. Dreams, trances, and ritual bathing were important aspects of maintaining contact with the spirit world. The spirits went away to foreign lands in the summer leaving the people free to concentrate on resource collection. Then, in the slower winter season when the food had all been stored, the spirits returned to the Northwest.

Supernatural beings were everywhere and affected peoples' lives by bringing good and evil. All illness people experienced had supernatural origins. Spirits also helped enforce good behavior in the society. For example, *Tsonoqa*, the Wild Woman of the Woods, roamed the woods eating any children she could catch and thereby presenting a good reason not to wander from the village. The Thunderbird lived on a mountain peak and brought thunder, lightning, and rain. Land Otter Man stole people, deprived them of their senses,

Masked dancers perform inside a communal plank house. Library of Congress.

and turned them into otters who tormented people. Raven was the always clever and mischievous trickster figure in the belief system.

Supernatural explanations made sense of the world. Every animal, plant, object, and location had a spirit connected to it, and humans had a relationship to them all. If these spirits were treated properly they could bring great bounty to humans. The salmon were a race of immortal men who lived in houses under the sea. In the late spring they assumed the form of fish and offered themselves to humans as food. Women stripped their flesh to eat, but returned the bones to the river so the men could be reborn the next spring. Obviously, these immortals had to be respected and honored, or a critical source of food would be taken from the people. There were similar, if less elaborate, rituals to appease the spirits of every resource humans used from game animals to trees. Certain animals were used as totems and they had a closer relationship to those in a clan using their image as a crest. That special relationship might make it easier for a clan member to kill his own totem species because he could talk the animal into giving its life for the good of the clan.

Ceremonials of all kinds were an important way of life on the Northwest Coast. Elaborate ceremonies held during the winter served to honor spirits, and reinforce community ties and shared beliefs. The Northwest Coast tribes had a highly developed system of drama, which included songs, music, dancing, and elaborate costumes, props, and performance. All ages gathered to witness the spectacle held in a dimly lit house, which refreshed everyone's familiarity with the supernatural world and the proper behavior of humans within it. The most intriguing of these ceremonies was the potlatch, an ancient ritual of redistribution. The post-Columbian historic potlatch, with its outrageous displays of disregard for wealth, seems to have been a reaction to European values and the availability of manufactured goods. When banned by the Canadian government in the nineteenth century it had become an exaggeration of a longstanding Northwest Coast tradition.

Potlatch

The potlatch was a characteristic event of Northwest Coast society that served several purposes. It was essentially a lavish feast of honor. It united families and lineages, validated rank and power, and redistributed wealth. The word potlatch derives from the Chinook word *patshatl* meaning to give away. In this unique celebration the host gave away lavish gifts to his guests to impress them with his wealth and thus validate his rank. The most important aspect of life in all tribes in the region was a person's status. This ceremony announced and confirmed that status. A high-ranking family undertook the hosting of a potlatch ceremony to commemorate a change in their lineage, most often the ascension of a new chief. Different groups chose different times in the cycle to memorialize that change. The Tlingit did it as a mourning ritual for the deceased chief, the Tsimshian, as a celebration of the new chief, and the Haidas noted the growth of the young man who would become chief someday.

Although the lineage's leaders and elders decided to host a potlatch, it involved every member of the household. It would take months and perhaps years to plan a large celebration. The feast would go on for up to 10 days and entertain more than 100 people. They invited both neighbors and high-ranking members of other villages who might travel days to attend. Special messengers went out with the invitations, giving the guests plenty of time to prepare the songs and dances they would be expected to perform at the

event. Meanwhile the entire host household worked to ensure a successful celebration. There had to be so much food that guests could not finish it all. Each guest would receive a gift according to his or her rank. The most valuable gifts might represent years of hunting, fishing, and trading on the part of the giver. A chief might have to borrow from other groups or call in debts to acquire enough goods. All of this had to be prepared and stockpiled in advance. In addition, ceremonial masks and costumes had to be readied and songs and dances practiced for the event's performances.

The etiquette of a potlatch was strict. Guests arrived via elaborate war canoes at the host beach where they were welcomed with songs, which they then had to reciprocate. The first days were dedicated to feasting to the extreme, almost gorging on fish, meat, oil, seaweed, and berries, as well as watching performances. With the social aspects completed, the hosts turned to the real purpose of commemoration. The host lineage donned regalia that displayed their family crests and through songs, dances, and stories recounted the families' history. They established their claims to symbols, honors, privileges, and resource territories through their connections to the supernatural beings. All of the group's wealth and status was on display for their visitors to acknowledge and validate. Then the gifts were brought forward for distribution and their history, worth, and meaning were described. They were carefully chosen to reflect the rank of the recipient. At the lowest level, actual resources like dried salmon or cedar bark were given away. Value increased to furs, blankets, robes, carved items, boxes, canoes, and even slaves. One of the iconic potlatch gifts was a copper. These shieldlike objects of pounded copper displayed a crest etched into a darkened background. The bestowal of these metal plaques flaunted the wealth of the giver and honored the recipient. By giving away so much of their material wealth, chiefs proved their worth to the community and thus verified their rights to privilege.

Artistic Tradition

Many of the gifts given away at the potlatch showcased the incredible artistic skill of Northwest Coast society. Artistic expression reached remarkable heights in this culture that valued the beauty of everyday objects. Virtually no item was left undecorated, including spoons, dishes, house posts, canoes, boxes, and hats. Except for coppers, and bone and some stone implements, most Northwest Coast artifacts were made from plant material. This

region is the heartland of North American twined weaving technique, and it reached one of its highest expressions here. The Tlingit and Haida women were the best weavers. First they had to prepare their materials. They took long, narrow pieces of the inner bark of the cedar tree and split it into strips that could be woven into matting. Another technique was to use spruce root and cedar bark cordage in a twined pattern. The cedar bark was beaten until shredded and then rolled into long flexible fibers; the spruce tree roots were split into strips. This technique was used for mats and hats, as well as baskets. Skilled weavers produced such a tight weave that the object was actually waterproof. Many items, especially hats, would incorporate complex geometric designs.

One of the best-known examples of Northwest Coast weaving can be seen in the famed Chilkat robes produced only by the Chilkat tribe. They have been called outstanding expressions of Northern Coast textile art. These highly valued robes were traded throughout the Northwest Coast for chiefs to wear. Of interest, the production of a Chilkat robe was a joint venture between men and women that might take a year to complete. Men hunted or traded for the mountain goat wool, made the half loom, and planned the design on a painted board that woman followed as they wove. The women washed the wool, leaving some of it natural color and dying three other colors: black with hemlock bark, yellow with lichen, and blue with copper. They then twisted the goat wool around a core of twined yellow cedar bark creating a weaving fiber. Following the pattern designed by the men, the women wove a blanket in separate panels that were then joined with sinew or wool and bark cord into a trapezoidal shape. The striking product of this long process is one of the few ancient artistic products that is still made today.

Whereas women excelled at weaving, men carved wood. They made bowls, spoons, house screens, masks, storage boxes, canoes, and totem poles. Each item was adorned with the characteristic stylized designs of the Northwest. Some were extremely elaborate, such as the masks used for ceremonies. These wooden carvings depicted sprits in often grotesque exaggerations. The very detailed carving of the creature came complete with hair. Some masks were hinged to open and reveal another carving below, allowing the dancer to transform in the middle of the performance. Because the masks depicted the supernatural, they were powerful items that had to be treated with respect.

Even mundane items like food bowls for daily use were ornamented with intricate carvings. They created truly huge bowls for

Chilkat robes were highly valued by chiefs.
Library of Congress.

potlatches whose intricate shapes were really more like a sculpture than a utilitarian item. The boxes they made to store extra clothing and food supplies were remarkable. A carver took one cedar plank and grooved it on three lines. He then steamed the wood until it was pliable enough to bend into a box shape. Three corners had no seams; the fourth was sewn shut creating a watertight seal. A bottom was fitted on with a groove for the sides to sit in and then pegged and sealed. Designs were usually carved in each panel to decorate the box. The resulting box was so tight it could hold fish oil. The Haida also carved beautiful boxes and bowls from argillite, a fine-grained black stone.

The Haida were also known as the best canoe carvers. Each canoe was a dugout made from a single log. The shape and size varied with the purpose of the vessel, ranging from small fishing canoes for two men to war canoes that held 50 people. A special canoe maker went to the forest to choose the proper tree for his project. After offering his thanks to the tree, he had it cut down, debarked, and split in half. He would then spend weeks or months working to shape

This dancer is fully costumed for a ritual
performance. Library of Congress.

the canoe. Adzes and wedges chipped away wood to give shape
to the bottom and sides. Once the walls were the proper thickness,
the builder would build fires around the outside of the canoe and
heat water on the inside to soften the wood so that thwarts could
push the sides outward. In the final steps, the hull was sanded and
polished, cedar gunnels were applied, and the canoe would be
decorated with paintings and carvings depicting the honors of the
owners. A ceremonial canoe also had carved figures attached to the
bow and stern. These enormous carved canoes made an impressive
sight gliding across the water.

Perhaps the most recognizable form of Northwest Coast art is the
totem pole. It is another art form that continues from ancient times
to the present. The poles varied in size and design depending on the
use and between regions. Again, the peoples of the British Columbia region, such as the Haida and Tlingit, excelled at pole carving.
A memorial pole was a freestanding pole in honor of a dead chief.
A mortuary pole had a cavity in the top for the cremated remains
of a chief. Massive posts in the interior and entryway supported

houses. Made of a single giant cedar tree, totem poles bore the stylized designs so characteristic of the culture.

These totems were also displayed on houses, blankets, clan crest
hats, and weapons. They were stylized representations of the spiritual patrons of families. They could be animals, humans, hybrids,
or natural features such as the sun and moon. They embodied the
sacred history of the family and were carefully guarded by the
families who owned them. Common designs were bears, wolves,
killer whales, beavers, and ravens. Each totem had its own characteristics and represented something in the ancestry of the family who owned it. Beavers were known for their industriousness
and their building skills, and Eagles were respected for intelligence
and power, as well as extraordinary vision. The killer whale was an
important crest and was commonly depicted. These majestic creatures were associated with strength, dignity, prosperity, and longevity. When placed in proximity to one another, as on a memorial
pole, these intertwined totems tell a story, revealing the ancestry of
a family. In many ways, the totem poles summarize the Northwest

Totem poles often depicted a family's lineage.
BigStockPhoto.com

Coast culture by bringing together artistic form and skill, reverence for ancestry, and display of wealth and status in the medium of the great cedar tree.

The Pacific Northwest Coast culture was one of the most unique in America. It developed independently in a region cut off from easy contact with the rest of the continent. Taking its cue from the natural environment, the culture was one of gigantic proportions. Tremendous salmon harvests, monumental dugout canoes, large cedar houses, and totem poles make this culture seem larger than life. Strict hierarchy, social and economic stratification, elaborate ceremony, and intricate artwork characterized coastal peoples. They lived bountifully from a few major resources—forest and river—and had no need for agriculture. Independent and unique, the people of the coast lived successfully for millennia.

FURTHER READING

Drucker, Philip. *Cultures of the North Pacific Coast.* San Francisco: Chandler Publishing Co., 1965.

Fladmark, Knut. *British Columbia Prehistory.* Ottowa: Archaeological Survey of Canada, 1988.

An Introduction to North America's Native People: Northwest Coast Culture Area. This site contains pictures, maps, and text explaining the culture of the Northwest coast. http://www.cabrillo.edu/~crsmith/noamer_nwcoast.html (accessed September 1, 2007).

Malin, Edward. *A World of Faces: Masks of the Northwest Coast Indians.* Portland, OR: Timber Press, 1994.

Matson, R. G., and G. Coupland. *The Prehistory of the Northwest Coast.* New York: Academic Press, 1995.

Native American Culture Map, Northwest Coast. The map shows the various tribes of the Northwest Coast. http://www.snowwowl.com/maps/mapnorthwest.html (accessed September 1, 2007).

Ruby, Robert H., and John A. Brown. *A Guide to the Indian Tribes of the Pacific Northwest.* Norman: University of Oklahoma Press, 1986.

Woodcock, George. *Peoples of the Coast: The Indians of the Pacific Northwest.* Bloomington: Indiana University Press, 1977.

7

The Arctic and Sub-Arctic

The farthest northern region of America is perhaps the least understood. Most people view it as an empty wasteland, far removed from the verdant eastern woodlands. It is perhaps one of the harshest climates on earth. Bitter cold persists much of the year with temperatures below minus 50 degrees Fahrenheit. Winds blow at gale force, storms lash the land, and the seas whip into monumental waves. For part of the year, the land is cloaked in constant darkness. There are no trees and little greenery. Yet, this unforgiving natural world also supports an abundance of natural resources. The cold Arctic seas are home to numerous species of seals, sea lions, walruses, and whales, as well as deep water fish like cod and flounder. The ocean shallows support shellfish and, in the inland river systems, freshwater fish and anadromous fish abound. Even on the adjacent mainland, caribou, muskox, lemmings, hares, Arctic fox, wolves, bears, and many nesting birds can be found. Farther south, woodland caribou, moose, bison, and many smaller animals inhabit the area. The resources exist despite challenging conditions. The story of human life in the Arctic is one adaptation to this unique and challenging environment.

The Arctic actually supports diverse environments and thus diverse human societies. Some areas have large mountains such as the Brooks, Alaska, and Aleutian ranges; others like the Canadian

shield are fairly flat. Because of the topography, few large rivers developed, although exceptions are the Yukon and Kuskokwin Rivers. Much of the region is in the tundra zone. In the summer the upper layer of soil melts, leaving plains of shallow ponds and wet areas that support grasses and sedges. Under that top layer is permafrost or ground that never thaws. Little precipitation falls, so little, in fact, that nearly desert conditions exist. The moisture that does come falls mostly as snow; however, the topsoil is always moist because the permafrost prevents precipitation from soaking in. In the southern edges and along the west coast, the permafrost is spotty, allowing spruce trees and shrubs to grow.

Perhaps surprisingly in this Arctic climate, western Alaska and the Yukon River drainage were not covered by glaciers; however, they were sometimes cut off from the interior by ice fields. This would have blocked people coming across the Beringia migration route from leaving the area. Then, when the glaciers in front melted allowing access to the interior, the rising sea levels blocked any return to Siberia. This may be why no group claimed the region as their homeland until about 3000 B.C., when we believe the common ancestors of the modern Eskimos and Aleuts arrived.

The understanding of human habitation in the far north continues to generate controversy and disagreement among anthropologists. The region experienced a series of migrations from the west. According to the most accepted understanding of America's origin, all the migrants crossed to the continent via the Bering Land bridge in the Arctic. One theory proposes two subsequent waves of migration of peoples who stayed in the north. The first wave brought NaDene or Athabaskan speakers from Siberia around 12000–10000 B.C. The second wave of Eskimo/Aleut ancestors came before the land bridge flooded permanently. Of course, evidence of habitation on the land bridge to support these theories would now be submerged. Some experts assert that humans occupied the area by 25000 B.C. These exceptionally early dates are as controversial as similar assertions for other American regions. The earliest indisputable evidence of habitation dates from 9000–6000 B.C. at the Old Crow site in the Yukon. People here fit a paleo-Arctic pattern and left behind stone blades associated with the bones of modern animals. These interior hunters must have exploited large land mammals like bison.

Another ancient site was home to people who did not have access to such mammals. Beginning around 6750 B.C. and continuing for at least 500 years, people made their home at Anangula at the tip of

the Aleutian Island chain. (It is now a national historic landmark.) This outpost on the edge of the Bering Sea at first would seem to have little to recommend it. It was a barren landscape with no trees or plant life apart from a few berries and indigestible grasses. The Anangula settlement sat on the shoreline looking out to the only source of life—the ocean. There is no existing evidence of boats at the site, but it seems unlikely that the inhabitants did without them in this environment. At this ancient time, the sea level would have been lower and thus travel between areas easier. The surrounding sea was home to hair seals and sea lions all year and fur seals and whales during migration seasons. The availability of shellfish, fish, and birds would have made a fairly successful life for skilled hunters.

The Anangulan hunters must have been very good because they supported a permanent village of 75 people for hundreds of years. The people lived in small, semi-subterranean, oval houses only about 15 feet long, constructed of driftwood covered by matting and live sod. The artifacts left near the house sites support an idea of gender division similar to modern Aleut people. Women and girls worked in the house sewing and grinding pigments by the light of an oil lamp, and the men and boys crafted stone and bone tools atop the house where they could watch for marine prey. What must have been a strong communal society succeeded at Anangula until the site was abandoned around 5000 B.C. after being blanketed with volcanic ash.

The Anangula site was quite early and also fairly remote out on the Aleutians. This was the edge of the Bering Land Bridge, and their material life was similar to that of Siberia. Anangula and the nearby site of Chaluka contain tools that resemble implements found in Siberia and Japan. They are more stylistically Asian than later finds. The human remains from the sites are of long-headed individuals, quite different from round-headed Eskimos. So it appears that these earlier migrants from Asia were later pushed out or absorbed by the Aleut who came to dominate the islands.

In the centuries after the Anangula habitation, people of the Arctic began to develop regional variations. As elsewhere in the paleo-Indian period, variety in resources caused people to adapt and develop distinct lifestyles. Between 5000 and 2500 B.C. in the far north, hunters produced differing tool kits depending on their needs. Those people living on islands and bays exploited marine resources; those in the interior adapted to their own terrestrial resources. Once sea levels stabilized around 4000 B.C., humans living on the coast began to adapt to the new landscape and conditions. They hunted

marine mammals like sea otters, hair and fur seals, and whales, as well as catching ocean fish. Hunters used skin kayaks to hunt on the open water and multibarbed harpoons to bring down large marine mammals. In the Kodiak Island region, we call this the Ocean Bay tradition that lasted until about A.D. 1000. The term *Kodiak tradition* refers to a more southern derivative of Ocean Bay at the same time period. These people added salmon fishing and caribou hunting to their sea mammal resources. The Kodiak people of the Kachemak period (500 B.C.–A.D. 1000) must have been successful. They left more tools, more elaborate burials, and simply more material remains, which indicates greater population density. The later Koniag tradition continued the evolution of technology and adaptation.

Change continued in the Arctic, especially around 2500 B.C. in the northern part of the region. The culture we later identify as Eskimo began to take shape. The most important element of this development was the Arctic small tool tradition. This is what archaeologists have termed the technological advancement of using one-half- to three-quarter-inch chisel-like blades to carve wood, bone, and ivory. It has been described as a "distinctive, miniaturized toolkit of

Hunters in the Arctic have been using kayaks and harpoons for thousands of years. Library of Congress.

delicately chipped tools." In some areas like the Kodiak Peninsula, toolmakers began grinding and polishing slate rather than chipping it as was still done elsewhere. The Arctic small tool tradition, which may have originated in Siberia, is an important benchmark in the cultural traditions of the region, marking the beginning of prehistory.

These migrants introduced the bow and arrow to the Americas. It spread quickly through the maritime zone, although not among the Aleuts. The groups who used the tradition appear to have balanced marine and terrestrial game exploitation. Their houses were small, square, and semi-subterranean. Each sod dwelling had a downward sloping entrance to conserve heat, which was provided by driftwood or fatty animal bone fires. In eastern Canada the hunters used more temporary skin tents as they moved about. They hunted caribou, musk ox, polar bear, seal, and walrus, as well as salmon and trout if they were available. After 500 years, however, the focus shifted to greater use of marine resources and the small tool tradition disappeared by 1600 B.C. in some areas.

THE LAST MIGRANTS

By 2000 B.C., a divergence occurred in the Arctic that produced the distinct cultures of the region to the present day. Initially the ancestors of the two groups we call Aleut and Eskimo (Inuit) migrated from Siberia in the last wave of immigrants. They inhabited the islands and coast of Asia and then crossed the Bering Sea to Alaska. They spoke a language we call Eskaleut, which has clear connections to Siberia. The Aleut people split from the Eskimos fairly early; some believe that the division began in Siberia. This group settled in the Aleutian Island chain and developed independently of and farther away from the Eskimo culture.

Living in the islands the Aleuts naturally became marine specialists, exploiting the natural resources of the ocean. They hunted whales, sea lions, walrus, and sea otters and harvested sea birds from island rookeries. Their techniques for marine hunting evolved into an amazing system. The Aleuts used a detachable harpoon that was at once a masterpiece of technology and artistry. The weapon was made in three parts: a lower main shaft, an upper foreshaft about one-third to one-half the main length, and in between a small shaft with a socket on either end. The whole system was joined by lashing. The harpoon head had a slot on top for a sharpened point and a long spur that caught in the animal and caused the point to

turn in the wound. The line attached to the head allowed the hunters to maintain contact with the wounded animal. Other specialized gadgets such as sealskin floats, drags, and wound plugs completed the hunting kit. Archaeologist Dean Snow declared that this system "may well be the most sophisticated weapon system ever devised by a prehistoric hunter." The Aleuts used their ingenuity to manufacture many specialized items to assist in hunting. Because their skin boats sat so low, in the ocean the glare off the water could blind a hunter. Special hats with long, tapering brims decorated to resemble sea mammals became standard hunting gear. The Aleut culture did spend energy on decorative arts, as well as personal decorations such as stone labrets, but in general they produced less flamboyant art than the Eskimos. In later periods the Northwest Coast styles exerted strong influence on the Aleut culture.

As the Aleut culture settled into a consistent tradition based on successful exploitation of their rich locale, their relatives the Eskimos continued to improve their subsistence skills. As the Arctic small tool tradition waned and disappeared, other technology developed. The small tool tradition had been a successful adaptation; however, a climactic cooling trend that altered animal populations may have stressed small communities beyond the possibility of survival. Beginning in 1600 B.C., the region experienced a few sharply colder centuries that made survival a challenge. Groups in the extreme north retreated southward and westward, probably following changes in caribou locations. Different cultures grew out of the small tool tradition, such as the Choris on the west coast and the Sarqaq in the Canadian Arctic. Development and innovation continued as two new cultures came to dominate the Arctic, one in the east and one in the west. East of the Mackenzie River a group known as Pre-Dorset arose from the Sarqaq culture around 2000 B.C. They spread eastward and survived a continued cooling trend. After 500 B.C., their successors, the Dorset, spread eastward, using areas uncovered by retreating glaciers.

As they moved, the Dorset altered their lifestyle to meet new needs. Their housing could vary from shallowly excavated round houses with paved stone floors, to skin tents supported by whale bones, to sod block houses. They also built snow houses that they could heat and light with the new technology of stone lamps burning sea mammal oil. The Dorset hunted both seals along the coast with the help of kayak and umiaks, and caribou in the interior. Other terrestrial resources like stone appear in Dorset artifacts. Because they were so disconnected from Siberia, they did not have the

pottery that other groups adopted from Asia. They used meteoric iron when they found it and native copper for knives and points. Objects all had ornamentation and many items were made purely for adornment. The Dorset are famous for a highly developed artistic tradition of carved wood, bone, and ivory depictions of humans, animals, and spirits.

They also started making specialized tools designed for Arctic survival such as snow knives to cut blocks for building, ice creepers to improve foot traction, and protective snow goggles. These people, however, lacked technology that other groups had including harpoon floats, dog sleds, cold-trap entrances for houses, and bow and arrows.

The Dorset expanded and contracted with the conditions. For about 500 years they lived in Newfoundland, leaving around A.D. 600. We know little about the reasons for Dorset disappearance by A.D. 1000. Some suggest that their reliance on seals and caribou doomed them in a period of climate change. The remnants of the culture were swamped by rapidly expanding Thule Eskimos.

In the western portion of the Arctic, a dynamic new culture emerged independently of previous occupants. The Norton culture

Sealskin containers provided waterproof storage. Library of Congress.

was named for archaeological finds in Norton Bay. It began along the Bering Sea and spread northward to cover more than 2,000 miles of coastline. Although some items of Norton technology go back to the Arctic small tool tradition and the Norton developed from the Choris culture (1000–500 B.C.), most of their tools represent new adaptations to the environment. By 500 B.C., the Norton people were thriving throughout the Bering Sea region by balancing hunting and fishing. These hunters tended to focus more on marine resources than terrestrial ones, hunting sea mammals year round and fishing intensively. Therefore they built more permanent settlements along the coast, which could be fairly large; Cape Nome held 400 residents. A large 40-foot long building was probably used for community activities and as a communal workspace. The Norton people had the first pottery in the Arctic, which was fiber-tempered, stamped pottery in a style they learned from Asia. They made flat-bottomed pots that were not particularly strong because of air spaces in the clay. Other technology proved more successful. The earliest toggle harpoons helped these hunters be more effective as they paddled their kayaks and umiaks in the frigid waters. The Arctic ulu knife with the handle above the blade proved effective at cutting up sea mammals for meat and blubber.

One major village, Ipiutak at Point Hope, Alaska, in the northern range of the Norton culture, represents the later stages of the tradition. Ipiutak had semi-subterranean houses along the coastline. These were square buildings excavated 20 inches into the earth and covered with pole and sod roofs. There were also some larger ceremonial dwellings where people communed with the supernatural through song and recitation. This lifestyle drew from both land and sea. From the interior came birch-bark containers and antlers from the caribou hunted with bow and arrow. On the coast, elaborately decorated harpoon heads were used to kill seals and walrus. Fish and birds were a minor part of the diet. The site is famous for highly decorated artifacts. It seems that every item from knife handles to ornamental beads was highly embellished with designs. They also sculpted animals out of ivory and antler, some of which had elaborate inlays of ivory and jet. The 138 excavated burials yielded elaborately made grave goods, suggesting ritual burials and the practice of cults and shamanism. Amazing openwork carvings, as well as animal and miniature human figurines attest to the skill of the artisans. Ipiutak also shows evidence of early iron smelting, which must represent contact with Asia. The Ipiutak people lacked elements thought to be typically Eskimo such as slate tools, pottery

and oil lamps, and harpoon floats. By A.D. 1, the Norton tradition hunted from the Bering Sea to the Yukon; however, it was soon to be replaced by an even more widespread lifestyle pattern.

THULE TRADITION

In the first millennium A.D., people began to abandon land mammal hunting and turn most of their energy toward the ocean. They realized that in this harsh landscape, the coasts, islands, and surrounding waters are more productive than the land. So the people known as Thule became expert walrus and whale hunters. Arising on the Siberian and Bering Strait islands, the Thule crossed to the mainland and spread rapidly. They reached their success partially through the use of technological devices. They used bone, ivory, and polished slate to craft projectile heads, knives, and the characteristic *ulu* or transverse bladed knife. Thule hunters became masters of the sea. They hunted sea mammals from an *umiak* or skin-covered boat. These could be made quite large to carry many people. Captains of

Ivory carving has long been a traditional form of artistic expression. Library of Congress.

such boats were known as *umialiks* and became quite respected in their communities for their hunting, leadership, and ritual skills. The umiak created a stable platform for whale and walrus hunting. A whale hunter would thrust a toggle harpoon into a whale. The new toggle design would cause the head to detach from the harpoon shaft and twist and turn inside the animal's wound, causing further damage. The line attached to the harpoon head could be tied off to a chunk of ice, which the wounded whale would pull as it swam away. The boat stayed with the whale until it tired and could be safely killed. This was not a safe occupation considering the strength of the prey and the frigid, wet conditions humans faced. Walrus hunting was also hazardous. The animals were considered mysterious and malevolent because they would sometimes flip and maul boats. The amount of meat, hide, ivory, and bone they yielded made the unpredictable walrus a worthwhile prey. Hunters also pursued seals from shore for eight hours a day in winter temperatures of 50 below zero.

This lifestyle obviously required excellent adaptations to the environment. People constantly modified things to improve life, such as developing cold trap doors to make their homes more livable. One of the most important adaptations was clothing. Without proper protection from the harsh elements, humans could not have survived for long. The clothing the Thule made was light and warm. They learned to dress in layers of carefully tailored clothing. For example, they might wear two caribou fur parkas, with the fur facing inward on the under parka. Wolverine fur framing the parka's hood created an ice-free tunnel of air to breathe. Each garment had to be dried carefully after use to preserve its insulating and waterproof qualities. Footwear, *uguruliks*, were made from caribou and sealskin. A knee-high caribou fur shaft with a sinew drawstring was sewn onto a seal skin sole with sinew. A strip of sealskin sandwiched between helped insulate. Socks and caribou skin liners added warmth for the harshest weather. Aesthetics were as important to the people as utilitarianism. Everything was finely crafted with beautiful finish and ornamentation, from harpoon heads to sewing kits.

The Thule people's successful adaptation helped them to spread across the north. In a little more than 100 years, they reached from the Bering Sea in the west, across the mainland to Greenland in the east. Between the tenth and eleventh centuries, the Thule culture had to contend with a major weather change, a warm-up. This warm trend resulted in the breakup of pack ice offshore so whales, walruses, and seals migrated on a wider path. Bowhead whales came to the Beaufort Sea to feed and the Thule hunters pursued

Sealskin parkas help protect hunters from the harsh Arctic conditions. Library of Congress.

them eastward. Hunters eagerly exploited this newly available resource because one whale kill every two years could provide a village with nine daily pounds of meat and blubber. With whales as the linchpin of village success, whale captains came to dominate village life. Judging from historical practices, the captains would have built, equipped, and maintained a boat. The boat and gear were stored at one of the village's men's houses, which also served as ceremonial center. It was probably the captain's duty to support his crew of six or seven men and their families.

By the twelfth and thirteenth centuries, the Thule had settled on islands and coasts of the central Canadian Arctic. They subsisted on seals, fish, and land mammals in Greenland, Labrador, and Baffin Island. This Thule culture now spread more than 6,000 miles from Siberia to Greenland. One expert wrote that the Thule represented the "greatest linear distribution of any people in the world." Beginning around A.D. 1200, cooler temperatures returned and the Thule began moving onto the ice in the winter. They lived

in snow houses on the edge of the icepack and stalked seals at their breathing holes in the ice. People moved over the frozen landscape with the aid of sleds. In the summer caribou and river fish fed the families. In the western portion of their territory, hunters pursued whales from the ice again and great whaling villages grew up, some of which still exist.

The Thule people were flexible in their adaptations to changing conditions, which is what made them so successful where other groups failed. In their dispersal, they overran and replaced the existing Dorset culture. The Thule modified their lifestyle to handle the stresses of climactic change. During warm trends they exploited bowhead and beluga whales, walrus, caribou, seals, and polar bear; but when the whales and caribou waned in the warm period, hunters switched to other prey such as seals and broke into smaller living groups that were easier to support. On Baffin Island in the northeastern Arctic where other cultures had barely supported 150 people, the Thule supported 250 people for a long time. In the eastern region, the Thule ran into Norsemen who called them *skraelings* or barbarians. The Europeans traded iron for ivory and seal meat, but often clashed with the indigenous people. Norse artifacts such as chain mail and iron boat rivets have been found at a fourteenth-century indigenous site. Eventually the Norse settlements collapsed, perhaps pressured by the Thule. The Norse were gone but the remarkable adaptations of the Thule culture would live on in the Eskimo (Inuit) culture that dominated the northern Arctic.

After the climactic changes of ancient times, the environment in the far north stabilized and allowed the development of two distinct lifestyles that continued for millennia up to, and to some extent through, European contact. The two major groups inhabiting the Arctic were the Aleut and the Eskimo—the latter preferred to be called Inuit. As discussed previously, these peoples probably migrated from Siberia in one extended wave of migration and then diverged as they remained in America. The Aleut claimed the islands of the west coast of Alaska, which bear their name; the Inuit spread along the coastal regions of the west and north. Although sprung from a common culture, the Aleuts and Inuits developed quite distinct adaptations to their new homes.

ALEUT CULTURE

The people known as Aleut who called themselves Unangan or "the people" lived in the 1,300-mile-long chain of volcanic islands

of the Aleutian archipelago, which arcs westward from Alaska toward Siberia. They were united by a language with only two dialects, Unalaskan and Auttana, and a shared cultural adaptation to the maritime environment. Their homeland was a series of more than 100 treeless islands in a cold, damp, foggy climate surrounded by the frigid waters of the Pacific, flanked on one side by the Gulf of Alaska and the other by the Bering Sea. The entire life of the Aleuts was oriented around that resource-rich ocean.

The Aleuts were intimately connected to the sea. They chose village sites along the rocky coasts, often in bays with gravel beaches that provided safe landings for boats. The location usually boasted a freshwater stream for water supply and salmon fishing. The availability of driftwood, access to stone for tool-making, and an elevated area for lookouts made a good site into a great one. The waters of the bays rarely froze, so this location provided access to sea mammal hunting year round. Each village had defined territories from which they could harvest resources. Their communal housing was oblong with semi-subterranean floors and whale bone frames, both of which were covered with sod and grass. A village would look like a series of green humps in the landscape. The entrance was in the roof via a ladder like the southwestern pit houses.

These traditional winter houses were called barabara or ulax and held up to 40 families within their 90-foot length. Inside, the quarters of each family were defined by woven grass mats. Each family had sleeping and storage spaces, assigned according to rank, as well as excavated hiding places that might be linked to secret escape passages. Like most communal houses, these served as gathering places for ceremonial, social, and production activities. Houses and their activities were guided by an elder of the kingroup. This was a communal society that valued cooperativeness and punished improper behavior with banishment, which could be a death sentence in this environment. This was not an egalitarian society, however; instead, like the Pacific Northwest people, Aleut society followed a class ranking. Chiefs, together in consultation with the nobles, ruled the commoners and slaves. Kinship and thus hereditary rank passed through matrilineal decent. High status was displayed with highly decorated clothing and possession of dentalium shells, amber, and slaves.

The Aleut culture was completely attuned and amazingly well adapted to the sea. They gathered everything they needed from the rich but harsh marine environment, from food to building materials. The men hunted sea mammals from kayaks, which were

unique in the region for their split bows that increased seaworthiness and speed. Long days on the ocean exposed hunters to difficult conditions, one of which was unrelenting glare off the water. They developed a wooden hunting hat with a long vision to protect the eyes. It also reflected the ranked society of the Aleuts—a short visor was worn by the young and inexperienced hunters, an elongated visor by the rank-and-file, and open-crown long-visored hats by important mature men. Sea lion whiskers adorned the hats and the number of whiskers indicated the wearer's success in hunting.

Sea lion, sea otter, and seals were favorite prey. These animals provided meat, fat for heat and light, and skin and gut to manufacture clothing. Naturally in such a wet, cold climate, the Aleut clothing had to be warm and waterproof; however, it was more than functional. Women decorated clothing with colorful natural dyes, feathers, and puffin beaks and even elaborately carved ivory, bone, or wooden figurines. They also wove hats and baskets of spruce roots and grass in incredibly fine weaving with up to 2,500 stitches per square inch. Plant fibers and animal products provided whatever the people needed, being made into cords, cables, and fishing line.

The Aleut traded with other groups for resources they did not have, such as terrestrial products. They traveled widely in skillfully made boats that could hold a large group. Contacts with other people provided both exotic items and new ideas. Many elements of Aleut culture mirror those of the Pacific Northwest, reflecting the continued interaction of the regions. Like the Northwest Coast culture, Aleuts dedicated their winter season, after sufficient resources had been gathered in the summer and fall, to celebration and ceremony. They held both spiritual ceremonies to give thanks to the spirits for their continued success in survival and social celebrations of life events such as marriages. During these rituals the Aleut looked much like Northwest Coast performers with body paint, tattoos, and elaborate wooden masks.

The Aleuts had good reason to thank the spirits of their world. They had a successful, stable lifestyle in a challenging environment. The Aleuts showed remarkable ability to adapt to their surroundings and to continue their lifestyle virtually unchanged for thousands of years. The Aleutian island chain is not a huge territory, and the Aleuts did not expand beyond it; but within their homeland, the Aleut culture remained dominant from 2000 B.C. up to European contact. They remained independent of the larger, expansive Inuit population to their east.

INUIT CULTURE

The developments of the Norton, Dorset, and Thule cultures in the Arctic were precursors to a remarkable society that has long captured the imagination. The people commonly called Eskimo, but more accurately referred to as Inuit, built and sustained a unique lifestyle that allowed them to survive in one of the harshest regions on earth. The people who practice this Arctic adaptation are spread out over more than 6,000 miles across the top of the North American continent, which made Inuit the most widespread aboriginal population in the New World. Although there are numerous small villages and kin groups in this territory, Inuit culture shared these characteristics: similar languages, similar physical and genetic characteristics, and, to a lesser extent, possession of a common cultural base. The culture is essentially an adaptation to Arctic and sub-Arctic maritime environments. All the aspects of pursuing and hunting Arctic marine animals, including the technological, social, and ritual practices, are the primary focus of Inuit life. Thus Inuit groups separated by thousands of miles across the Arctic will still have more in common with each other than they do with immediately adjacent Indian groups such as Athabaskans who are their closest inland neighbors.

The Inuit can be roughly divided into western or Alaska Inuit, central or Canadian Inuit, and eastern or Greenland Inuit. Each group was influenced by its slightly different environment and by neighboring groups like the Aleut in the west. There is some difference between Inuit group's survival techniques. Those on the coast exploited primarily marine resources, whereas those living in the interior hunted land mammals, primarily caribou. Some groups, however, migrated between the regions to exploit both sets of resources. They also adapted housing styles to best fit their needs; however, they had more in common across the Arctic than they did with other indigenous people in America.

One of the characteristic icons of Inuit culture is the snow house or igloo. These were not the permanent houses of any of the Arctic groups, but rather winter seal hunting camp dwellings for the central Arctic Inuit. This group ventured onto the frozen sea in the winter to hunt seals. They needed an easily constructed, sturdy, insulating dwelling and the remarkable ice house met their needs. The style and construction evolved over the years to a nearly perfect system for winter camp. Once at a chosen campsite the men of the group began building ice houses for their families. They needed

firm snow that had fallen in one storm, which they found by prob-
ing through the softer surface snow with a caribou bone. Once the
proper snow layer was identified, a builder drew a 9– to 15–foot
diameter circle in the snow with his snow knife and began work.
From within the circle he shoveled off the softer snow and cut rectangular blocks from the harder layer. The roughly 20 × 24 × 4 inch
blocks were set up on a ledge in an ascending spiral. As each row
was tamped into place, it jutted inward, creating the characteristic beehive shape. Women shoveled soft snow against the growing
outside wall to hold the blocks with an insulating layer. A long narrow corridor beneath the snow led to a round porch. A ventilation
hole in the roof and a clear ice block window completed the structure in about one hour.

Inside the snow house, the family had a bench covered with skins
for sleeping, resting, and playing during the day. The wife set up
a stone lamp on an ice block "kitchen" table. The lamp was a shallow stone dish filled with pounded blubber, which ignited a ring of
moss wicks. This simple but effective technology provided both a
cooking fire and light for the snow house. The heat from the flames
slightly melted the roof of snow, producing a thin layer of melt
water that ran down the walls and refroze, thus adding stability
to the structure. Clothes hung on drying racks and personal items
on pegs stuck in the wall. Extra food could be stored in the snow
porch, which protected it from predators. Overall, the snow house
provided a safe and comfortable shelter for an Inuit family during
the dark, cold Arctic winter.

In the summer and among Inuit like those in Alaska who did not
hunt on the oceans in winter, a sod house was common. The design
was similar to the snow house. It was a dome-shaped structure
supported by a whale bone or driftwood frame and covered with
layers of sod. It, too, had a long subterranean corridor entrance. One
large semi-subterranean room served the family for all activities.
Light came through a window of clear ice or sea mammal intestine
and from the stone oil lamp. Most Alaskan villages grouped the
homes around a larger sod structure that served as a communal
men's house and ceremonial center.

Both villages and camps of the Inuit were organized around family groups. Families traced relatives for three generations on each
side. They moved frequently, coming into contact with other kin
groups, and thus created an extensive network. Because survival
depended heavily on cooperation, Inuit also created quasi-kinship
groups through the use of fictive kinship terms. This practice

extended the responsibilities of sharing and cooperating to a much larger network. One famous aspect of this extension of obligations is the practice of wife exchange. Two men who were good friends might trade wives. The children of both families were then bound by a special relationship that had definite obligations.

All children enjoyed a fairly free upbringing by tolerant parents. They were doted on and only punished for serious infractions. Children tended to follow closely the parent of their gender. Girls learned to tend stone lamps, cook, sew clothing, and care for infants from their mothers. Seen as less valuable because they did not grow up to be hunters, baby girls were killed by some Inuit groups, especially during hard times. Grown girls typically married early and indicated their readiness with a chin tattoo. Eligible women could be in great demand because of the gender imbalance created by infanticide. Men might seek out wives from other groups or even steal married women by force. There was no marriage ceremony; a couple simply started living together. Boys played at hunting with toy sleds and harpoons made by their fathers. They would be ready for a real hunt by the age of 10 when their fathers determined they were ready and could begin to wear a labret to indicate their maturity. Young children might be adopted by elderly individuals who hoped they would care for them in years to come. Elderly people were respected, but it was difficult to be old and infirm in a harsh, nomadic culture, so some of them had to be left to die on long difficult journeys if they could not keep up.

Not surprisingly, there was a great deal of tension in an Inuit village. The arduous conditions, long dark nights of winter, and close proximity to others stressed even well-adjusted people. Mental instability was common and occasionally someone deemed a threat to others had to be killed by relatives for the good of all. Gossip and feuds abounded in the close quarters of camp, and jealousy, fear, and hatred led to fights, property destruction, and murders. Some institutionalized practices provided a safety valve for intense feelings. Rival men could challenge each other to a fistfight held in a prescribed fashion. They might also engage in a song duel performed in front of an audience, which judged the winner.

Song also had a positive, joyous side. Inuit so enjoyed singing that two men might be song partners for life. They would meet in the winter at the ceremonial house and sing to the drumming of others. One partner could honor the other by composing a special song that his wife sang in front of the whole camp. Close song partners might cement their bond by exchanging wives. Music

helped to pass the long nights of winter and to provide pleasure in an otherwise strenuous life. Storytelling served a similar purpose and also helped to pass on aspects of history and tradition in an oral culture. The narrator of a story usually had a decorated story knife depicting images of creatures. As he acted out roles, the storyteller carved scenes in the snow. Everyone in the village gathered to hear stories in the ceremonial house, and families told them in their homes as well. Artistic skill also enlivened Arctic life. Even everyday objects—knives, lamps, parkas—would be decorated. Some students of Arctic culture argue that artistic expression was an essential part of Inuit life that was created for its aesthetic value. Others believe it was created for survival, in order to please the spirits that governed Inuit life. For example, a harpoon with a skillful depiction of an animal pleased the *inua* or spirit of that animal and thus ensured good hunting.

Spirituality

Spirits and the supernatural figured prominently in the Inuit world and directed much of their behavior. Life in the Arctic had many misfortunes and tragedies that could not be explained without resorting to a supernatural source. Modern Inuit have been described as an extremely credulous people, and it appears that their ancestors readily believed in spirits. The creation story generally common to all Inuit involves Sedna (or Nuliajunk), a beautiful girl who married a seagull. Unhappy in seagull land, the girl called for her father to come and save her, which he did by killing the seagull husband and fleeing in his boat. The mourning of the gulls at the loss of their friend can still be heard today. The seagulls pursued Sedna and her father and caused a great storm to come upon the boat. Hoping to appease them, her father flung Sedna overboard. When she clung to the edge of the boat, he cut off the first joint of her fingers, which fell into the sea and became whales. When he cut off her second joints, they swam away as walruses. The cut off stumps of Sedna's finger turned into seals. Sedna herself went to dwell in the bottom of the sea where she became the sea spirit and mother of sea animals. Depending on the behavior of men, she would send out animals as food or withhold them and cause humans to starve.

Other spirits also interacted with men and determined their fate. Narssuk the giant baby who controlled wind and snow hated humans. Tatqeq the spirit of the moon could bring men good hunting luck and women fertility if he chose. For some Inuit the moon

spirit also ruled the souls of game animals so his good favor was critical. Humans also had souls that could get lost or stolen and lived on after the body's death and could turn into wicked spirits. Properly treated, death spirits would go to one of three Inuit afterworlds depending on their conduct during life. With all of the problems that spirits could cause, the people naturally spent a great deal of time observing ritual and taboos intended to keep them happy. Like most indigenous people, the Inuit attempted to maintain harmony in the mortal and supernatural worlds. Disharmony in their demanding environment meant certain death, so their ritual became quite intricate. Many taboos on the preparation of animal meat governed the butchering, cooking, and serving of game animals. For example, land and sea animals could not be killed with the same weapon, prepared in the same pot, or consumed from the same plate. Powerful animals like the polar bear had equally powerful spirits that required special handling. Inuit maintained links to the supernatural world through strict taboos, amulets, masked ceremonies, and the services of shamans.

Hunting

Most of the Inuit concerns with the spirits were connected to successful hunting. Most of their worries, stress, and daily life also focused on the hunting that kept them alive. There was little vegetation in the Arctic and thus in the Inuit diet. Undigested greens obtained from a caribou's stomach were a treat. Humans in the Arctic primarily consumed meat. Each season brought different opportunities for killing animals, and each was critical to survival. In winter most Inuit groups turned to the frozen sea for sustenance. Nomadic groups trekked long distances to reach suitable hunting grounds. Dog sleds assisted in transporting gear, but all the adults walked and often had to pull the sleds over rough patches. They were looking for good seal hunting territories, determined by the number of seal breathing holes that they could find. As the ocean ice grew thicker, seals kept small holes open in the ice. They needed to surface through these holes about every 20 minutes to breath air. The hunters, led by a camp leader, chose a likely area to search for seal holes, which often were covered by a thin layer of snow. Dogs often helped sniff out the holes for hunters who probed the snow to determine the shape of the opening.

Seal hunting required great patience, as the hunter kept watch on his chosen hole, sometimes for hours. When the seal finally surfaced,

Sleds pulled by dogs helped people transport goods over the Arctic ice. Library of Congress.

the hunter had to strike quickly with a harpoon with a detachable head. Eventually tired out by thrashing below the ice with a wound, the seal could be pulled to the surface and killed. The seal carcass was then offered a drink of water, and mittens were placed on it so that the seal spirit would report good treatment and encourage other seals to offer themselves as prey. While on the ice, the hunter might encounter another predator waiting at seal holes—the polar bear. The great bear was a formidable opponent, and to kill one required great tenacity but also brought great honor.

Seals could also be netted in their holes, harpooned from kayaks, or killed from a blind (a structure that concealed the hunter), while out sunning on the ice. Kayaks, an Arctic invention, provided fast, light, quiet transportation for seal hunters. With a driftwood frame and skin covering, the watertight craft could be propelled long distances with a single- or double-bladed paddle. Kayaks could also be used for hunting caribou. Inuit hunters used them to approach caribou crossing shallow waters.

By the end of a long, cold, dark winter, Inuit families were tired of seal meat and looked forward to the variety brought by the spring thaw. Now men fished for cod, trapped foxes and squirrels, and hunted birds. As the snow houses melted, the winter camp broke

up. The families had coalesced during the winter to provide sufficient human power for seal hunting, but now they dispersed into smaller groups living on land in sealskin tents. Families still hunted seals from the edge of the ice, with women and children helping by scaring seals from some air holes thus forcing them to surface at a hole manned by hunters. For some Inuit groups, spring brought the whaling season. Different coastal groups pursued different species of whale. Northern Alaskans hunted bowhead whales feeding in the Beaufort Sea, Canadian Inuit pursued belugas, and Greenlanders sought the exotic narwhal. All the whales were powerful and dangerous, but provided massive amounts of meat, blubber, and ivory and baleen. Whaling was not undertaken lightly. The communal hunt was surrounded by ritual, tradition, and taboos. Typically an experienced hunter guided the effort. In many villages that hunted from umiaks, the captains of the boats gained great honor and respect from their years of successful leadership. Preparations for whale hunting often began months ahead of time with ceremonies and organization of gear. When the lookouts spotted the first migrating whales in the spring, all was ready. As the boats were launched from the ice edge and paddled furiously toward the whale, the most skilled harpooner prepared to stab the animal in the short interval when it came to the surface for a breath. He aimed for the head and spinal cord where the toggle-headed harpoon point would do the most damage. Sealskin floats attached to the line helped keep the wounded animal on the surface where hunters from the other boats could help dispatch it with lances thrust into vital organs. Finally, the dead whale was towed to shore where it was offered water from a specially carved bowl, so its spirit would be assuaged. Butchering the behemoth engaged the whole community, which shared the labor and the reward of a successful hunt. It was dangerous work for men in flimsy boats to approach a powerful and then wounded whale, but the rewards were immense, both in resources and honor.

Whaling was always a communal hunting activity. The other critical game species in Inuit life, the caribou, was often pursued communally. Inland groups hunted caribou all year, and coastal groups traveled to the tundra to exploit the caribou herds. Like other major grazing species, caribou congregated in large herds for part of the year. They came together in the spring and fall to make long migrations to and from tundra feeding grounds. After the proper ceremonies and ritual observances, Inuit hunters united to drive the herd to a killing place. They used cairns and concealed women and children to scare the animals toward the intended site. Once trapped

by a cliff, corral, or even a lake, the caribou could be killed with arrows. The carcasses yielded important meat supplies, valuable hollow hair for warm clothing, antlers for weapons and tools, and strong sinews for sewing. Other land mammals like the musk ox, which could be hunted with the aid of dogs, wolves, and wolverines, provided a variety of fur, hide, and meat for the Inuit.

The Inuit diet was rounded out by the addition of fish. Most groups used fish resources to some extent, and those along major rivers in the Alaska Peninsula relied heavily on the salmon runs. Spawning salmon could be easily confined and collected with simple traps. Other freshwater fish were speared or netted. In the winter some fishermen chiseled through six feet of ice and sat patiently at the hole dangling a fish decoy for hours. On the ocean, 600-pound halibut could be caught on 900-foot long seaweed fishing lines. Because meat was the sole basis of the Inuit diet, even small birds were worth pursuing when they came north to nest in the short Arctic summer. Species like auks could be roasted and their bills used to adorn clothing.

SUB-ARCTIC

In contrast to the development of proto-Eskimo culture from the Bering Sea north and eastward over the millennia is the domination of the interior sub-Arctic by Indians. The sub-Arctic is a vast region that covers most of Canada and the interior of Alaska. It touches the ocean only on the eastern edge along the St. Lawrence River and on Newfoundland, so it is primarily a terrestrial habitat. The southern portion of the sub-Arctic was covered with boreal forest stretching unbroken from the Atlantic Ocean to the Rocky Mountains. This was dark woodland of pine, spruce, aspen, and birch. To the north the forest gave way to the treeless tundra dotted with small ponds, lakes, and streams. Frozen solid in the winter, the tundra blooms verdantly for a short summer season that attracts caribou, as well as voracious mosquitoes and black flies.

According to the theory mentioned earlier, that two major waves of migration peopled the Arctic, the peoples of the first wave are considered Indians rather than Inuit (Eskimos). These earlier migrants were forest hunter gatherers from Siberia who crossed the land bridge between 14,000 and 12,000 years ago. They spread south to the Northwest Coast as ancestors to the Tlingit and Haida, to the Kodiak Islands, and into the interior where eventually the Athabaskans made it to the American Southwest as Navajos and

Apaches. Those that stayed in the far north pursued a different lifestyle than did later Arctic migrants.

The main block of Athabaskans remained in the western boreal forests and forest–tundra border region, expanding and contracting their ranges with the climactic changes. Before 5000 B.C., the forest expanded southward with the retreat of the glaciers, creating more territory for forest dwellers. Little evidence remains of these hunter gatherers who moved frequently and dwelled in temporary structures. Their lifestyle followed a northern Archaic pattern of local resource exploitation, and in the west the main prey would have been caribou. In the central sections of the Canadian interior, Athabaskans came into contact with expanding northern Plains Archaic culture hunting the roaming bison herds. From these groups they learned the technology of side-notched projectile points, a style that then spread northward, reaching Onion Portage in the Yukon by 5000 B.C.

The Athabaskans lived in small bands of related people. Their social life and organization revolved around their extended families. The land supported just a low density of human population, so they came together into groups of 200 or more only occasionally. Such communal gatherings would have offered opportunity for courtship outside the family group, sharing of resources, and renewal of cultural ties. An unbalanced gender ratio often led to polygamous marriages to accommodate everyone into a family. There was actually little to bind these people together, as they had no overall political entity, elaborate ritual system, or complex trade network. At best they shared linguistic similarities and cultural adaptations. Their mobile lifestyle left little mark on the land. They used birchbark to craft canoes, tipis, and containers, which were often decorated. When the interior of the bark was faced outward, the red skin could be scraped away to produce designs. They also used flattened, dyed porcupine quills to embroider embellishments on clothing. The hunter-gather lifestyle of these interior Athabaskans remained relatively unchanged for over 5,000 years until European contact.

The Chipewyan people offer a look into the lifestyles of Athabaskans in the centuries before European contact. The Chipewyan know their world intimately through long residence as well as worldview. Their creation belief explains their landscape and their place in it.

In the center of their primordial world a woman lived in a cave and subsisted on berries. A doglike creature entered her cave one night and

slept with her. She had a dream that the creature turned into a handsome man with whom she made love and became pregnant. Then a giant man appeared who was the creator. He took a stick and outlined lakes and rivers which filled with water, and he created mountains and forests. He tore the doglike creature into many pieces which he flung about. As they landed the pieces became animals. The internal organs became fish, the flesh was caribou, moose, wolves and other forest animals. The creature's skin turned into birds when he threw it in the air. The creator commanded the new beings to multiply and thus provide the woman and her descendants with food, clothing and shelter.[1]

This story explains much about Chipewyan life as they hunted the northern forests and maintained a special relationship with dogs, the progenitors of their people.

Sub-Arctic Hunting

Central to the lives of all sub-Arctic hunters was the caribou. This deerlike animal that traveled in huge herds played the same role in the sub-Arctic as the bison did on the plains. It provided meat and fat for sustenance, skin for clothing and shelter, and bones and antlers for tools. The patterns of the caribou, like the bison, dictated the patterns of the people. The animals came together in herds upwards of 100,000 individuals that traveled from the forests to the tundra to feed on newly emerged plants. At this time only a communal hunt could be effective. In the winter when they dispersed into small groups, the caribou were better hunted by individuals. The caribou were nomadic as were the people.

Caribou hunting was a male activity. In the summer, men would work together to kill many members of a large herd. To detain the animals for killing, they had to drive them into water or into a surround, which was a wooden pen. Permanent surrounds, over a mile and a half around, dotted the tundra. Once contained the caribou could be shot. In the winter a man would stalk a single caribou, often using a decoy to get close enough to kill it. After the kills the real work began. Women had to butcher, skin, and prepare the carcass. The meat that was not eaten immediately was dried for storage. Pemmican, which was a staple of hunters, was made by pounding dried meat and mixing it with fat to be stuffed into caribou intestines. The skin had to be scraped clean, dressed with a paste of brains, and massaged for hours to render it soft enough to use. Women then sewed it into clothing, blankets, or tent covers. Untanned caribou hide could be used for containers and cooking

vessels. The bones often served as tools, although the Chipewyan used copper for knives, lance points, and scraping tools. They mined it along the Coppermine River and likely traded it to other groups without access to copper deposits.

The Chipewyan and other caribou hunters had to live a nomadic lifestyle as dictated by the animals' migration. Like other nomads, they did not build permanent structures. A caribou skin tipi with a floor insulated by spruce boughs and skins served as a portable, comfortable shelter when heated by a central fire. In the farthest northern areas, people constructed domed winter houses of skins and banked the outside with snow. The temperature in the northern regions could reach 70 degrees below zero, so a winter camp had to be well insulated and the inhabitants well covered with warm clothing. Tailored, layered clothing with attached moccasins and mittens helped protect vulnerable flesh from extreme cold.

Winter camps were often set up near a lake or river to exploit fish resources. Fish were caught in nets woven from strips of caribou hide or willow. Buoyed by floats, the nets stretched across narrow streams. The nets warranted special attention, as they were believed to have personalities and would be jealous if strung one to another. Charms on the corners gave the nets special power to attract and hold fish. Fish could also be caught in weirs, speared, or shot with barbed arrows. Fresh fish, and sometimes fresh kills of caribou, moose, or small game, added to stores of dried meat to get a family through the winter.

Life was difficult in the sub-Arctic and not everyone survived. Although the caribou proved to be a life-sustaining resource, little else was available. The Chipewyans and their neighbors ate virtually no vegetables. Some moss and berries made it into the meat diet. If times got exceptionally tough, people could eat their caribou skin clothing and even eventually their own dead if there was nothing else. Cannibalism was neither regular nor acceptable, but it could happen.

Most sub-Arctic people lived their whole lives within the confines of a small family group. Like other nomadic groups, they came together in large gatherings only occasionally. For the Chipewyan this was at the caribou spring migration. Hundreds of people would come to an area where caribou crossed a river or woods edge. The Chipewyan followed a set ritual of telling each other the misfortunes of the year and receiving formal condolences; then the socializing could begin. Young men and women of marriageable age might come to an agreement. A girl married after her first menses around

age 12, often to a much older man. Marriage was not formal; a couple simply began living together and the ties were not strong. In some Athabaskan groups, a challenger could wrestle a husband for the right to his wife. Within the family setting the father was the leader. Each individual had a role in the success of the family and dissent was uncommon. In fact, the Chipewyan rarely engaged in warfare, counting only Inuits and Cree Indians as enemies. These two groups were considered enemies because of the belief that their shamans could cause sickness among Chipewyans. Athabaskan shamans worked hard to protect their people from malicious interference by others with supernatural powers.

The Cree shamans feared by Chipewyans were part of another non-Eskimo group that inhabited the eastern portion of the north. These people belonged to the Algonquian language group and spread northward from the northeastern woodlands. There was a great deal of diversity of language within the group, which suggests early divisions among the people. Only the Montagnais and Naskapi of Labrador and the Cree of Quebec form a similar language group. The culture known as Shield Archaic began in 5000 B.C. and continued relatively unchanged until A.D. 1500. This group formed a block spreading from Labrador west to Manitoba. Again, the acidic northern soil preserved little of the wood, bone, and antler objects these people would have relied on, so we know even less about them than the Athabaskans. Algonquians hunted, trapped, fished, and gathered in the forest and tundra edges. They traveled in birchbark canoes in the summer and on snowshoes towing sleds in the winter. They lived in conical tipis, which could be easily moved. From their Inuit neighbors, some groups adopted the style of tailored clothing, which was a successful adaptation to the cold. The Beothuk on Newfoundland, who may have been Algonquians, hunted with Inuit harpoons, indicating another area of contact; however, contact and exchange of ideas does not mean harmony. The Beothuck appear to have been mistreated by Inuit, Norsemen, and later Europeans. In fact, the English and French settlers shot these "Red Paint" people for sport.

There was little change in the sub-Arctic hunting-gathering lifestyle over the millennia. The people had worked out an Archaic-style adaptation to their environment that worked well enough for them to survive, but not to thrive in the manner of other richer resource regions. Life continued in a pattern of seasonal migrations by family-based kin groups in order to exploit major natural

resources, especially caribou. Some years were harder than others and some groups experienced starvation in lean times. The system was stable enough, however, to sustain an ancient way of life for thousands of years until European contact unraveled the entire cultural adaptation.

The Arctic and sub-Arctic regions are incredibly harsh and it would be understandable if they remained uninhabited; however, this difficult northernmost region was home to specialized cultures. The Aleut and Inuit carved out viable existences for themselves. Part of the later waves of migrants to the continent, these latecomers remained in the northern land of ice, snow, and darkness. They developed fascinating adaptations to this world, both practical and aesthetic. Inventions like toggle-head harpoons and stone oil lamps made life bearable, and intricately carved ivory made it more beautiful. More than any other group, these far northern residents had to master specific skills for survival. Once these had been achieved, their lifestyle continued for thousands of years.

NOTE

1. James Maxwell, ed., *America's Fascinating Indian Heritage* (Pleasantville, NY: Reader's Digest Association, 1978), 330.

FURTHER READING

Arctic Circle: History and Culture. This site from University of Connecticut includes a virtual classroom about the Arctic. http://arcticcircle. uconn.edu/HistoryCulture/ (accessed September 1, 2007).

Arctic Studies Center. The Smithsonian Institution's Arctic Studies Center offers many resources. http://www.mnh.si.edu/arctic/index.html (accessed September 1, 2007).

Boas, Franz. *The Central Eskimo.* Lincoln: University of Nebraska Press, 1965.

Dumond, Don E. *The Eskimos and Aleuts.* London: Thames and Hudson, 1987.

Laughlin, William. *Aleuts: Survivors of the Bering Land Bridge.* New York: Holt, Rinehart and Winston, 1980.

Looking Both Ways: Heritage and Identity of the Alutiiq People of Southern Alaska, An Interactive Exhibit. This site focuses on the Alutiiq people who live in southern Alaska. http://www.mnh.si.edu/looking bothways/ (accessed September 1, 2007).

Malin, Edward. *A World of Faces: Masks of the Northwest Coast Indians.* Portland, OR: Timber Press, 1994.

Maxwell, Moreau S. *Prehistory of the Eastern Arctic*. New York: Academic Press, 1985.

McGhee, Robert. *Ancient People of the Arctic*. Vancouver: UBC Press, 2001.

Peregrine, Peter N., and Melvin Ember, eds. *Encyclopedia of Prehistory*. Vol. 2: Arctic and Subarctic. New York: Kluwer Academic/Plenum Publishers, 2001.

Bibliography

Aikens, C. M. "Archaeology of the Great Basin." *Annual Review of Anthropology* 7 (1978): 71–87.

Ames, Kenneth M., and Herbert D. G Maschner. *Peoples of the Northwest Coast: Their Archaeology and Prehistory.* London: Thames & Hudson, 2000.

Axtell, James, ed. *The Native American People of the East.* West Haven, CT: Pendulum Press, 1973.

Ballantine, Betty, and Ian Ballantine, eds. *The Native Americans.* Atlanta, GA: Turner Publishing, 1993.

Borden, C. C. "Peopling and Early Cultures of the Pacific Northwest." *Science* 203 (1979): 963–971.

Bragdon, Kathleen J. *The Columbia Guide to American Indians of the Northeast.* New York: Columbia University Press, 2001.

Caffrey, Margaret M. "Complementary Power: Men and Women of the Lenni Lenape." *American Indian Quarterly* 24, 1 (Winter 2000): 44–63.

Chance, Norman. *The Inupiat and Arctic Alaska: An Ethnography of Development.* Fort Worth, TX: Holt, Rinehart and Winston, 1990.

Coe Michael, Dean Snow, and Elizabeth Benson. *Atlas of North America.* New York: Facts on File, 1986.

Coupland, Gary, and R. G. Matson. *The Prehistory of the Northwest Coast.* San Diego: Academic Press, 1995.

Delcourt, Paul A., and Hazel R. Delcourt. *Prehistoric Native Americans and Ecological Change: Human Ecosystems in Eastern North America since the Pleistocene.* New York: Cambridge University Press, 2004.

Dye, David, and Cheryl Anne Cox, eds. *Towns and Temples along the Mississippi.* Tuscaloosa: The University of Alabama Press, 1990.

Erdoes, Richard, and Alfonso Ortiz, eds. *American Indian Myths and Legends.* New York: Pantheon Books, 1984.

Fagan, Brian M. *Ancient North America.* London: Thames and Hudson, 1991.

Fitzhugh, Ben, and Junko Habu, eds. *Beyond Foraging and Collecting: Evolutionary Change in Hunter-Gatherer Settlement Systems.* New York: Plenum Publishers, 2005.

Fowler, Loretta. *The Columbia Guide to American Indians of the Great Plains.* New York: Columbia University Press, 2003.

Frison, George C., ed. *Prehistoric Hunters of the High Plains.* San Diego: Academic Press, 1991.

Galloway, Patricia, ed. *The Southeastern Ceremonial Complex: Artifacts and Analysis.* Lincoln: University of Nebraska Press, 1989.

Gladwin, Harold S. *Excavations at Snaketown: Material Culture.* Tucson: University of Arizona Press, 1965.

Gregonis, Linda M., and Karl J. Reinhard. *Hohokam Indians of the Tucson Basin.* Tucson: University of Arizona Press, 1979.

Gumerman, George J., ed. *Exploring the Hohokam: Prehistoric Desert Peoples of American Southwest.* Albuquerque: University of New Mexico Press, 1991.

Haynes, Gary. *The Early Settlement of North America: The Clovis Era.* Cambridge: Cambridge University Press, 2002.

Heizer, Robert F., ed. *The Handbook of North American Indians: California.* Vol. 8. Washington DC: The Smithsonian Institution Press, 1978.

Hoffecker, John F. *A Prehistory of the North: Human Settlement of the Higher Latitudes.* New Brunswick, NJ: Rutgers University Press, 2004.

Hudson, Charles. *The Southeastern Indians.* Knoxville: University of Tennessee Press, 1976.

Jablonski, Nina, ed. *The First Americans: The Pleistocene Colonization of the New World.* Berkeley: University of California Press, 2002.

Jones, Terry L., ed. *Essays on the Prehistory of Maritime California.* Davis, CA: Center for Archaeological Research, 1992.

Josephy Jr., Alvin M. *The Native Americans: An Illustrated History.* Atlanta, GA: Turner Publishing, 1993.

Justice, Noel D. *Stone Age Spear and Arrow Points of California and the Great Basin.* Bloomington: Indiana University Press, 2002.

Kallen, Stuart A. *Native Americans of the Northeast.* San Diego: Lucent Books, 2000.

Kantner, John. *Ancient Puebloan Southwest.* New York: Cambridge University Press, 2004.

Kehoe, Alice. *North American Indians: A Comprehensive Account.* Upper Saddle River, NJ: Pearson Prentice Hall, 2006.

Kopper, Philip. *The Smithsonian Book of North American Indians.* Washington, DC: Smithsonian Books, 1986.

Kroeber, Alfred. *Handbook of the Indians of California.* Washington, DC: Bureau of American Ethnology, 1925.

Laughlin, William. "Aleuts: Ecosystem, Holocene History, and Siberian Origins." *Science* 189 (1975): 507–515.

Mann, Charles C. *1491: New Revelations of the Americas before Columbus.* New York: Alfred Knopf, 2005.

Milner, George. *The Moundbuilders: Ancient Peoples of Eastern North America.* London: Thames and Hudson, 2004.

Nies, Judith. *Native American History.* New York: Ballantine Books, 1996.

Pauketat, Timothy R. *Ancient Cahokia and the Mississippians.* New York: Cambridge University Press, 2004.

Plog, Stephen. *Ancient Peoples of the American Southwest.* London: Thames & Hudson, 1998.

Power, Susan C. *Early Art of the Southeastern Indians: Feathered Serpents and Winged Beings.* Athens, GA: University of Georgia Press, 2004.

Pringle, Heather. *In Search of Ancient North America: An Archaeological Journey to Forgotten Cultures.* New York: John Wiley & Sons, 1996.

Scarry, John, ed. *Political Structure and Change in the Prehistoric Southeastern United States.* Gainesville: University Press of Florida, 1996.

Sita, Lisa. *Indians of the Northeast: Traditions, History, Legends, and Life.* Milwaukee, WI: Gareth Stevens Publishers, 2000.

Snow, Dean. *Archaeology of North America.* New York: Viking Press, 1976.

———. *The Iroquois.* Cambridge: Blackwell Publishers, 1994.

———. *The Archaeology of New England.* New York: Academic Press, 1980.

Stanford, Dennis. "Paleoindian Archaeology and Late Pleistocene Environments in the Plains and Southwestern United States." In *Ice Age People of North America,* eds. Robson Bonnichsen and Karen L. Turnmire, 281–339. Corvallis: Oregon State University Press, 1999.

———. "Paleoindian Archaeology and Late Pleistocene Environments in the Plains and Southwestern United States." In *Ice Age People of North America,* eds. Robson Bonnichsen and Karen L. Turnmire. Corvallis: Oregon State University Press, 1999.

Tankersley, Kenneth. *In Search of Ice Age Americans.* Layton, UT: Gibbs Smith, 2002.

Thomas, David Hurst. *Exploring Native North America.* New York: Oxford University Press, 2000.

Turnmire, Robson Bonnichsen, and Karen L., eds. *Ice Age People of North America.* Corvallis: Oregon State University Press, 1999.

Underhill, Ruth. *Indians of the Pacific Northwest.* Washington, DC: Bureau of Indian Affairs, 1945.

Wede, Waldo Rudolph. *Toward a History of Plains Archaeology.* Lincoln: Center for Great Plains Studies, University of Nebraska, 1981.

West, Frederick Hadleigh, ed. *American Beginnings: The Prehistory and Palaeoecology of Beringia*. Chicago: University of Chicago Press, 1998.

Wood, W. Raymond, ed. *Archaeology on the Great Plains*. Lawrence: University Press of Kansas, 1998.

Woodcock, George. *Peoples of the Coast the Indians of the Pacific Northwest*. Bloomington: Indiana University Press.

Index

About the Author

CLARISSA W. CONFER is an Assistant Professor in the Department of History and Political Science at California University of Pennsylvania.